SIR JOHN SUTTON

A Study in True Principles

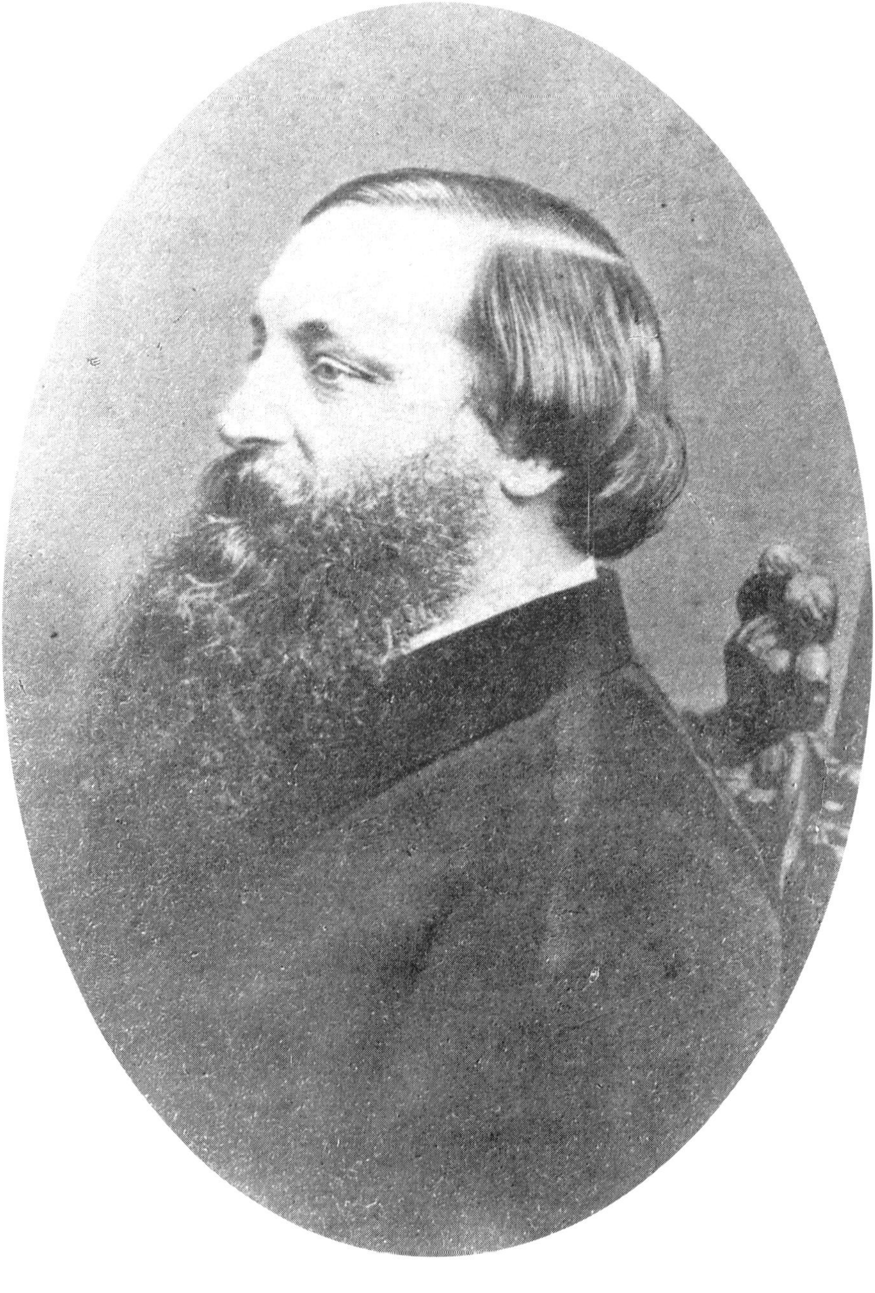

SIR JOHN SUTTON
A Study in True Principles

C. H. Davidson

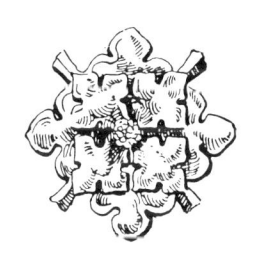

POSITIF PRESS • OXFORD

Frontispiece: Sir John Sutton, Bart., 1820–1873 (*photograph: Chorstift Kiedrich*)

Thanks for the German summary to
Mrs Linda Lyon and Prof Friedrich Riedel

Designed and produced by John Brennan at the Positif Press, Oxford.
© C. H. Davidson and Positif Press 1992. All rights reserved.
No part of this publication may be reproduced or transmitted in any form or by any means, electronic or mechanical, including photocopy, recording or any information storage and retrieval system, without permission in writing from the publisher.

Positif Press, 130 Southfield Road, Oxford OX4 1PA

ISBN 0 906894 20 4

Typeset in Bembo by Parchments (Oxford) Ltd and Positif Press
Printed and bound by Biddles Limited, Guildford and Kings Lynn

CONTENTS

Illustration sources	6
References	7
Acknowledgements	9
Introduction	11
The Sutton Family	13
Chapter I	15
Sir John Sutton – Some Dates, Places and Formative Influences	
Chapter II	36
Sir John Sutton – Organ Lover	
Chapter III	110
Sir John Sutton – Restorer of Churches	
Chapter IV	138
Sir John Sutton – Musician	
Chapter V	170
The Anglo-Belgian Seminary	
Chapter VI	183
Sir John Sutton and the Poor	
Chapter VII	186
The Sutton Circle	
Conclusion	197
Zusammenfassung	198
Bibliography	215
Index	218

ILLUSTRATIONS

The Author and Publisher would like to thank the following for granting permission to use photographs and drawings appearing in this book:

p.10 Chorstift Kiedrich; p.16 Author's collection; p.25 Westvlaamse Gidsenkring vzw; p.20 Schneider letters; p.31 Kna-Bild, Frankfurt/Main; p.46 Schneider letters; p.50 *Country Life*; p.55 Jim Berrow; p.57 Author's collection; pp.58, 61 and 63 Jim Berrow; p.64 Béthune Archive; p.69 S.W. Harvey; p.71 N. P. Mander Ltd; p.74 Author's collection (*Stowe Catalogue*); p.76 B. B. Edmonds; p.78 John Brennan; p.81 Franz Bösken (from *Die Orgel von Kiedrich*); p.83 Verlag Orgelbau Kuhn; p.86 Kna-Bild, Fankfurt/Main; p.88 Paul Smets, Rheingold-Verlag; p.89 Westvlaamse Gidsenkring vzw; p.91 (top) Author's collection (bottom) Positif Press (from: A. G. Hill, *The Organ and Organ-Cases of the Middle Ages and Renaissance*, London, 1883); p.92 Author's collection; p.93 Author's collection (from: John Norbury, *The Box of Whistles*, London 1887); pp.94 and 96 John Brennan; p.98 Royal College of Organists; p.103 Positif Press; p.111 Myer's Collection; p.114 Roy Tricker; pp.116 and 117 Author's collection; p.120 RCHM; p.125 *Country Life*; p.127 Verlag Horst Ziethen, Köln; p.128 Schnell, *Kunstführer 1465*, (München 1984); p.130 Author's collection; p.132 Rheinische Kunststätten; p.135 Béthune Archive; p.136 Hed. Barth; p.138 Author's collection; p.151 Bernhard & Staab, *Kiedricher Chortradition...* (Kiedrich, 1965); pp.154 and 155 Chorstift Kiedrich Archive; p.158 Rheinische Kunststätten; p.163 Collection of the late Mrs Clifton-Brown; pp.174, 177 and 179 Béthune Archive; p.185 Kalle-Folie (Manfred Boersch); pp.189 and 192 Andrew Freeman collection.

REFERENCES

Short Form	Full Reference
BIOS Journal	*British Institute of Organ Studies: Journal*, pub. annually from 1977 (Oxford: Positif Press).
BIOS Reporter	*British Institute of Organ Studies: Reporter*, pub. three or four times a year from 1977.
Bösken	Bösken, Franz, art. "Die Orgel von Kiedrich", *Acta Organologica* VIII (Berlin: Merseburger, 1974).
Dictionary of National Biography	*Dictionary of National Biography*: (London: Macmillan, 1921-2).
Elvin	Elvin, L., *Bishop & Son, Organ Builders* (Lincoln: 1984).
Father Smith	Freeman, A., *Father Smith* (London: Musical Opinion, 1926) revised Rowntree, J. (Oxford: Positif Press, 1977).
Ferrey	Ferrey, B., *Recollections of A. W. N. Pugin*, 1861: republished with Introduction by Clive and Jane Wainwright (London: Scholar Press, 1978).
History of Jesus College	Gray, A., and Brittain, F., *A History of Jesus College Cambridge* (London: Heinemann, 1960).
Hopkins and Rimbault	Hopkins, E., and Rimbault, E., *The Organ* (London: Robert Cocks, 1855).
Pearce	Pearce, C. W., *Notes on English Organs* (London: Vincent Music Co., 1905).
Rainbow	Rainbow, B., *The Choral Revival in the Anglican Church, 1839-1872* (London: Barrie & Jenkins, 1970).
Rembry	Rembry, E., *De Bekende Pastoors van St. Gillis te Brugge* (Bruges, 1896).
Schepens	Schepens, L., art. "Het Engels Seminarie te Brugge" in *Handelingen van het Genootschap voor Geschiedenis* (Bruges: 1967).

Staab	Staab, Josef, *Die Kiedricher Chorbuben und Ihre Tradition*, Chorstift Kiedrich, 1985.
Stanton	Stanton, P., *Pugin* (London: Thames & Hudson, 1971).
Stones and Story	Morgan, I. and Morgan, G., *The Stones and Story of Jesu College Chapel, Cambridge* (Cambridge: Bowes & Bowes, 1914).
The Organ	*The Organ* – periodical pub. quarterly, from 1921 (London: Musical Opinion Ltd.).
Thistlethwaite	Thistlethwaite, N., *The Organs of Cambridge* (Oxford: Positif Press, 1983).
Tricker	Tricker, R. W., *St. Mary's West Tofts Norfolk, History and Guide* (pamphlet) (Ipswich, 1984).
Venn	Venn, John, and Venn, J. A., *Alumni Cantabrigienses* (C.U. P., 1924).
Wainwright	Wainwright, Clive, *Notes for the Victorian Society's Tour of Norfolk, 1978* (typescript).
Zaun	Zaun, J., *Geschichte des Ortes une der Pfarrei Kiedrich* (reprinted: Gemeinde Kiedrich, 1979).

Manuscript Sources

Béthune	Letters of Sir John Sutton to Baron J. de Béthune, at the Béthune Archive, Kasteel Marke, Kortrijk, Belgium: no. 1230.
Bishop	Records of Bishop & Son, Organ-builders, at Beethoven Street, London.
Conclusion Book	Jesus College Conclusion Book, Jesus College Old Library, Cambridge.
Hardman	Letters of Sir John Sutton to John Hardman & Co., Hardman Archives, the Central Library, Birmingham.
Schneider Letters	Letters of Sir John Sutton to Prälat Schneider, at the Staatliches Hochschulinstitut für Musik, Mainz.

ACKNOWLEDGEMENTS

As with all historical work, many people have contributed material, suggestions and corrections to this book. Prominent among them have been the owners of letters and documents quoted:

M. le Baron de Béthune and his family, for hospitality both of their archive and house while I worked at Marke:

the Hochschulinstitut für Musik at Mainz, and Professor Toussaint who sent me copies of Sir John Sutton's letters there many years ago (they have since been moved to the Bischöfliches Diözesanarchiv):

the Master and Fellows of Jesus College, Cambridge:

the Warden and Fellows of New College, Oxford:

the Cambridge University Library:

Pusey House Library, Oxford:

the Birmingham Central Library and its staff, for many searches in the Hardman Collection:

the Norfolk and Northamptonshire Record Offices and their staffs:

the Kiedrich Chorschule and a former Chorregent, Herr Kurt Erkes, for copies of the foundation documents of the Chorschule, and Mrs. Mary Dittrich who photographed them.

In the organ world, I have had memories, information and encouragement from many friends, notably Canon Gordon Paget, the Revd. Bernard B. Edmonds, and Messrs. Stephen Bicknell, Laurence Elvin, Michael Gillingham, Dominic Gwynn, Noel Mander and Austin Niland.

On the architectural side of things, Mrs. Alexandra Wedgwood has been most generous, even though she does not agree with all my theories; Mr. Clive Wainwright of the Victoria and Albert Museum has been unfailingly sympathetic.

Dr. W. H. Brock and other members of the Victorian Studies Centre of the University of Leicester have introduced me to the historical method of dealing with the material, and made many helpful suggestions.

The late Mrs. Robina Clifton-Brown was most generous with her family memories, and hospitality.

There are many friends in Kiedrich who have shared their knowledge, their memories and their homes with me and my wife:

the lapse of time between beginning this work and its appearing in print has meant that several of them have died, and I must mention Hochw. Dekan Wilhelm Klippel, former Pfarrer of Kiedrich, and Herr Weil, who lived in the house which once belonged to Sir John Sutton. I owe a great debt of gratitude to Hochw. Hans Bernhard, former Chorregent and now Domkapellmeister at Limburg, who first introduced me to Sir John's achievements in the village.

Mrs. Sibyl Phillips of Roade has done far more than just type the text: a sharp eye for omitted references, mistakes and inconsistencies has saved me from all sorts of errors that would have drawn down the wrath of reviewers and students alike.

My wife has been my most constant encourager, and has endured piles of books and papers, constant untidiness and a great many searches for references, with exemplary patience.

To all of them I offer my best thanks: and this must also go to anyone whose names have been unintentionally omitted from the list.

C.H.D.

Sir John Sutton

INTRODUCTION

There were many men and women who lived between 1840 and 1900 who did not find a place in Lytton Strachey's *Eminent Victorians*, but who were at the same time very well-informed, very capable, and did or had done excellent work in their own fields. Some of them achieved local fame, and a few local notoriety; quite a lot have memorials on the walls or floors of their parish churches, and many more have stained-glass windows placed in their memory, for it was a church-going age. Some had a social conscience and tried to do something for the poor and aged of their districts. A good many were skilled in painting or sketching, and were ready to take their part in the home-made musical or vocal entertainments which took place in many households during the winter evenings.

Sir John Sutton, the third Baronet, of Norwood Park near Southwell in Nottinghamshire, was one such: he has no entry in the *Dictionary of National Biography*, and only appears in a few paragraphs of the architectural histories of his Cambridge college, and occasionally in writings about the nineteenth-century history of the organ and its decoration, in our own country. His memory is far brighter in the Rheingau district of Germany, for he was one of the many Englishmen of his time who carried out most of their life's work abroad. But he was no colonial administrator, nor planter of the Union Jack in unexplored territories; he worked where he found himself, and where he found work he felt he alone could do well.

To anyone interested in the historical and archival side of organ-building in Britain, Sir John Sutton is something of a household name because he published one of the first books about organs in the language. Like some other small books, it had a very long title [*A Short Account of Organs built in England from the Reign of King Charles the Second to the Present Time*: London, 1847.] which is often abbreviated to the *Short Account*; and in it he argued forcibly against the development of large and powerful organs in the middle years of the nineteenth century. Hardly anything, though, has been known about him; the sole published works about him were two articles in *The Organ*, one of which described organ-cases "of the gothic renaissance" in England, and the other dealt briefly with work Sutton did in Kiedrich, a village between Wiesbaden and Rüdesheim in Germany. So it seemed worth-while to try to gather enough information about him for a biographical article.

This dissertation is the result, for he was one of the people closely concerned with the early days of what may be called the Cambridge end of the Oxford Movement – that side of the revival of Anglican church life of the mid-nineteenth century which concentrated on the study of medieval church-building, architecture, arrangement and furnishing, with of course the worship offered there, and the reasons why things were as they were. Social conventions in England used to be such that it was not considered manly to be interested in embroidery, the furnishings of a church or the choice of anthems or hymns for a service; and the fact that John Sutton became a Roman Catholic and spent – or over-spent – nearly all his income on things of this sort meant that his immediate family kept his memory neither bright nor cherished. Further, his going to live abroad for the last eighteen years of a fairly short life meant that few in England outside his family noticed his death, and so no biographical obituary notices appeared in the newspapers.

Research, however, has revealed that he has an importance all his own. In architecture he was a friend of Pugin, and carried out a good deal of work right in the spirit of that single-minded genius. Pugin introduced him to Jean de Béthune, a practical and hard-working enthusiast for gothic furnishing, stained glass and architecture in Belgium, who became a very firm friend and with whom Sutton planned and executed some works – including one or two in England – much admired today. In organ-building he was much influenced by the late seventeenth-century Bernard Smith's organs in England, and by the fifteenth-seventeenth century organ of Kiedrich in Germany; he saved the German Kurmainzer "dialect" of plainsong from extinction; he very nearly accomplished his aim of re-founding a complete ecclesiastical collegiate body at Kiedrich; and he founded, and planned extensively for, a seminary to train Roman Catholic priests in Bruges. Such a list of achievements deserves recognition; and it was made possible by an annual income of between £40,000 and £50,000, of which only the amount necessary for his own, and two or three servants', keep was spent upon himself.

Valuable collections of his letters still exist at the Bischöfliches Diözesanarchiv in Mainz, at Kasteel Marke, home of the de Béthune family, in Belgium, and in the Hardman Archives at the Central Library in Birmingham: and biographical material is to be found in two Belgian works about other people, and the magisterial nineteenth-century parish history of Kiedrich written by Canon J. Zaun.

This work is offered as a tribute to a man of deep religious feeling, who did what he could for God in spite of many emotional and psychological troubles: and did it well.

THE SUTTON FAMILY

Many scholars and researchers have been confused by the fact that there were seven Sutton brothers, and that three of them were very active in the revival of the gothic style of building churches, in organs and their lore, church music and glass-painting. Two of them will appear in this study: the third has been written about elsewhere, but has an importance all his own. In addition, there was a clergyman of the next generation who continued a little of the work and looked after his uncle's art collection at Brant Broughton Rectory. It seems sensible then, to tabulate them here to avoid further confusion.

1. *Sir JOHN Sutton*, the third Baronet, 1820-1873, the subject of this study. He was the friend of Augustus Welby Pugin and to a lesser extent of his widow and son, Edward Pugin. He was deeply concerned in the restoration and the life of Jesus College Chapel in Cambridge and paid for most or all of the restoration and re-building of West Tofts church in Norfolk, with the two Pugins as architects. In 1854 or so he went to live on the Continent and after that carried out no substantial work in England. He wrote *A Short Account of Organs Built in England...*, which was published in 1847.

2. *The Revd. AUGUSTUS Sutton*, 1825-1885, Rector of West Tofts and later Canon of Lincoln. He had the joy of seeing his church made into "one of Pugin's finest accomplishments"[1], and fully appreciated it. He was a great bell-ringer, a choir-trainer and organist, something of an architect, a glass-painter and designer, and acted as liaison between local clergy and the church-furnishing firm of Hardman in Birmingham, as letters in their archives testify.[2] He was also a great expert on tower clocks, collecting ancient and disused ones from churches, restoring them and presenting them to other churches. He made the house called Caston Hall at West Tofts into the Rectory and was an excellent parish priest, regularly noting congregations of over a hundred both morning and evening from a population of only about two hundred and fifty people. He is epitomised in the *Diary* of the Revd. Benjamin Armstrong of East Dereham as "The Rev. A. Sutton, son of Sir Richard, who is famous for bell-ringing, organ-playing and clock-making, came to Dereham for the grand inauguration of the newly cast bell."[3]

3. *The Revd. FREDERICK HEATHCOTE Sutton*, 1833-1888, Vicar of Theddingworth in Leicestershire and then Rector of the family living of Brant Broughton in Lincolnshire from 1873 until his death. He was also a Canon of Lincoln. He published *Church Organs and Organ-Cases* which began in 1866 as a description of the organ at Old Radnor in Wales, and went through four editions, the last being in 1883. At Theddingworth he bought an eighteenth-century organ, had it restored and replaced its case with a gothic one designed by himself, and decorated the chancel. At Brant Broughton he restored the whole church, using his friend G. F. Bodley as the architect, and kept a very valuable diary of the work. He filled the windows with stained glass of his own making and had the village blacksmith make all the iron-work to his designs. He collaborated with his brother, Augustus, in making many stained windows for Lincoln Cathedral. He designed quite a number of excellent organ-cases, mostly working with Bodley and Garner, and acted as adviser to clergy and nobility all over the country in matters of church restoration, interior arrangement, organs and furnishing. He was another fine Tractarian parish priest, caring for everyone living in his parish without distinction. He made a valuable collection of medieval paintings and other *objets d'art* on his regular journeys to the Continent, and provided a home for the chamber-organs his eldest brother left behind at his death.

4. *The Revd. ARTHUR FREDERICK Sutton*, 1852-1925, son of Augustus; Rector of West Tofts 1885-1888, of Brant Broughton 1888-1924, and of Earls Colne in Essex 1924 to his death, and Canon of Lincoln. He continued the enrichment of Brant Broughton church, adding the chancel screen, and the organ-case in 1909, and cared for Frederick Sutton's collections, which were only dispersed at his death. His obituary stated, "Upon him his uncle's reputation, though not his mantle, descended."

REFERENCES

1   Stanton, p. 139.
2   Hardman.
3   The Revd. Benjamin Armstrong,
    A Norfolk Diary, 19 July 1864:
    edited A. C. T. Armstrong
    (London: Faber 1947).

CHAPTER I

Sir John Sutton – Some Dates, Places and Formative Influences[1]

John Sutton was born on 18 October, 1820, eldest son of Sir Richard Sutton, Bart., of Norwood Park near Southwell in Nottinghamshire, and of Mary Elizabeth his wife[2]. She was the daughter of Mr. and Mrs. William FitzWilliam Burton, of Burton Hall, County Carlow in Ireland. This first child was actually born at Sudbrooke Holme in Lincolnshire which was a house Sir Richard rented for the shooting season; as will be seen, not even the imminent arrival of a possible heir would make this great sportsman give up more shooting than necessary!

Sir Richard Sutton, the second baronet (1798-1855), had succeeded to the title at the age of three[3]; and careful husbanding of his estates by trustees during his minority made him one of the richest men in England. Educated at Eton and Trinity College, Cambridge, he married a few days after his twenty-first birthday and settled down to raise a large family and to pursue the sports of fox-hunting, shooting and fishing with single-minded ardour. He was Master successively of the Burton, Cottesmore and Quorn Hunts, and is remembered as having spent £300,000 on fox-hunting during his life[4]. But there were other sides to him, for he played the flute, was a lover of books, and certainly paid for the building and decoration of a chantry at West Tofts church to his wife's memory. He was alive to his eldest son's nervous shyness, bought an organ for him, and arranged for Christopher Bird to have him as a pupil. To his children, relatives and friends, he was always generous. He built a school at West Tofts for the children of his estate workers and maintained it until his death, which took place at his London house, 94 Piccadilly. He was buried a week later, on 21 November 1855, at West Tofts, and tradition says that a fox howled all night upon his grave.

Lady Mary Elizabeth Sutton, John's mother, remains a shadowy figure, fully occupied with her duties as wife and mother, for the couple had eight sons, one of whom died in infancy, and four daughters[5]. We know from Zaun[6] that her eldest son always spoke of her with the greatest love and respect, and the fact that he restored West Tofts church in her memory, rather than his wife's, speaks volumes.

We know nothing of John's early life but we can assume that

Sir Richard and Lady Mary Elizabeth Sutton with John, c.1821

with the very large income enjoyed by Sir Richard there were plenty of people available to give him amusement and training. For a while, the rapidly-growing family had a private tutor and then John went to what we would now call a preparatory school at East Stoke near Newark in Nottinghamshire, no trace of which remains now[7]. In 1834, John and two brothers, Richard and Augustus, went to Eton College[8]. He stayed there for two years only. We have no evidence about the reasons for so short a time but we may speculate that to a quiet, sensitive boy with a passion for music, Eton could well have been something like a bear-garden. Assistant masters' duties in those days only embraced teaching itself and even in the eighteen-nineties, life in the boarding-houses was described as "a regular routine of sadistic orgies"[9]. Sir Richard saw the damage that was being done and arranged that he should board with Christopher Bird, a private tutor, in Northumberland. It was quite common in those days for country clergy to take residential pupils, partly to improve their income and partly to keep their own teaching abilities active – and incidentally providing a useful service to moneyed families who preferred to have their sons educated with as much personal teaching as possible, or whose children were not suited to normal school education.

The Revd. Christopher Bird, Vicar of Chollerton near Hexham (1778-1867) was a man of many parts[10]. He held degrees from both Oxford and Cambridge; extremely capable in both classics and mathematics, he was at home, and listened to with respect, in almost every subject. He was a contemporary and close friend of Lord Brougham (Lord Chancellor in the Whig Government of 1830) and helped him with able pamphlets on Catholic Emancipation: and he was keenly interested in the education of the middle and lower classes, and the improvement of the dwellings of the poor. He was a very able preacher and to the last, let nothing interfere with his parochial duties:

> "On foot, or mounted on his pony, with a plaid on his shoulders, he was indifferent to the roughest weather; he would go *qua via difficilis est et qua nulla via*. The year before his death he spent a long day without food, ministering with his own hands to the necessities of a poor old woman he found sick and deserted in a hovel on the moor."

He took the Sutton brothers on their first trip up the Rhine as far as Basle, and most probably visited Kiedrich with them.[11]

Sutton spent nearly five years at Chollerton and from his own account came to know William Henshaw, "perhaps the first Cathedral Organist in England", pretty well. Henshaw's dates are 1791-1877, and he was organist of Durham 1813-1862. Sutton's extensive knowledge of the cathedral organ there, and the fact that he was able to make a copy of the original contract for its building, suggests that he was friendly with, and perhaps a pupil of, Henshaw. It is said that Henshaw was a "skilful though not a showy performer"[12] and *The Parish Choir* stated that:

> "The choir at Durham had long enjoyed a high reputation. The men's voices ... were of good quality, and the boys were well instructed. Their attendance at the daily services was enforced, so that there was not at Durham the contrast

between Sunday display and week-day negligence that disgraced many cathedrals..."[13]

Henshaw is mentioned several times in *The Life and Letters of John Bacchus Dykes* but with no notice of his musicianship.[14]

John Sutton was admitted Pensioner of Jesus College, Cambridge, on 6 July, 1840: he matriculated in Lent 1841, so presumably took up residence in October of that year[15]. Why he went to Jesus College is not clear; his father, Sir Richard, had been at Trinity – but as the various brothers all seem to have had their university education at different colleges, it would be wrong to read too much into it. On 1 January, 1842, Lady Mary Elizabeth Sutton died in childbirth at Hake's Hotel in London[16]. She was buried at West Tofts, in the churchyard in the middle of Sir Richard's favourite estate. Why, though, did she die at an hotel when the family had a London house of their own? The reason is that from 1837 this house was let to the Duke of Cambridge, seventh son of King George III (Adolphus Frederick, 1774-1850). He had been Governor-General of Hanover from 1814, and Viceroy from 1831 to 1837, when Queen Victoria succeeded to the throne of England and the Salic Law made it necessary for the eldest surviving son of George III (the Duke of Cumberland) to be crowned King of Hanover[17]. This is why the house (later the Naval and Military Club) was called Cambridge House. Sir Richard and his family made Lynford Hall near West Tofts their principal seat, though the baronet himself moved about a good deal according to the seasons of the year and the sport he happened to be following; and, when in London, they stayed at hotels.

The Oxford Movement and the Cambridge Camden Society

By the time Sutton arrived in Cambridge in 1841 the great revival of English church life and enthusiasm known as the Oxford or Tractarian Movement was firmly established. Its history is well known[18] but to ensure parallels of dating, Tract 90, *Remarks on Certain Passages in the Thirty-Nine Articles* by the Revd. John Newman (later to be Cardinal) which unleashed the full force of opposition, appeared in the same year, 1841. So during nearly all Sutton's adult life in England there was religious controversy and by his English church building and furnishing work, he showed clearly that he was on the Tractarian side.

The Oxford fathers were primarily theologians with little or no interest in architecture, or church ornaments, or music: by contrast, the Tractarian-influenced Cambridge Camden Society's primary aims were in "aestheticks" [sic][19]. It was founded in 1839 by two undergraduates, J. M. Neale (1818-1866) and Benjamin Webb (1819-1865), and its motto was "*Donec templa refeceris*" (until the churches are restored). Members were keenly interested in architecture, church arrangement and decoration, liturgy and music; and were encouraged to inspect, sketch and report on medieval churches near the town. The Society's aims were to restore the medieval appearance of the English parish church, both inside and out, and there are few churches in the country today that do not show some feature heavily influenced by it. Sutton joined the Society during his first year at Cambridge[20].

John Sutton took no degree at Cambridge; perhaps his nerves would not have stood up to examinations, or he was thought not to be good enough at mathematics, then a *sine qua non* – judging by the state his affairs were in at his death, this is quite possible! But his time was certainly used fully, for he became a very fair classical scholar, did the groundwork for his book, *A Short Account of Organs* which was to be published in 1847, and became known to the Master and Fellows of his college as an enthusiast for the architecture and furnishing of churches. He also formed a friendship with Thomas Attwood Walmisley (1814-1856) Professor of Music at Cambridge from 1836 to his death[21]. Walmisley was taught music by his godfather, Thomas Attwood, organist of St. Paul's Cathedral, "in youth Mozart's pupil in Vienna, in old age Mendelssohn's host and friend in London". He was appointed organist to Trinity and St. John's Colleges in 1833 and later was deputy to the aged incumbent, Pratt, at King's College and the University Church as well; and all the time that Sutton was up, had rooms at Jesus College. He was the first professor to introduce musical lectures illustrated by practical examples and was a fine improviser in various styles on both piano and organ. He wrote a good deal of music for church and concert hall and directed at least some of the concerts Sutton arranged in his rooms for his Cambridge friends. Attwood's pupils may have formed something of a circle in London and if Sutton was admitted to it, it would explain how he was able to play and examine so many London organs for *A Short Account.*

Although there are no sources to indicate what Sutton may have read during his formative years, his membership of the Camden Society is a fair indication that he absorbed the general atmosphere of romantic medievalism which flourished during the early Victorian period – particularly among certain aristocratic families of the eighteen-thirties and eighteen-forties.[22] One influential source of such medievalism was *The Broadstone of Honour: Rules for the Gentlemen of England* which the Roman Catholic convert, Kenelm Digby (1800-1880), a contemporary of Sir Richard Sutton at Trinity College, Cambridge, had published in 1822[23]. The title is a translation of *Ehrenbreitstein*, the name of one of the most romantic castles on the Rhine, and the book was directed towards the restoration of the outlook of medieval chivalry among the noble and moneyed classes of Britain. In 1836, A. W. N. Pugin had unfavourably compared contemporary architectural practice with that of the Gothic Middle

Ages in *Contrasts*; while, echoing the provocative message of Carlyle's *Past and Present* (1843), in his novel *Sybil* (1845), the young politician Benjamin Disraeli blamed the development of Britain's "two nations" of rich and poor upon the failure of Church and Aristocracy to play the rôles which they had assumed in medieval society. Whether or not Sutton read Digby, Carlyle or Disraeli – we can be certain that he read Pugin – as a spiritually-minded aristocrat sensitive to the "condition of England", it must have been inevitable that he would be drawn into this cult of medievalism.

On 23 December, 1844, his undergraduate career in Cambridge having ended in the June of that year, John Sutton married Miss Emma Helena Sherlock, daughter of Colonel Sherlock of the King's Hussars and his wife, at Southwell Minster in Nottinghamshire. Here is the great tragedy of his life, for his new wife died after only a month of marriage, on 26 January, 1845, and was buried at West Tofts a week later. Nobody can ever know the full effects of such a shock on any young man, even though, after the fashion of those times, probably very few people outside the Sutton and Sherlock families, and John's own few close friends, knew that he was a widower for twenty-eight years. The romantic tradition of Digby decreed that a man of honour would spend his entire life in the service of one woman, whether she was available to receive and return his love or not, and while Sutton was as much at ease in women's company as in men's and could, for instance, discuss a young woman's marriage with a friend in writing, it does not seem that he ever had the remotest intention of finding another partner himself. "*Nach dem Tode seiner jungen Frau wollte sein Herz nur nach Gott und der Kirche gehören* (after his young wife's death, his heart desired to belong only to God and the Church)." This comment of Canon Zaun's is probably itself a little romanticised; but after some months, an opportunity arose for Sutton to busy himself to some purpose.

In 1845 the Master and Fellows of Jesus College, Cambridge, decided to have some work done on the college chapel. No formal minute of their decision remains, but at some time during the autumn an indirect approach was made to Sutton, suggesting that he might like to return to the College and take some part in the work. A note survives in the College Archives[24] from Edmund Randolph, a life-long friend of Sutton's and eventually his brother-in-law:

> "I heard from Sutton yesterday – he promises to do all he can in the money way for our Chapel – and seems to like the idea of returning to Jesus College. He thinks of writing to you on the subject.
>
> Edmund Randolph.
>
> He is staying at University College, Oxford."

Quite why he was asked, apart from sympathy with his bereavement, is not clear; an eminent architect, Anthony Salvin, had been appointed already and both the Dean and Chaplain were competent in Gothic. Anyway, John returned to rooms in Jesus College and in the following year the College regularised his position by appointing him a Fellow-Commoner: he would pay double the fees of an ordinary undergraduate but would be on equal terms with the senior members — including access to their cellar! This position he retained until the day of his death, so making a contribution every year to the college's finances. It seems that, while he was there, he lived rather apart from normal college life — "Sir John Sutton?" said a very aged man to the Revd. B. B. Edmonds, "Why, he was almost a recluse!" He emerged from his rooms to deal with the restoration of the chapel, to play the organ for the services in the Hall while the chapel was out of use, and to train and teach the boys' choir he recruited in the town.

The two Fellows of Jesus College with whom Sutton worked closely in the restoration of the chapel deserve mention: Osmond Fisher, 1817-1913, Fellow 1844-1858, was by inclination a geologist[25], but numbered archaeology, architecture, music and rose-growing among his interests. John Gibson, 1818-1892, Fellow 1842-1857, was equally interested in archaeology and architecture, and had the foremost part to play in the restoration of the chapel — "to his consummate taste and judgment the successful accomplishment of the enterprise was in large measure due"[26].

Both these men designed organ-cases — Fisher the one now at Harlton church near Cambridge[27], and Gibson that at King's Stanley church in Gloucestershire (and a copy of this is now in the Roman Catholic parish church at Stroud).[28] Gibson became Chairman of the Cambridge Architectural Society, the Camden Society's successor in the town and university, and in later years was to design the new organ-gallery at Kiedrich[29].

Augustus Welby Northmore Pugin, 1812-1852, had come into Sutton's life a little earlier: we can be certain that he had met some of the family in October 1844 when he went to West Tofts to receive instructions about Lady Sutton's first Chantry, but his earlier work at Oxburgh Hall quite nearby may well have attracted the attention of the neighbouring gentry. In any case, by the time work was begun on Jesus College Chapel in 1846, he and Sutton were firm friends. His own fame as architect, designer of furniture and enunciator of principles is assured[30]. His career began in 1835 and in the following seventeen years he designed more than a hundred buildings, wrote eight major books, and founded a prosperous business in the production of metalwork and stained glass windows from his own designs[31]. He became a Roman Catholic in 1835 and could see little good in any architecture produced after the fifteenth century because he felt that men then ceased to design or build for the glory of God. His own style was modelled on medieval examples and he travelled widely to collect them or to make drawings of them: he wrote, "I strive to *revive not invent*"[32] – and broadly speaking this was true. Though generally intolerant of those who disagreed with him, Pugin could be wonderfully persuasive when he chose, and all his life Sutton followed Pugin's principles of architecture and decoration. Pugin may be said to be the most famous of Sutton's English friends, and when he encouraged him to go to the Continent to see the treasures of Gothic to be found there, he gave him an introduction to the most famous man who befriended him in Belgium.

Jean-Baptiste-Charles-François, Baron de Béthune, 1821-1894, was of similar aristocratic background to John Sutton and of deeply convinced Roman Catholic faith.[33] From Sutton's many letters to him he appears as utterly dependable, sensible and loyal – a true friend. He was a church furnisher, designer of stained glass and a reluctant architect. His buildings are few – but he was a great propagator of Gothicism through the Saint-Luc school of architects and the Guild of St. Thomas and St. Lutgard, which he founded[34].

One can trace several aspects of John Sutton's character back to one or other of these men: the single-mindedness in following his chosen path he must have inherited from his father; his grasp of the classics, and regard for the poor, from Christopher Bird; the copying of medieval features in church architecture and furnishing from Pugin.

We take up the narrative again: Sutton and Edmund Randolph went to Europe in the summers of 1847 and 1848, and during the 1848 tour Sutton gave Béthune a copy of his book, *A Short Account*, which had been published the previous year and contained drawings by Pugin illustrating how Gothic organ-cases should be designed.

On All Saints' Day 1849, Jesus College Chapel was re-opened with choral Mattins and Holy Communion: the Professor of Music, T. A. Walmisley, played the organ Sutton had presented and which he had designed in the style of the seventeenth-century instruments – and it is certain that he had a great influence on the design of its case, although Pugin was responsible for the detailed drawings. Walmisley also wrote an anthem for the occasion – *Ponder my Words*, for four boys' voices – and Sutton himself must either have directed the choir or listened to the whole effect from the congregation. This service must have been one of the high spots of his life, for the college chapel held a great place in his affections and he had spent much time and work upon its restoration.

Meanwhile, work had begun upon the church at West Tofts (with Pugin as architect) as Sutton's memorial to his mother. It must be assumed that the first Chantry had been finished three years earlier, as a bill from Messrs. Hardman for painting it and the tomb it contained is dated 5 December, 1846. Work was commenced on the foundations for the new north aisle of the church itself on 26 April, 1849, and this and the new south porch were completed and taken into use the following year. The cost of the north aisle only, according to the Faculty issued for the work, was to be £1,320 and, though the drawings for the rest of the church are dated 1850, it is understandable that a halt was called to the actual building work for some time. It was not to be resumed until 1855.

Sutton himself remained in Cambridge for a while and must often have pondered his future. He seems never to have had any interest in the sporting life, or in managing an estate, which were really the only occupations open to a baronet then: his interests and gifts were in ecclesiology and music, and while his brothers, Augustus and Frederick, were able to exercise the same interests to a great deal of purpose in the priesthood, it was really not *done* for a baronet to seek Holy Orders. 1854 was the year in which he left England, except for visits. There is evidence of some spiritual or nervous crisis in the Béthune letters, but nothing detailed enough upon which to base a diagnosis. He may have had some disagreement with his father – and indeed, on his own evidence, Sir Richard's last years were coloured by fits of rage "at times fearfully resembling insanity"[35]. He may have felt that there was little to keep him in Cambridge and, within a couple of years, his two collaborators in the Jesus College work had both left university life for country parsonages. He may have felt that, on Pugin's death in 1852, the mantle of collecting and collating evidence of Gothic design and practice in Europe had to fall on somebody and, as he was free of marital ties, it might as well fall upon him. Earlier visits to the Continent would have shown him that it was far simpler to gain access to the churches and their treasuries if he was himself a Roman Catholic; and certainly if he needed music, dignity in worship and a relatively liberal and parochial outlook in his religion, it was pointless to search for it in the British embassy or consular chapels controlled by the Colonial and Continental Church Society, in those days a firmly Protestant body.

There has never been any hint that the reason for John Sutton's leaving England was some sort of scandal: numbers of men left the country in those days because of debts or marital irregularity, but he was not among them. The decision to become a Roman Catholic would not be understood by his father or the rest of the family: Cambridge friends and acquaintances would regard him as something of a renegade, for very few Cambridge men had "gone over to Rome" in the wake of Newman and Ward of Oxford. There is a tradition in the Béthune family that Sutton's change of faith was due to his talks with Felix Béthune, and certainly he received instruction from him, but we can look to Augustus Pugin for the original influence behind the decision. Sutton embraced the Roman Catholic faith before Canon Felix Béthune at Roeselare in 1855, and was confirmed by Bishop Malou of Bruges (incidentally, a different diocese – but the Bishop was related to the Béthunes) the following day. He seems then to have left Belgium and gone to Bonn for a while, for there are several letters in the Béthune collection from that town, and then to have taken rooms in Freiburg-im-Breisgau where there was "a tolerable piano".[36]

Sir Richard Sutton died suddenly on 13 November, 1855 (so if John had wanted to return and take up life again in England, he had every opportunity to do so). As always where landed estates are concerned, there was a great deal of business for the eldest son and although, as he said, his father had left a "most just" will, a great deal of cash was needed to carry it into execution (for instance, each son except the eldest was left £40,000 on reaching the age of 25). The new baronet was needed to give his consent to what the trustees and agents felt were the best decisions in the circumstances – the immediate sale of the hunting pack of hounds, the stud of horses, and the whole Lynford estate (it had been bought by Sir Richard anyway in the eighteen-twenties and was no part of the ancient Sutton heritage), and 94 Piccadilly was let again, this time to Lord Palmerston. This work must have occupied John in England for most of 1856.

In 1857 he returned to Germany and settled in the *Pfarrhaus* or rectory at Kiedrich in the Rheingau (between Wiesbaden and Rüdesheim). He knew of the ancient organ there, either by hearsay or by a previous visit, and although it was unplayable, his inspection of it convinced him that it was quite possible to have it restored, made musical again, and altered back to what he felt its medieval appearance must have been. Having somehow, without any fluency in German, convinced the parish priest of his good intentions, he supervised the dismantling of the organ by a Belgian organ-builder – and then all disappeared to Bruges.

Meanwhile his brother, Augustus Sutton, was noting progress on the church at West Tofts: on 27 June, 1855, the foundations for the new chancel were begun, and at Christmas the following year the chancel and second Sutton Chantry were completed and the whole structure was thrown into one "to my great dilight" [sic][37]. Furnishing, including the building of an organ, occupied another seven months, and then on 31 August, 1857, there was a great service of dedication. There is no evidence that John Sutton was there – or that he was not, but judging by his later behaviour at the Assize Sermon in Nottingham, it seems most likely that he stayed in Belgium.

By 1858 he had bought two old houses in the Gouden-Hand-Straat in Bruges and was writing detailed instructions to Béthune about the alterations, painting and furnishing of them. In fact he never

The back of Sir John Sutton's house in Bruges overlooking the Golden Hand Canal. On the wooden loggia was written: Ave Maria grā. plena

lived in the one he had altered for himself, as the old couple who were tenants at the time of purchase were poor and he had no intention of turning them out. He lived, then, in the next-door house, altering both to give a complete Gothic atmosphere ("... down to the very bindings of the books", says Zaun[38]) to the dwelling he really wanted.

Most of his life after this date was spent either at Kiedrich – where he bought three properties in 1869 and had them made into a single house for himself – or Bruges, or in long journeys around Belgium and Germany in search of Gothic features, furnishings, stained glass or whatever, for copying. His aim in these journeys is expressed by a letter from Gibson, the former Dean of Jesus College, Cambridge, to Béthune:

> "22 May, 1861... If Sir John has taken to travelling during the winter and spring months, I think he will be now a long time before he returns for any length of time to his home in Bruges. But I think he does well to explore as he (illegible) service in doing what architects have little time to do – and in bringing to light undiscovered works."[39]

The choir-school of Kiedrich received its endowment, and therefore the legal re-founding documents, in December 1865; its progress from that date was neither uneventful nor entirely satisfactory, but by the time of Sutton's death nearly eight years later, it was clear that the plainsong of the ancient archdiocese of Mainz was re-established there on a firm foundation, and supported by the diocesan authorities (of Limburg-on-the-Lahn) and the enthusiasm of the Kiedrich people.

In 1867, Sutton was appointed High Sheriff of Nottinghamshire: as such, it was his duty to protect and support Her Majesty's judges whenever they visited the county town for the Assizes, and to be their host at dinner. George Mann wrote to Béthune on 23 January 1867:

> "Sir John Sutton is name[d] 'High Sheriff' for the County of Nottingham this year, and in the month of March our friend Sir John will go to Nottingham and accompany the Judges every day to the court of Assizes in his own Carriage with six horses and give a grand dinner every evening. Mgr. Boone will be the Chaplain of Sir John..."[40]

The local press did not make much of the High Sheriff, probably because most people's attention was concentrated on a particularly unpleasant murder case, but the *Nottingham Journal* for 4 February, 1867, reported:

> "Sir John Sutton, Bart, the new High Sheriff for Nottinghamshire, is, it is said, at present in Rome. Sir John is the son of the late Sir Richard Sutton, of Quorndon, near

Loughborough, and brother of Mr. R. Sutton, the owner of the celebrated race horse Lord Lyon, the winner of the Derby, the St. Leger and the Two Thousand Guineas last year. Sir John is a patron of four livings, but as he is a Roman Catholic, the presentation to them during his lifetime is vested in the University to which they belong. Sir John, who was educated at Eton and Cambridge, married in 1844 the daughter of Col. Sherlock K.H., and succeeded to the title and estates on the death of his father in 1855."

On 12 March the same paper reported:

"... on the bench near the Judge, besides the High Sheriff and Under Sheriff, there were an Italian priest (Father Boone of Rome, domestic chaplain to Sir John Sutton), and Mr. G.B. Eyston, of London (Sir John's agent) ... From the Guild Hall his Lordship proceeded to St. Mary's Church, escorted by the borough and county officials. Sir John Sutton accompanied the learned Judge to the church doors, but then returned to his carriage and drove back to his hotel ... As the High Sheriff has not appointed a clergyman of the Church of England to be chaplain, the assize sermon was preached by the Rev. Prebendary Morse (Vicar of St. Mary's)..."

There is no indication in any of the surviving documents that Sutton spent any more time than odd days in England after 1855, in spite of Zaun's statement that he remained friendly with his family; and when the only visit by a brother that we know of took place in November 1865, he left for Kiedrich – letter from George Mann to Béthune, 20 November 1865:

"... It is very probable that the Revd. Frederick Sutton may come this week and I must entertain him ... Sir John started for Kiedrich this morning..."[41]

One would have thought that even if business called, as it must have done when the *Chorstift* documents were being drawn up, a day or two spent in his youngest brother's company would have been the least that brotherly affection, and politeness, demanded.

All these years work was going on both in Kiedrich, in the restoration of the church, and in Bruges with the establishment and provision of three consecutive homes for the *Seminarium Anglo-Belgicum* founded by Sutton to provide Roman Catholic priests for England, and especially for her sea-port towns. It was this last work that provided the chief grounds for the bestowal on Sutton, by the Pope, of the decoration of Knight Commander of the Order of St. Gregory the Great[42], in 1870 (the petition by Canon de Hearne,

Rector of the Seminary, is dated 8 May of that year, and the papal document 3 June). Weight was added to the Belgian petition by the Bishop of Plymouth, in England, who wrote that Sutton had supplied many of the needs of his diocese – which explains Zaun's otherwise unsupported statement that half Sutton's income remained in England, partly for the building of churches and convents. In the absence of any records of money coming from Sutton in the diocese of Plymouth it must be assumed that the donations were made in strict secrecy, so we are unlikely ever to know which churches and convents benefited from them.

Sutton was invariably kind to his servants, though like many people whose main concern was with the Church and related things, he had in fact very few – only two are ever mentioned: "old Sistra" the cook-housekeeper in Bruges, and "my man" who seems to have gone everywhere with him. A cook would hardly be needed in Kiedrich, as when he was there, Sutton always went to the parish

Letter from Sir John Sutton to Prälat Schneider

priest's house for the mid-day meal, and perhaps the man-servant was provided for there too. Sutton was alive to their faults; he once described Sistra as "a rum-tempered 'un" when inviting George Mann to stay and, if Roman Catholic servants were required in the nineteenth century, they often had to be Irish. With the poor diet which was all Irish people could manage then, they could rarely be robust. Hugh Quillan, for instance, was buried in Sint-Kruis cemetery in Bruges in 1868, aged 25, and the care of his successor, unnamed, occupied Sutton for the whole of the winter of 1872-73. They went to Amilie-les-Bains in the south of France so it is likely that the man was consumptive. By May 1873 he was fit to travel and they returned to Bruges. But now Sir John himself caught a cold which rapidly developed and turned into rheumatic fever and the doctor "could only recommend complete rest". Saddened by the fact that several of his projects, especially the English Seminary, were left unfinished, Sir John Sutton, third Baronet, died on 6 June 1873.

"Almost all Bruges mourned"[43] – as well they might, for no poor person was ever turned away from his door. If Kiedrich tradition was that he kept a leather bag of sovereigns on the table from which every beggar reeived a golden pound, it is likely that Bruges had the same treatment. He was buried on 9 June. Ten pupils of his seminary carried him from his house to St. Gillis' church where the Requiem was celebrated by the parish priest M. van Coillie. The Bishop would have officiated himself but for a confirmation tour on the other side of his diocese. The music was directed by M. Amandus Leun, the choirmaster whose salary was paid by Sutton, and was sung by the seminary students[44]: the coffin was surrounded by a hundred and six candles embellished with the Sutton arms, and the choir and sanctuary of the church were hung with black. After the service, a hearse with six horses conveyed the body to Sint-Kruis cemetery where it was buried in a side-chamber of the family grave of the Boones (Mgr. A. A. Boone was in charge of a great deal of business for Sutton in Belgium, and did his best to grapple with affairs after his death). The same day, twelve hundred three-pound loaves were distributed to the poor of Bruges, and the same number a month later.

Sutton had, in fact, intended to prepare a vault for himself and Canon Zaun in Kiedrich churchyard under the Crucifixion group, but never got around to doing the work. His wish, however, was carried out a century after his death: the *Chorregent* at the time, Herr Kurt Erkes, asked the author where the Belgian grave was and, after a visit to the Aldeburgh Festival in England, at the invitation of Mr. Benjamin Britten (as he then was) the choir paid a visit to the cemetery of Sint-Kruis and sang at the grave. Long negotiations with the Bruges authorities followed and eventually, on 22 October, 1974, the coffin was exhumed and driven to Kiedrich where it was laid in the choir-school. A new outer coffin was made of century-old oak by a local craftsman and on All Souls' Day, 2 November, Sir John Sutton's body was re-interred on the north side of Kiedrich churchyard after a solemn Requiem in the parish church, celebrated by the Assistant Bishop of Limburg, with the assistance of former *Chorregents* and several priests of the district. The grave-stone, designed by Jean de Béthune, was also transported from Bruges and re-erected over the grave; it reads:

> *Pray for the soul of Sir John Sutton, B*^{art}
> *of Norwood Notts. England: who, full of good works*
> *died on June 5*th *1873, aged 53.*
> *On whose soul and all Xtian souls may God have mercy.*
> *Amen.*

On high days, when a procession goes round the churchyard, a visit is always paid to the grave of Kiedrich's *grösster Wohltäter* (Kiedrich's greatest benefactor) and the following prayer is recited:

> "Lord, we pray Thee for the soul of our benefactor John Sutton. His life was dedicated to Thy glory and the service of his neighbour. His heart belonged to the poor and needy; bodily and spiritual necessity found with him an open ear and an open hand. Our churches where Thou art worshipped, owe him thanks for restoring their dignity and beauty: he gave new life to the venerable Mainz plainsong for the celebration of the liturgy, through the founding of our choir, and so ensured its living on until today. For all this, our district of Kiedrich has owed him thanks for more than a century. With our gratitude and respect, his mortal remains were brought home to us. We promise to play our part in all his legacy to us by faithful service to, and enrichment of, the holy liturgy. We pray Thee, though, O Lord, that he himself may be granted the joy of taking part in the heavenly praises before Thy throne for ever. Through Christ our Lord, Amen."

It seems right to insert here a few quotations which throw light upon Sutton's spiritual life in his mature years on the Continent. Naturally there are not many, for the English nobility of the time wore neither their spiritual nor moral hearts on their sleeves. But there are glimpses here and there:

> letter to Mgr. Schneider, 24 February 1870:

> "... There is a good deal of snow, and I have not been to Mass for 3 days, as I get my feet wet in going to the Church, and then catch cold at Mass in the cold church..."[45]

SOME DATES, PLACES AND FORMATIVE INFLUENCES

*Sutton's tombstone on the north side of the churchyard at Kiedrich.
It was designed by Jean de Béthune*

which makes one think that he followed the example of a good many ordinary people in those days, and attended the early Mass every day. A couple of months earlier he had caught himself out in a serious breach of good manners:

> "Coblenz, Decr. 27th., 1869.
>
> Dear Herr Schneider, I have just read your letter over again, and am shocked to find that I have neither observed, nor thanked you, both for saying that you intend to say Mass for me tomorrow and also for your kind gratulations for my feast Day (27 December is the feast of St. John the Evangelist) – This shews how much more I think of this world and my common occupations, than of the next, and of things really belonging to the Catholic Religion, it is very wrong of me, but it is also a *lesson* for me as it shews me the real state of my mind, and how much it is *preoccupied*, by things that interest me. However you must have patience with me, the Old Choral, which I have played several times over and the Lettner affair, and its *possible* consequences, have filled my mind to the exclusion of more serious thoughts. Again thanking you very much for the Mass, and also for remembring [*sic*] my Feast day,
>
> Believe me yrs. very much obliged
> J. Sutton."[46]

We will not be far wrong in assuming that Sutton found his deepest spiritual satisfaction either in buildings restored or built according to true principles and furnished richly for worship, or in the actual liturgical worship offered in them, prepared with care and sung as well as scholarship and musicianship could manage. At Bruges and Kiedrich this worship was rich enough on Sundays, with the Kurmainzer plainsong in one place and Palestrina's music in the other, and for week-days, physical work on the churches or mental work in planning the seminary, arranging for the restoration of something medieval, or an organ, or writing his detailed letters about these sorts of things, was all hallowed by the daily Mass.

One further note: Canon Zaun testified

> "*Oft hörte ich ihn sagen, 'Ich bin kein Theologe, aber ich weiss, dass die Kirche unfehlbar ist und sein muss: das ist mir genug, um Alles zu glauben, was die katholische Kirche lehrt.'* (I heard him say often, 'I'm no theologian, but I know that the Church is infallible, and must be; that is enough for me to believe all the catholic Church teaches.')"[47]

Infallibility was in the air: the Vatican Council of 1869-70 dealt, among other things, with the infallibility of the Pope, and it must have been talked about for some years beforehand, and certainly up to the time of Sutton's death. The sentiment was commonplace enough in the mouths of laymen at the time[48], and its propaganda value should not be forgotten, but in fact Sutton must have heard, if not absorbed, plenty of theology from Pugin, the Camden Society, the senior Common Room at Jesus College, the de Béthune brothers and the Bishop of Bruges. But he had chosen his place behind the scenes, and confined himself firmly to his own principles of action.

What sort of companion was John Sutton to his friends? – for he led a very retired life at all times, even going to the length of having letters sent under an assumed name (Schmidt!) to an accommodation address in Kiedrich[49] to conceal his presence from the villagers. But to his friends, especially to those who shared his interests, he was probably a delightful, gently humorous companion. Walking in the "Inspruck" [*sic*] and Salzburg countryside with his brother-in-law Edmund Randolph[50]; writing to thank Béthune for a little supper party:

> "Antwerp 19 February 1856... Will you tell Madame Béthune, that her Protestant Friend desires to be very kindly remembered to her, but that he fears she is a terrible bigot, and that during one of his visits she will blow him up with Gunpowder, in short that she has *revived in him* all his *childish fears* of Popery, and that he fears if he *eats too much supper at her house*, his dreams will be of *Gunpowder Plot, Sicilian Vespers* – and Mass$^{cre.}$ of Bartholomew etc. etc..."[51]

And in contrast to his brothers, who always wrote to Hardmans in the third person, he sent "best wishes to Mrs. Hardman and the children"[52].

These are small quotations, but all we have to show how Sutton communicated with his friends. If we add to them the politeness, directness and enthusiasm of the other letters, we can make up an attractive picture of an English gentleman with just a few unusual tastes for the age he lived in: and if we add to this the influences he came under in his formative years, the people he met and the large income he enjoyed, we can understand how he was able to accomplish the work described in the following chapters. Canon Zaun, writing in *Geschichte des Ortes und der Pfarrei Kiedrich*, described him thus:

"Sir John was a nobleman in the authentic sense of the word. His heart was pure, without haughtiness or bearing a grudge; he had no vulgar feeling, still less any capability of underhand dealing. Never did he break his given word. Carefully and conscientiously fulfilling everything which duty and justice seemed to demand of him, he hated deceit and a deceiver as much as any other fall from goodness. Whoever tried to appear otherwise to him than he really was, and did not escape his sharp eye, was to him a *humbug*, and lost for ever any hope to know him better, or to reach any relationship with him. His great unselfishness and generosity was often abused by work-people and beggars, which he knew and saw completely through; often because of their circumstances, he bore this silently, but with the sort of people who tried to cheat him intentionally, he broke off all communication for ever. Whoever asked for anything from him without actually needing it, certainly obtained it; but with the gift came an end of giving, because he found all self-seeking insupportable. He did not easily allow strangers into his company, so as not to be troublesome himself, and not (in his turn) himself to be troubled. When anyone won his confidence, it was unlimited, steadfast and high-minded. He arranged for the wishes of his friends and acquaintances to be carried out with gentle persistence; and sought in the most moving way, without wounding human sensibilities, to satisfy them – even if this cost him a great deal in money or effort. He was always grateful for the smallest attention or service from others. Used to a simple life himself, he rejoiced from his heart when he could spend some hours in the company of friends and acquaintances. He would entertain them with musical performances, and was himself foremost in presenting the best pieces. His own organ- and piano- playing was enchantingly lovely (*bezaubernd schön*) and deeply felt, especially when he improvised in the style of the great classical composers. He loved Handel, Beethoven, Mozart and Sebastian Bach the best. He mixed happily with the people on pilgrimage and at other festal times in order to know their philosophy and thoughts. He delighted the children and himself on these occasions by throwing them small coins, with which he had previously filled his pockets. He also made sure that there was enough to eat and drink on those days, especially for the poorer pilgrims. With all his noble birth and riches, Sir John was above all things modest and self-effacing. He never obtruded himself on anyone, or troubled anyone. Although he understood perfectly how to mix with the foremost of the nobility, he preferred (given the opportunity) the conversation of the simplest country people. In clothing and furniture, in eating and drinking, he was ever simple and sober. He never showed offended pride; even the ingratitude of rude people could never stop him doing them further good, because he looked for his reward for well-doing from God rather than from men."[53]

REFERENCES

1 Most of the biographical information in this Chapter comes from Zaun: *Geschichte des Ortes und der Pfarrei Kiedrich.*

2 Burke, *Peerage, Baronetage and Knightage.*

3 *Dictionary of National Biography*, and Burke, *Peerage, Baronetage*

and Knightage.
4 Obituary in the *Illustrated London News*, 24 November 1855, p. 611.
5 Burke, *op. cit.*
6 Zaun, p. 164.
7 *ibid.*
8 *Eton College Register.*
9 J. R. de S. Honey, *Tom Brown's Universe*, (Millington, 1977), p. 202.
10 The facts in this paragraph are taken from *A Memorial of The Revd. Christopher Bird*, a pamphlet privately printed and circulated in 1867. A copy is in the archives at Chollerton.
11 A copy of a lecture delivered to the Cäcilien-Verein at Cologne on 12 August 1873: *Kiedricher Zeitung* III, 1980.
12 Article by J. T. Fowler, *Durham Cathedral Quarterly*, Easter 1915.
13 *The Parish Choir* I (1846), p. 135.
14 J. T. Fowler, *Life and Letters of John Bacchus Dykes*, p. 52.
15 Venn.
16 *Complete Baronetage* V, p. 162.
17 Fulford, *Royal Dukes* (London, 1933), p. 302-3.
18 J. W. C. Wand, *A History of the Modern Church* (London: Methuen, 1952), pp. 205-220.
19 J. F. White, *The Cambridge Movement* (Cambridge University Press, 1962).
20 *Ecclesiologist* 1841 List of Members.
21 *New Grove's Dictionary of Music and Musicians* and Scholes, *Oxford Companion to Music*
22 The whole movement is best described in Mark Girouard, *Return to Camelot* (Yale University Press, 1981).
23 Kenelm Digby, *The Broadstone of Honour: Rules for the Gentlemen of England* (Rivington, 1822)
24 Jesus College Archives.
25 Obituary in *Ely Diocesan Remembrancer*, September 1914.
26 *History of Jesus College*, p. 158.
27 *Ely Diocesan Remembrancer, ut sup.*
28 A letter of 1876 in the Béthune Archive makes this quite plain.
29 Minute-book for the Society in Cambridge University Library: and Sutton's letters in Chapter II.
30 Stanton, pp. 10-12.
31 Stanton, p. 10.
32 Stanton, p. 11.
33 Jules Helbig, *Le Baron Béthune, Fondateur des Écoles Saint-Luc*, (Lille/Bruges, 1906).
34 Letter to the author dated 29 October 1985 from Andries Van den Abeele, Belgium.
35 Béthune.
36 Béthune.
37 *West Tofts Burial Register*, Norfolk County Records Office.
38 Zaun, p. 167.
39 Béthune.
40 Béthune.
41 Béthune.
42 Vatican Archives.
43 *Stones and Story*, p. 296.
44 Rembry, *De Bekende Pastoors de St. Gillis te Brugge*, p. 679.
45 Schneider letters.
46 Schneider letters.
47 Zaun, p. 173.
48 *ibid.*
49 Schneider.
50 Béthune.
51 Béthune.
52 Hardman collection.
53 Zaun, pp. 171-2.

CHAPTER II

Sir John Sutton – Organ-Lover

The organ is an instrument that gets into people's bones; those who love it can always talk about it, sometimes to the boredom to despair of their friends, and because no one organ is exactly like another there are endless possibilities of design of cases, variation of stops and position in buildings. We cannot know how or when John Sutton was first bitten by this particular bug, but his father began negotiations for an organ for him when he was only thirteen years old. Certainly he was very knowledgeable about the organ when he arrived in Cambridge in 1841, and he spent a great deal of his "career at Jesus in writing a book upon organs"[1] with the title, *A Short Account of Organs built in England from the Reign of King Charles the Second to the Present Time*.[2] Some critique of this book is necessary if we are to understand his outlook on organs which was very unusual for his time.

One of the results of the Oxford Movement was the publication of a great number of books. Those coming from Oxford itself were very learned in the academic sense – *The Library of the Fathers*[3] comes to mind at once – while those from Cambridge, under the strong influence of the Camden Society, concentrated on what J. M. Neale called "Aesthetics"[4] – matters concerning the fabric and furnishing of churches and the conduct of services. Neale, with F. Webb, published an edition of Durandus of Mende's *Rationale Divinorum Officiorum*[5] described as "a compendium of liturgical knowledge with mystical interpretation"[6]: on Durandus' mystical and symbolical precepts the Society, and Sutton, took their stand. It was followed by other books on members' chosen subjects, distinguished by thoroughness and accurate observation.

The quotation above at ([1]) is the first evidence we have that the *Short Account*, published anonymously, might have a discoverable author. In fact it seems to have been always an open secret that Sutton wrote the book: for instance, a footnote in the second edition of Hopkins and Rimbault's *The Organ, its History and Construction* says "the work is published anonymously, but its author is understood to be Mr. Sutton, of Jesus College, Cambridge".[7] Further on is another footnote: "There is great room for improvement in organ-cases in England. We may walk many a weary mile without seeing a truly catholic design... Of a far different character are the designs of the late

Mr. Pugin, appended to Mr. Sutton's *Short Account of Organs Built in England etc.,* 1847. But then these would be termed *Roman* Catholic."[8] – presumably because of Pugin's well-known Roman Catholicism. John Baron, in the second edition of *Scudamore Organs*, attributes the book to Sutton in a preface[9], and the first edition had a completely different note with the same object. Canon Dickson was also familiar with the idea of Sutton's authorship of the book[10], and indeed all authors who have quoted from it since Hopkins and Rimbault have simply assumed this, and have written as though it was an accepted fact. Sutton himself never disclaimed it, as far as is known, and indeed a copy of the book in the Béthune Archive at Marke in Belgium has written on the fly-leaf: "With J. Sutton's kind regards. Aug. 4, 1848."

There is a way in which the authorship of *A Short Account* may be proved. On pp. 54-55 the writer mentions two chamber organs by Bernard Schmidt in his possession and there is an illustration of the smaller one at the end of the chapter. This organ is now (1988) in the music room at St. Peter's Organ Works in London, and some years ago Mr. Noël Mander allowed a copy to be taken of the inscription glued inside the lid (written out *in toto* on p. 70). The handwriting is undoubtedly that of our subject and the obvious conclusion is that the people who attributed the *Short Account* to him are right.[11]

It is easy to see from the type, and the general old-fashioned appearance of the book, that it was printed by Charles Whittingham (known as *the nephew* to distinguish him from his uncle who bore the same name) at the Chiswick Press.[12] In 1843 Whittingham had caused an old-faced fount of great primer type cut originally in 1720 to be revived, and the first books to be printed with it were an Eton prize *Juvenal*, and *The Diary of Lady Willoughby*, both in 1844 (though, as will be seen below, the *Diary* was not actually published until 1845). The whole title of this second work deserves reproduction, because it so chimes in with Sutton's outlook upon organs in his book published a couple of years later:

> "So much of the Diary of Lady Willoughby as relates to her Domestic History, and to the Eventful Period of the Reign of CHARLES the First. Imprinted for Longman, Brown, Green and Longmans, Paternoster Row, over against Warwick Lane, in the City of London, 1845. The Style of Printing and general appearance of this Volume have been adopted by the Publishers merely to be in accordance with the Design of the Author, who in this Work personates a lady of the seventeenth century.
> Printed by C. Whittingham, Chiswick."

The inside appearance of this book is just the same as the *Short Account*, and subsequently several other works of an antiquarian flavour, such as the *Life of Mrs. Godolphin* (1848), the *Life of Nicholas Ferrar* (1852), Jeremy Taylor's *Worthy Communicant* and the *Works* of George Herbert (both 1853) were printed using the same type-face.

There is a copy of Sutton's work in existence[13] which has another publisher's name on the title-page – Richard Nichols, Birmingham, 1847. Both binding and paper give the impression of being a little later than the standard edition, in spite of the title-page bearing the same date.

Inside there is a *Preface* of eighteen pages giving an account of some of the work of one or two organ-builders "before the works of the celebrated Father Smith"[14] and then an *Introduction* of fourteen pages detailing the reasons for the writing of the book. Then follow chapters describing the organs of Bernard Schmidt, as he is now to be called, Renatus Harris (Ch. 2), Schreider, Schwarbrook, Byfield, Bridge and Jordan (Ch. 3), Snetzler (Ch. 4), Green (Ch. 5), Avory, England, Elliott, and then a section on Hill, Gray and Bishop (Ch. 6), and finally in Ch. 7 some remarks on organ-cases, leading to the five designs by A. W. N. Pugin.

The *Short Account* is an excellent example of the Camden Society's inductive method of deciding the best way to design a feature of a church. What was this? The founders and Committee were firmly convinced that medieval church building and furnishing was all done in accordance with certain discoverable principles, and that these principles could be discovered by examining as many unaltered examples as possible. "It must be remembered that Ecclesiology, like Astronomy and Geology, is an Inductive Science. No sound and truthful generalizations can be hoped for without a careful examination of particulars and for this work our Society is peculiarly adapted."[15]

How was the Camden Society so adapted? At least in its early days every member was bound to visit a church within four miles of the University Church weekly[16] and shortly this activity broadened out to include the whole country. It was not long before the Society published helps: *A Few Hints on the Practical Study of Ecclesiastical Antiquities for the Use of the Cambridge Camden Society* appeared for the first time in 1839, and *A Handbook of English Ecclesiology* in 1847. Probably the most important of these helps was the *Church Scheme*, or *Blank Form for the Description of a Church*, which was a check-list of the various features and arrangements which might be found in any parish church.[17] Four editions appeared in May 1839, and publication was continued for a long period. It contained a series of headings and spaces to be filled up by the church visitor, by the use of which, with sketches, a complete description of a particular church and of all its features and fittings could be built up. A tremendous amount of information was assembled from these *Church Schemes*, and it was possible to compare a given feature of similar date in any number of churches and so arrive at a rule for reproducing it in the mid-nineteenth century – for the Society believed that rules governing the design and placing of all manner of church items existed in medieval times, and that virtually nothing could be explained as occurring by chance, accident, or the personal whim of the craftsman.

> "It is plain, that the only way to arrive at any general principles of Ecclesiology, is to observe and describe the details and arrangements of unmutilated churches or parts of churches: and from a large collection of such observations, if carefully recorded, much advantage may accrue to the science."[18]

When the *Short Account* is read it is obvious that Sutton had absorbed this sort of philosophy and applied it to organs. He had gone on many journeys "taking" organs as other Camden Society members "took" a complete church and its contents; he must have made full notes on them for his own use, listing the stops of each one and commenting on its tone and touch, and sketching the cases. These details were worked up later into the descriptive chapters of the *Short Account* and, like many contributors to *The Ecclesiologist*, he could be very sharp in his criticism; even his favourite Bernard Smith did not escape.[19]

But more was required of a good Camden Society man than just criticism; he was expected to know how a given feature of a church should be designed according to the principles worked out by the inductive method. The Society had as its ideal the Decorated style of medieval architecture – "the Decorated style ... is that to which only ... we ought to return"[20] – and in architecture Sutton was at one with them, but it was impossible for anyone to return to the fourteenth century for authentic unaltered examples of organs, for none were known to exist in England by 1845. He took as his ideal the earliest organs known to him, those of the late seventeenth century, built by men almost universally admired among historically-minded musicians, Bernard Smith and Renatus Harris. Even here, though, there was tension between historic facts and Camden ideals in the actual size of organs, for the Society, in a weighty article, declared roundly, "We hope that no more organs ... may be put up in our beautiful old churches."[21] The reasons for this attempted ban seem to have been first, that the almost universal place for parish church organs in the middle of the nineteenth century was a west gallery – and the Society loathed galleries only slightly less than they loathed "pues" [*sic*]: secondly, the preferred place for an organ was to be on the floor of the church, at the west end of nave or aisles, but even then it must not obscure any window or ancient feature and therefore it must be small. The roomy, often twenty feet and more high, and above all classical (and hence pagan) organ-cases of the seventeenth and eighteenth centuries were obviously candidates for the axe.

In another article eighteen months later[22] the author observed about cathedrals:

> "The choral establishment is supposed to be sufficient by itself to sing the service; yet, if it should be wished to obtain greater solemnity, it would be perhaps narrow-minded to object to the use of a choir-organ ... Now, if the organ be restricted to this use, it will be seen that the great size of most modern examples is unnecessary and injurious. For no greater compass is required than would be sufficient to support or equal the vocal musick: to drown the voice is plainly most wrong and undesirable."[23]

– and the article went on to advocate two organs in cathedral and collegiate churches, one to accompany the choir and the second for use with "large assemblies of worshippers". A little later on, harking back to the previous article, the author observed:

> "We still believe that the former evil is mainly to be attributed to the increased size and greater importance given to the organ. The remedy of such cases is at hand: to augment the voices, or else to diminish or silence the instrument."

By the vocabulary and style the article does not seem to be by Sutton, but he was either much influenced by it or agreed with it already, because the argument of the *Short Account* is directly against the prevailing trend of his time in England – for the eighteen-forties and -fifties saw a great renaissance in British organ-building, led by William Hill the organ-builder[24], and his collaborator and enthusiastic adviser, Dr. Henry John Gauntlett[25]. The reason why Gauntlett advocated more powerful organs was that he had travelled to Holland and North Germany and had been much impressed by the hearty congregational singing there – something not common in Britain at the time. He believed that this uplifting sound was due to large, or at least forceful, organs in good acoustical surroundings, and determined to do all he could to promote a similar state of parochial church music in England. By 1847 he and Hill had provided organs of this sort at Christ Church, Newgate Street in London, St. Peter's, Cornhill, St. Olave, Southwark, Worcester Cathedral, Great George Street Chapel, Liverpool, Eastbrook Chapel, Bradford, and Ashton-under-Lyne Parish Church.[26] The visits of Felix Mendelssohn to London and Birmingham[27], and his playing of the works of J.S. Bach upon the few organs that were then suited to this music, contributed a great deal to the movement: however, it was so much due to the influence of the two Englishmen that a recent history of organ-building, Clutton and Niland's *The British Organ*, calls it "The Hill-Gauntlett Revolution"[28]. Other organ-builders were naturally not slow to follow where Hill led; the organs now being built contained manual choruses of power, brilliance and depth, supported by pedal departments whose complete tonal schemes were rarely, if ever, equalled until the nineteen-sixties. Pipes of new shapes, producing new nuances of tone, appeared and it became almost a fashion to employ William Hill to build a new organ or to rebuild an old one. However, James Bishop,[29] whom Sutton employed, did not really become a contender in these up-dating stakes, although he appeared to be so with instruments like St. Giles, Camberwell, in south London (1844)[30], for though there were many stops there was not the impressive power that Gauntlett and Hill sought. Soon after his death, in fact, the Editor of the *Musical World* wrote: "We can call to mind no large organ of his that, as a whole, is striking or satisfactory. He had, indeed, certain prejudices, certain adhesions to, not *old*, but *middle-aged*, doctrines as to tone..."[31] He went on to say that Bishop's great aim of all the stops mixing well "deprived the necessarily opposed qualities of organ tone of all distinct character". In other words, Bishop provided no stops with exotic tonalities and names like Viola, Vienna Flute or Tuba, however pleasant his organs sounded; and the decibel force of the *tutti* of a large Bishop organ was nothing like that of a Hill. To John Sutton, following the *Ecclesiologist* article just quoted and his own cathedral outlook, these would be virtues and were among the reasons which made him choose Bishop to build the Jesus College, Cambridge, organ in 1847.

The reason why this organ is placed in the triforium gallery to the north of the chapel is similarly old-fashioned. In 1848 the Camden Society published *Hierugia Anglicana, or Documents and Extracts Illustrative of the Ritual of the Church of England after the Reformation* (though it came out in sections earlier, and was thus available to members) and this book showed how many medieval ceremonies and customs lingered on right up to the Commonwealth. Perhaps it mirrored Oxford's *Library of Anglo-Catholic Theology*, begun in 1841. Sutton, disliking the very luke-warm advice given in the *Ecclesiologist* on the positioning of organs, found two books illustrating instruments in north triforia – Dugdale's *Monasticon Anglicanum*[32] and Sandford's *Description of the Coronation of James II*,[33] both of which dated from the sort of times *Hierugia Anglicana* described, and were therefore of equal authority with it. On this basis both the organs he provided in England – Jesus College, Cambridge, and West Tofts – were in this sort of position. He was followed on this point to some extent by his brother Frederick and completely by John Baron in *Scudamore Organs*[34].

But to build an organ in a Gothic church, whether ancient or contemporary, meant that it must conform in outward appearance to the standards of the Gothic organ-builders if it was not going to be utterly out of line, and in Chapter VII of the *Short Account* Sutton states roundly that there are ancient organ-cases remaining on the Continent which "would furnish very good models for new ones."[35] Even here there was a starting-point in the *Ecclesiologist* article just quoted – the suggestion is made that:

> "... the large group (of pipes) be made, where it is possible, in the middle; and then let the pipes be arranged, from large to small, in order on each side, giving a pyramidal outline to the whole. This form will be found more graceful, and more suitable for a pointed church ... Then by adding doors, we get the effect of a triptych. The leaves may be painted inside or outside, or both; so that, whether shut or open, the organ is made quite a decorative feature in the church."[36]

– and there is mention of a suitable model to be found in the church of San Salvatore, Venice. Sutton in his turn wrote at the end of the *Short Account* "the appearance when open will be very much that of a triptyc [sic] as the inside of the doors is painted."[37] He omitted to say that a triptych could be taken as symbolical of the Holy Trinity, making it doubly significant to a Camden Society man, and that organs built in this way mirrored the medieval winged altars found all over the German lands, and of which he himself became something of a collector, as many letters in the Béthune Archives witness. In the event, nearly all organs with which he was involved had case-doors of one shape or another, as we shall see when we come to consider them individually.

To sum up: here we have a book that was advocating a different approach to organs from that of nearly all contemporary thought, which was moving fast towards a position best described as the bigger the better. Financial considerations usually restricted parishes to some extent but even here Sutton, with ample money at his disposal, insisted on an instrument no larger than was necessary to accompany music barely adequately. His extra money was spent on clothing the organ with a Gothic case, ornamented and coloured in accordance with the ancient principles he had observed, and which he felt had been most likely used in Gothic times. Further, he was violently opposed to the wholesale destruction of ancient organs of warm, singing tone and with classical cases that were acceptable at the very least "because nothing half so good can be procured at present".[38]

It was to be expected that his words fell on deaf ears. The application of machinery to organ-building meant some reduction in the cost of parts that could be mass-produced to some extent, and so it was possible for slightly more powerful organs to be afforded. Moreover, if an instrument was to be placed in a "chamber" off the chancel, it could be argued that an ornamental case would not be appreciated – and so a further considerable financial saving could be made: more pipes could be crammed in, or the money could be spent on other features or furnishings of the church. The movement towards large, uncased organs was on its way, and has been thoroughly discussed by Mr. James Berrow in the *Journal of the British Institute of Organ Studies*.[39]

It is both interesting and heartening to note that, at the time of writing (the late nineteen-eighties) there is a powerful movement back to Sutton's ways of thinking, pure Gothic outward appearance excepted. Organs are no longer as large as money can buy, their tone is gentle and singing, they are decently and sometimes elaborately encased, and they are placed in positions of maximum musical usefulness.

Pugin's drawings of organ-cases at the end of the *Short Account* deserve mention. To those familiar with large French organs the first three give the impression of having been seen somewhere before – and indeed in Béthune's copy they have pencilled notes: "Strasbourg", "Fribourg" and "Amiens – porte de l'ouest". One cannot quite accuse Pugin of copying (though if one did he would not have been displeased) because certain alterations and additions have been made, but the likenesses are quite unmistakable. Where Pugin has been original, in the other two specimen case-drawings, he cannot be said to have been successful. The first, which Sutton suggests would be suitable for a village church, has every display-pipe of the same speaking length – something of an absurdity, and the second, "suitable for an oratory", would be about fourteen feet high – not always easy to fit in.

Oddly enough, John Norbury copied some of these drawings a good deal later in the century and his versions, published in *The Box of Whistles*, are rather more plausible than Pugin's because he was able to give some depth to them, and to separate the Positive cases from the larger portions.

On page 15 of the *Short Account* is the first of the *Vignettes*, as Sutton calls them, and it has generally been assumed that he drew them himself. But at the lower right-hand corner of this first example can be seen faintly the name 'Measom'. George Measom (1820-1880) was a professional illustrator and railway guide compiler. He produced the pictures and notes for the *Official Illustrated Guides* to, for instance, the Great Northern Railway in 1857, the London and North Western Railway and the London and South Western Railway in 1858, and the Great Western Railway in 1860. He was associated with other books, but like the railway guides they are all after 1847 which was when the *Short Account* was published. Is this another case where Sutton was helping a young man with "a great talent"?

Among the Schneider letters at Mainz is this fragment in Sutton's handwriting. By other letters there it would seem that August Martin [the painter who did most of Sutton's decorative work] had the idea of a joint publishing venture – he would produce drawings of ancient organ-cases, and Sutton would provide the accompanying text. These few sentences seem to have been the beginning of Sutton's part; they would have needed much developing, particlularly as he goes off at a tangent that was obviously occupying his thoughts at the time of writing.

"Origin of the Church Organ.

Much may be found in old Books on this subject in Mersenus &c &c [Mersenus – Marin Mersenne 1588-1648: author of *Harmonie Universelle*, Paris, 1637.] on this point I have not much read. But the Organ as an accompaniment to the Choral, seems not to have been in general use till the 2nd. half of the 15 century. The Gothic Organ Cases which still remain, all from the end of the 15 and beginning of the 16 century, prove, that in the chief points, that at this time, the Organ was much the same as at present, having about 4 octs. of an 8 feet register in the front. I am inclined to believe that in many cases the Compass of the Organs extended downwards to FFF, as the pedal in the Front a Friburg [*sic*] in Breisgau, still is so far as the old *front pipes are concerned*, and has in our times been carried down to CCC by intruding other pipes behind in the case – also in the Great Organs at Strassburg and Lübeck, there were pipes in front the longest of which were 27 or 28 feet long. The Organ at Strasburg was rebuilt by Silbermann, and the present front pipes are longer than 16 feet but only speak 16 feet tone, as they are cut behind at 16 feet, so that the last few feet do not affect the tone. At Lübeck the Organ was entirely renewed about 10 or 12 years since, and is only placed behind the Old case, but the old front pipes still remain though disconnected with the Organ. Before the Organ was last altered the lowest pipes in Front spoke, and was used as a 32 foot pipe though in reality it was only 28 feet long, probably this pipe spoke originally F, but when the very deep it is almost impossible to distinguish any note, and probably was not much detected by the ear. There was to be had formerly at Strasburg a little guide Book, in which was a short account of the Organ, and in this the length of the longest pipe of the original Organ was given, I think it

was about 27 feet long. In the Lübeck case, what I know, I had from a friend, who was informed on the subject, by the Dom Organist.
(*here a line right across the paper*)
It would be interesting to know the exact compass of the 15 century Church Organ, many of these organs still remain but have been changed from time to time so without some exact information from Books it is difficult to determine."
(*here another line*)

Then on another sheet of paper attached to the last is a sketch of the organ in Perpignan Cathedral, taken at a very oblique angle, and underneath:

"Gothic Organ in the Cathedral at Perpignan sketched from memory, for I had not time to stay long in the Church. Violet le duc [*sic*] has given it in one of his books, but without its position. I have not brought out the projecting part of the gallery far enough the effect of the original is better and bolder than I have made it.
(*overleaf*) The Cathedral of Perpignan, is a very late building, with one Nave and side Chapels, with an altar very low under it, I think Organ is as old as the Church probably about 1500 – it is oak or blacked wood and has no decoration in colour of any kind – or gilding."

A note following a cross at the side of the sketch reads:

"here gothic *pierced* panels over the Organist's head, in a deep recess I suppose for the clavier."

In the event, Sutton refused to have any more do with the book Martin planned: he felt the project would be expensive and did not trust Martin to carry out his part of the work punctually. He asked Mgr. Schneider to tell Martin that " ...I will have *nothing more to do with the idea.*"

Occasionally friends would tell Sutton about organs they had heard of or seen: there is a reply to news of this sort in the 1871-73 letter-file in the Bethune Archive:

"Bruges Thursday evening. I am very much obliged to you for writing about the old Organ at Rotterdam. I should like *very much* to have it. I hope it is not much broken and injured from being taken to pieces. It is the most interesting thing of the kind I ever saw. It is far too large a thing for our College Chapel, but perhaps wd. do for St. Giles's at Bruges. It is most suitable for a large Church, with 3 equal aisles, and should be placed as it was at Rotterdam before a shut

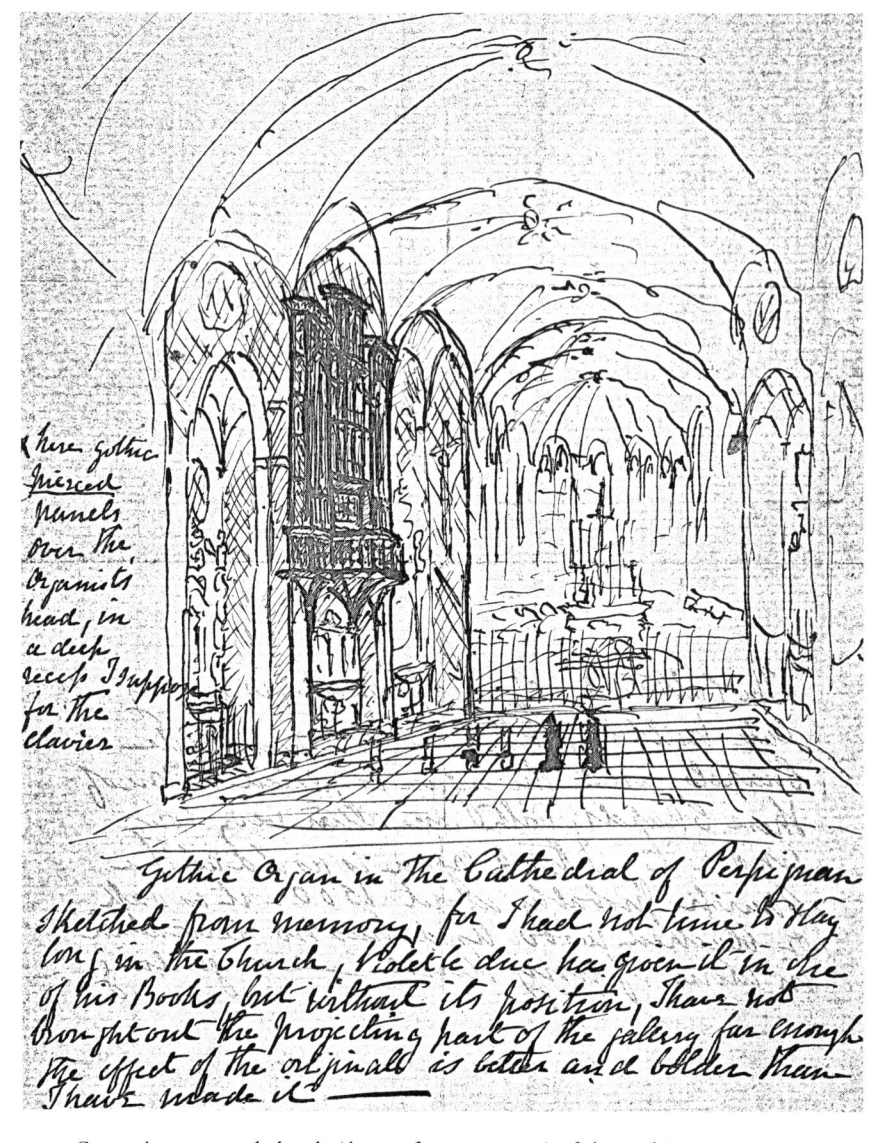

Sutton's notes and sketch (drawn from memory) of the gothic organ-case in Perpignan Cathedral

up window. If they will sell it to me I shd. like to go over to R. to see it carefully packed up & wd. take Hooghuys with me. ... If I have the organ I must have the whole thing, case and pipes and everything. I have an idea the case is put up in a museum at R. If I can have the whole I can put it together again as I have the plan of it."

Nothing seems to have come of this project, perhaps because the museum authorities did not want to part with a good exhibit. But it is interesting to note how far Sutton had moved from the Camden Society idea that an organ should never be placed in front of a window. (*Ecclesiologist* XXV, p. 1)

We now pass on to discuss the three English church organs presented by Sutton as they embody his principles so well.

Jesus College Chapel, Cambridge

When the restoration of the College Chapel was fairly under way, in about 1846, Sutton resolved to present a new organ. A decision must have been taken at this stage for there to be a choir, and choral services – probably under the influence of the Dean, John Gibson, and the Chaplain, Osmond Fisher: and Sutton's original intention was to obtain an organ by Bernard Smith, have it restored by J. C. Bishop, and to place it in the gallery built for it in the first arch of the north aisle of the chapel – a position approximating to the *Ecclesiologist's* triforium gallery.

He also decided how large it was to be:

"J. Sutton Esq. - Jesus College Cambridge – Mr. B. to look out for an Organ by Father Smidt to contain on the

Great Organ
1. Open Diapason
2. Stop do.
3. Principal   Mr. B. says he thinks the
4. Flute   Compass from CC to C in alt.
5. 15th.
6. 12th.
7. Sesquialtera

Choir
1. Stop
2. Principal   compass not particular
3. Flute

Arch – width about 14 ft.   Height abt. 20.
The instrument not required to fill it.

Address till end of Sepr.
    8 Guildford Lawn,
        Dover.

Mrs. Cooper to be called on about the book containing the accounts of the Old organs."[40]

No actual book belonging to Mrs. Cooper seems to be extant now: she must have been the wife of one of the two George Coopers who, confusingly, were not only father and son, but also sub-organists of St. Paul's Cathedral, and organists of St. Sepulchre's, Newgate Street in the City of London, in succession. The note-book was used for a series of articles in the *Christian Remembrancer*,[41] and no doubt gave details of the organs in many London churches with which the Coopers were familiar. As written in Chapter I, one would be very pleased to be able to tie John Sutton in with the group of men who were pupils of Thomas Attwood of St. Paul's, and who held influential posts in the church-musical life of London, and this note certainly points that way. It may be that Walmisley (who, although by this date living in Cambridge, was certainly a member of the group) gave Sutton the tip that Mrs. Cooper had a note-book about old organs, but it is just as possible that he had given Sutton an introduction to the Coopers because he knew of his antiquarian tastes in organs (and this was how he was able to examine so many London organs at a date when churches were locked all the week, and often only their organists held the keys to the organs); or Bishop himself, with his quite extensive acquaintance with London organists, might have suggested that he consulted the note-book. Perhaps it is hardly surprising that no such instrument became available in the time at disposal: though Mr. Elvin has shown that it was not unknown for J. C. Bishop at least to recommend the replacement of whole departments of Father Smith pipes by new ones of his own – "Mr. B. [sic] told the Dean of Durham a New Choir Organ would cost about £150 or £200."[42] – so the idea of an organ composed of Father Smith *pipework* was theoretically quite feasible. The next note appears in Bishop's 1846-54 Ledger like this:[43]

    1847.
    To a New Organ of the following description
    Compass from CC to C in alto. containg.

	Gt. Organ		Choir Organ
1.	Open Diap	1.	Stopt Dian.
2.	Stopt Dian.	2.	Principal
3.	Principal	3.	Flute
4.	Flute		
5.	15th		
6.	12		
7.	Sesquialtra		

    The pipes made of the best Materl. (Tin)

                                          £273 - " - "

There follows a list of extras and alterations which is more fascinating then the original specification:

Extras.	Mans [sic] time in altering Keys	5 - "
	1 new set of Keys	6 - " - "
	Open Dia Choir throughout, preparing for and applying	26 - " - "
	(A total of £305 - 5 - 0 was arrived at, and the extras continued on another page –)	
1847		
Sept –	To a New Double feeding Bellows with Compensation folds for evenness of pressure, with inside waste valve for silence, and J.C. Bishops [sic] invention for rendering the wind steady and free from Tremor –	10 - " - "
	To Packing case and Packing	15 - "
Sept. 28	To mans [sic] Journey to Cambridge to apply new Bellows to Organ altering Windtrunk, fixing Valve for steadying wind, Tuning Organ etc (Read)	6 - " - "
Octr.	To time and materials in making Music desk – Time in Packing Organ – Hire of 2 Vans, with 2 Horses each to convey it to Cambridge, with man's time and expenses in Journey to Cambridge to stow it away –	22 - 15 - "

Mr. Elvin added a further note: "Sutton himself furnished a Stopt Diapason and Flute (incomplete) for which he was allowed £5."[44] – which must obviously have been copied from another note elsewhere in the ledger

By the kindness of Mr. Stephen Bicknell and N. P. Mander Ltd., who rebuilt this organ in 1967, it is clear that two stops of the Great organ – the Stop Diapason and the Flute – and three registers of the Choir - Open Diapason, Stop Diapason and probably the Flute – are seventeenth-century work. The Great Flute is completed by some nineteenth century wooden pipes in the bass.[45]

The Choir Open Diapason is of wood and very soft. Was it perhaps proffered by Bishop from his stock of pipes knowing that John Sutton, with his predilection for seventeenth-century organs, would find it very hard to resist?[46]

The tradition has always been that the Stop Diapason and Flute on the Great organ came from Durham Cathedral when Bishop re-built the organ there. It is possible that the Stop Diapason did, for it was replaced in 1844 by Bishop, along with the Dulciana (both ranks in the Choir department)[47], but neither then nor in 1847, when the whole organ was removed to the north side of the choir, was any Flute stop (or any other stopped wood rank) replaced. So Sutton must have

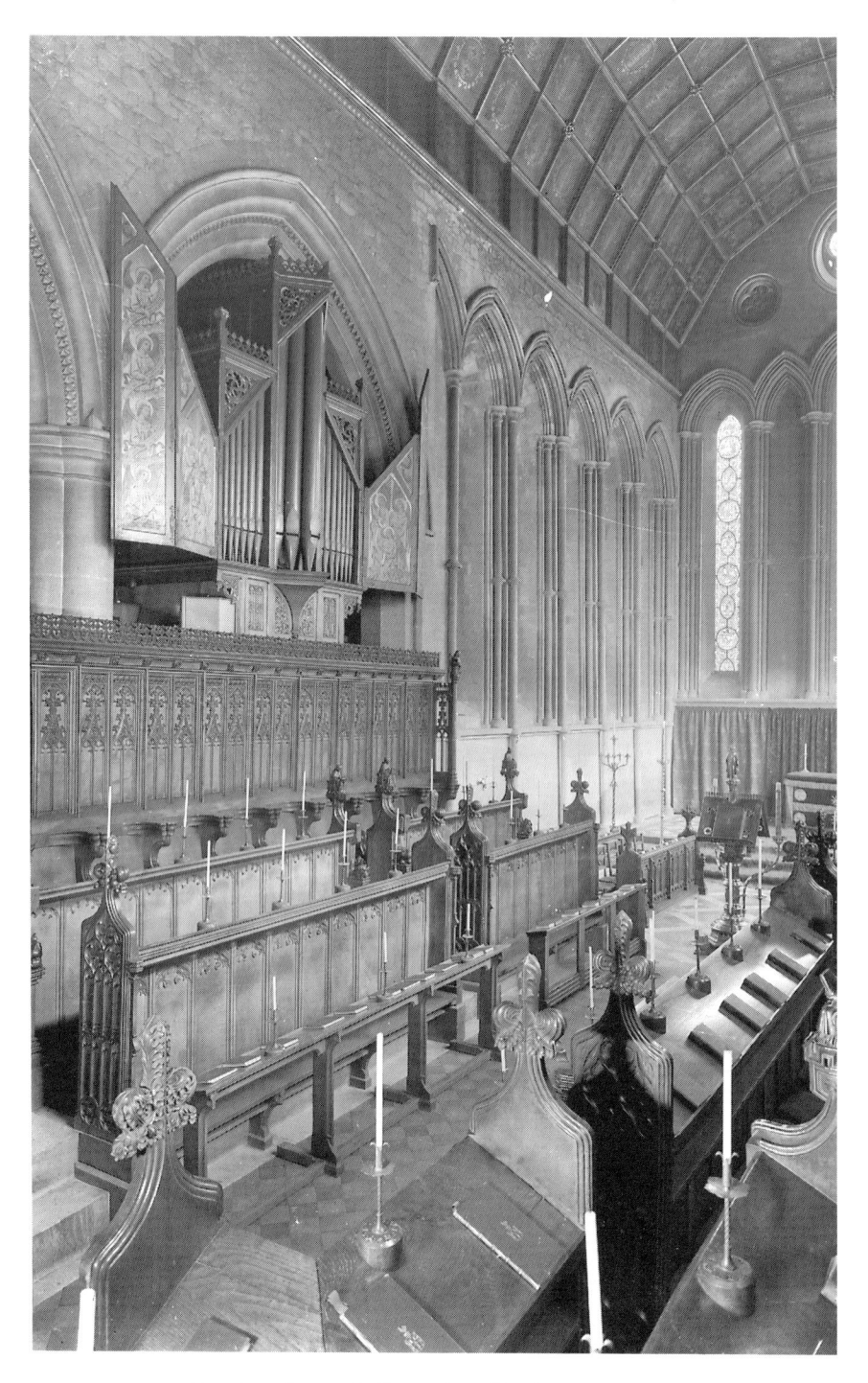

Interior of Jesus College Chapel looking north-east

obtained it from somewhere else – in spite of Mr. Bicknell's suggestion that pipes supplied by Dallam in 1662 were surreptitiously re-cycled by Smith and incorporated in his own instrument.[48] Did Sutton make friends with, for instance, William Hill, who was so active in Cambridge at this sort of time? – though even this does not explain the presence of two more ranks identified by Mr. Bicknell as seventeenth-century work. They must have come through Bishop, as they were charged for as new – further evidence that in this second quarter of the nineteenth century, many organs were by no means all that they seemed[49]. It does look as though, having been unable to lay hands upon a complete Bernard Smith organ, Bishop and Sutton between them produced something as near to the spirit and sound they believed Smith to have been aiming for, as they could. A principle was being followed.

Why was a new pair of bellows necessary when we must assume that a new organ would have a new wind system anyway? One need not take much notice of the self-advertising tone of the description in the list of extras, for Bishop normally wrote about his bellows in this way, as numbers of estimates attest.[50] Could it be, though – and this is an utterly unreasonable, fantastic guess – that Sutton originally ordered the antique style diagonal bellows, with only one large feeder worked by the blowing handle? If the whole organ was conceived on seventeenth-century lines, with its solid stop-handles, ancient pipe-work and lack of pedal pipes, would not seventeenth-century bellows be appropriate? When, on trying the organ in the factory he found the wind intolerably unsteady (for diagonal bellows were notorious for instability), we can well imagine John Sutton ordering the most modern wind-raising equipment, with every accessory that would contribute to the steadiness of the organ-tone.

It is equally difficult to account for a new set of keys being necessary: Mr. Elvin suggests that Bishop originally supplied keyboards with ivory naturals and ebony sharps, as on pianos, and Sutton had them replaced with the old-style ebony naturals and ivory sharps, as on the present east-side console[51].

It seems that the organ was stored in Cambridge until 1848 when a further entry in the ledger reads:

1848
Septr.   Putting up the Organ in Chapel.
        C.A.B.'s time and expenses   £11 - 0 - 6
        Read 7 days, Expenses   4 - 17 - 6
                                                             £15 - 18 - 0

It was evidently erected in the chapel a full fourteen months before the re-opening service on 1 November, 1849. This seems odd, because with at least carpenters, painters and cleaners about, there was sure to be plenty of dust and dirt, and one would have thought the organ was better left in store. Perhaps they were giving the instrument time to settle down in its new home and hoping that any further troubles would show themselves in time to be dealt with before it was needed every Sunday – which in fact they did, for the final account appears in October 1849:

> Oct. 8. Railway fare for Self and Man to Cambridge to
> tune Organ with expenses there   £5 - 5 - 0.
> Mr. S. paid fare back.[52]

and Bishops's diary for Tuesday, October 9 reads:

> "Compleated [sic] the tuning of Mr. Sutton's Organ in the Chapel of his College at Cambridge very much to his satisfaction it required regulating – we completed it in the course of the day and started with Mr. Sutton in a first class carriage at 8 o'clock for London."[53]

As actually built, the organ was not quite the same as the estimate-book specified. There was an octave of pedals permanently coupled to the Choir organ, with a Great to Pedal coupler, and the three-rank Sesquialtra on the Great was divided into a two-rank mixture of nineteenth and twenty-second at bottom C, and a Tierce through the whole compass.

Time has passed gently over this organ because when the Jesus College authorities sought to have more power and variety to their service accompaniments they bought another, second-hand organ and erected it on a west gallery leaving John Sutton's organ alone for the time being.[54] Then, when time dealt more hardly with the younger instrument, they disposed of it and instructed Harrison & Harrison Ltd. of Durham to add two more powerful manual departments, together with some pedal stops, to the Sutton organ, while retaining the original design and pipework unchanged. This resulted in a four-manual organ with pneumatic action, but with the virtue that, when N. P. Mander Ltd. were asked to restore it to nearly John Sutton's original conception in 1967, all the original pipes were there for re-use. *Nearly* Sutton's original conception, because the Choir Principal was transposed into a Fifteenth. Why this was done is not clear because there are ample "baroque" effects available on the new three-manual organ in the next arch if such are wanted – and the whole point of two unison and two octave stops on the Choir department of old English organs was to have a variety of unobtrusive accompanimental effects available. This concept is marred, though one can have no argument against Mander's addition of a standard

C-f¹ pedal-board and accompanying Bourdon.

The organ-case has been admired ever since it was erected: it must be the first since 1660 to be provided with shutters. This "tryptic [sic] effect" follows another principle and appears in all Sutton's cases. "His cases" advisedly, because it is likely that he was responsible for the basic design of all the new organs he was associated with. This statement demands proof and while absolute proof is not available, there is a good deal of previously unpublished evidence.

Several drawings, unmistakably in John Sutton's hand, are in the Béthune Archive in Belgium: they are small and rough (sketches would be a better title), but perfectly recognisable, and are of Kiedrich, Eltville, the projected organ for the Seminary chapel in Bruges, and of West Tofts in Norfolk. They give the impression that they were roughed out to show the architects concerned what was in Sutton's mind – something that could be used as a starting-point for a scale drawing and which he could explain at a meeting between like-minded friends.

Augustus Pugin, who has been credited with the Jesus College design up to now, was uninterested in organ-cases unless 'primed' by Sutton. There exists no Early English example he could copy – or at least none of his favourite period that he had seen, either in Britain or in Europe. As he strove "to revive not invent"[55] he felt inhibited. There are two organ-cases in this country that are claimed to be his work – Jesus College and West Tofts – and both of these were paid for by John Sutton. Not one of Pugin's Roman Catholic churches is provided with a proper organ-case. There is, of course, the design for the chapel of Ushaw College near Durham, first published by the Revd. Andrew Freeman in *The Organ* in 1939 but never carried out. The design deserves a hard look; it has been deservedly admired because it has shutters, and a Rood with the attendant figures of Our Lady and St. John and two candles incorporated in it. But take away these ornaments (which, contrary to Pugin's own rule, are not part of the necessary structure of the case) and what is left? – a quite ordinary 'organ-builder's Gothic' design on which quite a few organ-builders of that date could have improved. Did Pugin ask Sutton for an outline design for him to work up? – for the two men probably knew each other by 1843, when this design was produced. If so, Sutton's first attempt at an organ case was nothing marvellous.

This is not to say that Pugin did not try to produce organ-cases: there are some drawings in the Victoria and Albert Museum, and there are those he produced for the *Short Account of Organs*, again with Sutton heavily involved, but as Jean de Béthune noted in his copy, three of these last are just rather poor copies of large French and German examples, while a fourth is manifestly unpractical because nearly all the show pipes are of the same length.

It is certainly possible, then, that the basic design for the Jesus College organ-case was Sutton's own, ornamented, painted and perhaps improved upon by Pugin. It is a tremendous improvement on the Ushaw design, and the first example of shutters actually carried out since the Middle Ages makes the composition very impressive indeed, while the painted angels on their inside surfaces are fine examples of this early stage of the Gothic revival. From the *Sperling Notebooks* we learn that these doors were kept closed when the organ was not in use.

The tonal design is obviously what Sutton felt to be right for the accompaniment of a professional choir of eight boys and one supposes two men each for the alto, tenor and bass parts. It is quite possible to support the singing of a congregation in hymns with it while using most of its resources, but in fact it was not designed with hymn-singing or a great deal of organ-music in mind. As it has been through two organ-builders' hands since its beginnings, it does not help to try to describe what it sounds like now. Perhaps it is enough to record that Mr. Noël Mander, the organ-builder who dealt with it last, said to the author, "I made it sound as I thought it ought". The amount of seventeenth-century pipes it contains, though, makes it one of the important monuments of organ-building in the country and its size, position, tonal design and case make it a prime example of the positive principles worked out by Sutton from the writings of the anonymous Camden Society member.

West Tofts Organ I

There is a charming little organ now in the church of Great Walsingham in Norfolk, that tradition says was used in the church of West Tofts before the present organ came with the restoration of the chancel in 1857. If this is so, it would be in line with what was done at Jesus College and Kiedrich while the permanent organs were either under restoration or not yet built; and when West Tofts' own permanent organ came, this one went to Santon Downham church on the southern side of the estate, where it remained until the church was closed in the early nineteen-sixties, and Great Walsingham acquired it.

> "... there is a hand-written inscription inside the windchest behind the pallets: there is the initial G and the surname could certainly be Dawson, but the address which follows is clear: 34 Castle Street, Cambridge – this must be traceable in records to confirm the case. The windchest has not been renovated, so this must be the name and address of the original builder or workman."[56]

The West Tofts organ (I) now in Great Walsingham Church, Norfolk

Castle Street is certainly one of the addresses occupied by George Dawson, so it seems right to attribute the organ to him.

There is also plenty of evidence in the instrument itself to connect it with John Sutton – the solid doors that close over the front, the pipes, almost all of which are of wood, the trefoil patterns painted on the fronts of the keys, the linenfold panelling, and the diagonal lattice-work that hides the pipes. The four stops, worked by horizontal levers, are Stop Diapason, Principal, Twelfth and Fifteenth.

Might this have been a sort of test-piece, produced by Dawson to Sutton's order in the hope of larger commissions? It looks very much like the sort of thing produced by organ-building apprentices in Europe in our own day. Even though it is small, it was not intended to be a chamber-organ. The system of music under which Sutton and most contemporary village organists worked did not require the organ to do more than lead one or two metrical psalms, or hymns, during a service, and his own inclination being towards organs as small as possible for the duties they had to perform, one can understand this organ being as small as it is. West Tofts church, before the Pugin restoration, was of nave and short chancel only, and the chancel was shut off from the nave by a wooden screen, so it was almost a one-room building. Andrew Freeman, in his diary, observed that the organ was perfectly adequate for a small church[57]; and to a good Camden Society man, the smallest organ was better than a collection of musicians in a singing-gallery. As the organ-builder's assistant, Mr. N. Walmsley, has said,

> "Overall the case has been crudely and tastelessly repainted: where the re-painting round joins etc. is slap-dash, and on the untouched top of the case, it is clear that the original colours were 'Victorian Pink', olive green, white, red and gold. Very Camden Society!"[58]

There are a series of patterns around the edge of the grille that hides the pipes, and around the keyboard, delicate and artistic in themselves, of which the merest traces can still be seen: they must have added considerably to the attractiveness of this little organ when it was new.

This diagonal grille is so similar to that at Kiedrich – where it was placed behind the main organ to protect the *Positiv* and Pedal departments – and that at St. Giles, Cheadle, in Staffordshire (A.W. Pugin's most elaborate Roman Catholic church) where it fills the opening of the organ-chamber, that one wonders whether there is any connection other than John Sutton. Had the feature only appeared at Kiedrich and West Tofts, there could be a connection through the Hooghuys firm; if it were at Cheadle and West Tofts and not at Kiedrich, there is a possible link with Bishop, used by so many Roman Catholic churches during this period as their organ-builder, and by

ORGAN LOVER

Gt. Walsingham, Norfolk, Chamber Organ: Details of Original Decoration before repainting.

This pattern was repeated 12 times on the part of the case that runs from the keyboard to the top of the case at 90° to the grille facade. It occurs 12 times each side, and stands out in relief inspite of the crude overpainting.

This pattern occurs above and below the keyboard. Traces of white, red and olive green paint remain.

This quatrefoil motif is visible in relief around the edge of the grille. Crude overpainting has not obscured the fact that the quatrefoils were white edged with black on a gold ground.

The ends of the keys show this design in maroon on a gold ground which is obviously original.

Overall the case has been crudely and tastelessly repainted: where the repainting round joins etc. is slap-dash, and on the untouched top of the case, it is clear that the original colours were "Victorian Pink" olive green, white, red and gold. Very Camden Society !!!

Nick Walmsley 5/8/1986.

Sketches of the original decoration on the West Tofts I organ-case

West Tofts organ I

John Sutton at Cambridge: but how is it possible to explain the existence of such a rare and distinctive feature in three such diverse places, connected only by friendship?

The principles of the Camden Society were certainly being followed in this little organ: it most probably stood on the floor, it was no larger than the musical needs of the church containing it required, and it had a triptych case.

But who was George Dawson? He appears in no work of reference this author has ever seen, and for an organ-lover of Sutton's attainments to have employed him, one feels he ought to have had some distinction. He appears in several *Cambridge Directories* of the period (1847, 1850, 1853, 1858) as a music and musical instrument seller, at Castle Street or Magdalen Street. It is possible that he built the organ at St. Andrew-the-Less church in Cambridge, but like West Tofts II, this had to be re-built by Miller of the same town less than thirty years after its life began. He also restored the chamber-organ belonging to Osmond Fisher, the chaplain of Jesus College, under Sutton's direction, as an inscription inside it attests. If he did build any other organs, they do not seem to have survived, or had no name-plate displayed on them and so have sunk into the sea of anonymity.

It seems that John Sutton, without any children of his own, did his best to encourage young artists all his life. There was George Dawson in Cambridge, Edward Welby Pugin in Belgium, August Martin the painter in Belgium and Germany. Not all of them made good in the way their patron hoped, but that is the way of the world; and Sutton must have had the satisfaction of knowing that he had tried to bring them up to appreciate the true principles he himself followed so earnestly.

West Tofts Organ II

The origins of this beautiful organ have always been something of a mystery for, again, it bears no builder's name-plate. It has always been assumed that it was of English manufacture and that as A.W.N. Pugin was the architect of the church, he designed the case. When West Tofts church was closed on the district's being taken over as the Stanford Battle Area in 1941, it was taken down and stored. In 1950 it was given to South Pickenham church, a few miles away, where a new west gallery was built for it in 1963.

In the nineteen-seventies, work was carried out on it by Mr. Michael Russen, a Norfolk organ-builder, and in response to inquiries, he sent the writer a précis of a batch of letters of about 1856-7. The letters themselves have never been available in spite of extensive inquiries in England and the United States, so it is only possible to transcribe Mr. Russen's two undated letters.

(1) '... I have today received a short note from New York to say that the case was built in the Béthune workshops in Ghent whilst the restoration of the Kiedrich case was taking place. I wrote to David in New York about a week ago and have asked him if he would be kind enough to send me three photocopy sets of the documents relating to the history of this organ. It would appear from his first letter on the subject that they have letters between A.W.N. Pugin and Sir John, Hooghuys and Sir John, Zimmermann and

Pugin and Zimmermann to Bishops etc. in fact nearly the whole story. As soon as I receive these documents I will mail a set direct to you, no doubt it will take a couple of weeks for them to cross the Atlantic..."

(2) "Thank you so much for your letter of today which arrived with a letter from the U.S.A. which contains the details you need with regard to the above organ.

Sir John Sutton employed Pugin to build the case, Bishop & Sons to make up the pipework and Heinrich Zimmermann of Hooghuys to voice the pipework. Zimmermann was the head voicer of Hooghuys around 1857. The date of build is 1857. The Bishop pipework was ready for voicing on the fifth of March 1857 and Zimmermann came to West Tofts Church on April eighth and spent five weeks as the guest of Sir John during which time the voicing was carried out. The organ was completed on the twenty fourth of May 1857 the opening recital is said to have been given by the then organist of Norwich Cathedral. During the year 1881 Millers of Cambridge added the pedal organ of twenty pipes..."

It must have been Edward Pugin who wrote at this date as Augustus had died in 1852. The drawing of the organ-case in the Béthune Archive makes it almost certain that it was built in the Béthune workshops in Ghent and then shipped over to England and re-erected under Pugin's supervision as architect. There are certainly similarities of treatment between this case and that at Kiedrich, the main one being the very complicated shape of the sides of the case reaching up from the console to the main soundboard. Other similarities occur in the ornament applied to the small flats of pipes on the upper edge of the cornices at Kiedrich and the complete cornice at Tofts. There is also a strong similarity in the tone of the organ choruses, resulting in the West Tofts organ being unusually brilliant.

There is a letter from Sutton at Birmingham, directing that the ornamental iron bar that was to hold the front pipes in place be sent to "Mr. George Dawson, Organ-builder, Magdalen Street, Cambridge".[59]

Tonally, the design was a duplicate of that on p. 107 of the *Short Account* except that the Open Diapason was of wood, thus:-

Open Diapason	8
Stop Diapason	8
Principal	4
Twelfth	2⅔
Fifteenth	2
Sesquialtra	II

The second West Tofts organ as it now appears in South Pickenham Church

In 1881, eight years after John Sutton's death, Miller of Cambridge presented a bill for "building new organ according to specification and estimates" but the work done was not itemised in the bill itself. However, for the price charged (£88 - 10 - 0) it seems likely that the work was

(1) the addition of the second manual department in the tiny *Brustwerk* case under the main soundboard, of 37 notes and Gedact 8, Flute 4 and Hautboy 8;

(2) an octave of pedals and large-scale pedal pipes, for which space had to be provided at the top of the organ-loft stairs;

(3) the replacement of the wooden Open Diapason with a metal stop from Tenor C upwards – so well done that it fits perfectly into the chorus;

(4) the replacement of the seven *Brustwerk* display pipes in spotted metal;

(5) the necessary re-arrangement of the console.

The additions were a complete success and when the Revd. Andrew Freeman played it, he wrote, "I was struck by its *fire*"[60].

In its present home at South Pickenham it is difficult to appreciate the organ-case properly because some roof-beams cut across it. This is a great pity, for there is nothing quite like it in England, or for all practical purposes in Europe. It is a beautiful work of art and Sutton must have spent a great deal of money on it. There are forty-five pipes in display which corresponds to the old South German/Austrian/Italian compass of C with a short octave to c^3. Hundreds of organs in this area of Europe were built with this compass up to the end of the eighteenth century – but who in England of 1857 knew this to the extent of reproducing it in an organ-case but John Sutton?

The painted doors enclosing the pipes are signed *Bruno Boucquillon Antwerpen* 1856 on one and just *B.B.* on the other: the Béthune records show that he was one of the employees of the Ghent workshops. On the outside, both doors have elongated and elaborate, almost spider-like, hinges. The case is only about 40 cm deep which accounts in part for the force of the chorus. The Great organ keys have the same designs on their fronts as the keys of West Tofts I, now at Great Walsingham, but these are chamfered and incised instead of being merely painted; the Swell keys have the more usual Sutton trefoil design.

Sutton's series of sketches for this organ in the Béthune archive show all the features of the finished instrument – the polygonal gallery, the exotically shaped sides to the case, the shutters and the shape of the whole composition, towering up towards the roof, and even a suggestion of the *Brustwerk*. The scale is ingeniously suggested by a figure in the doorway to the gallery, and all in all, Béthune cannot have had much difficulty in producing the finished design.

ORGAN LOVER

Three views of the West Tofts organ (II) showing the doors painted by Bruno Boucquillon (open and closed) and the shallow depth of the casework

Sutton's sketch of the second organ for West Tofts

In its original home in West Tofts church, the organ had a gallery just to the east of the choir stalls, on the north side of the chancel. This was reached from the vestry below and the door to the small staircase was disguised as a cupboard. The back of the organ-case, as at Kiedrich, was against the plastered outside wall of the church, ensuring the maximum reflection of tone – necessary because of the double chancel arch and the wooden screen that filled the eastern one, if a singing congregation in the nave was to receive any support.

Once again, the principles were followed, with the only slight modification (parish churches have no triforia!) being the gallery, whose panels were painted in superb contrast to the organ itself. Here was a fusion of the principles with the copying of features from an organ of Sutton's golden period (about 1650-70) and even though the organ has been altered since, it remains an extremely successful example of what ample money and four firms could do.

These are the three organs that Sutton presented to English churches before he went to live in Europe but it would also seem appropriate to insert here some details of the English chamber organs he owned, or with which he was associated.

The English Chamber Organs

In English organ-lore, 'chamber-organ' means an organ, usually quite small, built specifically for use in a house. As it is intended for a smaller room than a church, and for use with a smaller number of either instruments or voices, the tonal outlook and output are generally much smaller than those of the church organs. In fact, a good many chamber-organs have found their way into churches over the years, but because of their gentle tone, they are not often an unqualified success in this very different rôle.

The Lynford Hall Organ

Sir Richard Sutton encouraged his son in his love for the organ, for negotiations were opened in 1832 with J. C. Bishop of London for an instrument to be built in one of the family homes – most likely Lynford Hall for reasons which will appear later. No doubt Bishop was approached because he had just completed repairs and additions to the organ in St. Paul's Cathedral, and Sir Richard would be most likely to ask Thomas Attwood, the organist, for his advice on where an organ for his son to play upon at home could be obtained. The top families dealt only with top people in those days! Added to this, Bishop enjoyed an excellent reputation as a builder of chamber-organs.

The first piece of evidence we have is from the Bishop records and is part of a long letter from the foreman, James Eagles (who was later to set up in business for himself in the Hackney Road) to James Bishop, the head of the firm. As a working organ-builder all his life, Bishop was very often away from home erecting or repairing organs and kept in touch with what was happening at his factory in Lisson Grove South by frequent letters. This letter is dated 21 June, 1832:

> "... Sir Richard Sutton and his Lady called today and gave the order for the Organ for his son. I showed them the last letter you received from him, at the back of it was the answer you returned in shape of an Estimate. Great Organ. Op Dia to Gam. St. thro. Pr. 15. Trum to Fdl G and octave of large scale Stopt Diap. for the Pedals. Swell to Middle C. St. Dia. & Hautboy. for 200 £1."

(At this point the page is torn and I have completed the lines conjecturally – CHD.)

> "Sir Richard says he shall not mind going to 50 *£1 above this* to make the instrument a good one, he thought *another stop in* the swell would be desirable, he wishes to have a *selection* of Cases that he may chuse ... you will send word about any addition that may be made to the instrument and what size, and feature of case you intend to put as they are about leaving town and wish to decide before they go, they are now at the Clarendon Hotel. I can make out a plain sketch or two if you think proper, something after the form of Clapham or any other you may suggest, with respect to the inside I suppose it may be set about forthwith..."[61]

For some reason the decision about this organ was delayed and the next we hear about it is in a letter to Eagles from J. C. Bishop, dated May 1833:

> "When you go to Sir R. Sutton with a Design or Sketch it must not be an expensive one and you may inform him that if the Swell was to be carried down to Fiddle G with a principal in addn. and Coupler Movement, it would very much Improve the General Effect, the whole of the Expence would not exceed the £60 he proposed or a dulciana introduced to play through and 5 composition pedals and principal in addition to the Swell if it only went to Middle C would be about the same Expence – let me hear from you before any part of it is put in hand..."[62]

One gets the impression that Sir Richard Sutton was not entirely ignorant of organs, from his suggestion that another stop in the Swell department would be a good thing – as it certainly would have been to balance the two manual departments up a little. It is to be wondered,

ORGAN LOVER

too, whether the organ was built as a reward to the shy, nervous boy on his going to Eton College to continue his education – for he would have started life there in the Autumn of 1833. We can forgive James Bishop, without his files and at a busy year's distance from the previous correspondence, putting an extra £10 on Sir Richard's suggested cost of extras "to make the instrument a good one".

No doubt the organ was built fairly soon after this, probably in the Music Room at Lynford Hall – for a music room the house certainly had when it was advertised for sale in *The Times* soon after Sir Richard Sutton's death. This entry in the ledger of Messrs. Bishop, Son and Starr, p. 213, must refer to it:

"21 May, 1856. Revd. T. Jameson, Cambridge.

To a second-hand organ belonging to Sir John Sutton	£126		
Journey to Lyndford [sic] Hall to remove do. to Cambridge & erecting it in the Round Church, travelling & other expenses			
Tuning expenses Cost 6,8,4 beside time	14	14	-
Conveyance of Organ from Lyndford [sic] Hall to Brandon Station & from thence to Cambridge, assistance & attendant expenses	2	15	6
	£143	9	6

"[63]

The Round Church is the church of the Holy Sepulchre in Bridge Street but as far as we know, none of the Bishop organ was used in the new organ built for the church in 1879 by Forster and Andrews of Hull. No doubt the pipe-scales used in a chamber-organ of 1833 were felt by this German-influenced firm to be quite inadequate for a church organ of the eighteen-eighties, and the whole thing was probably scrapped.

However, to make sure that we know what John Sutton's practice-organ at Lynford Hall was like, here is the probable specification culled from the Bishop letters:

Great		*Swell*	
Open Diapason (gamut G)	8	Stop Diapason	8
Stop Diapason	8	(Dulciana	8)
Principal	4	Principal	4
Fifteenth	2	Hautboy	8
Trumpet (Fiddle G)	8	Swell to Great Coupler.	

An octave of pedals, pulling down the Great keys, with a set of unison stopped pedal pipes. Compasses are uncertain but it is likely that the

Great would be from GG to f³, 59 notes and the Swell was either from fiddle G or middle C to f³. Nor do we know whether the five composition pedals suggested by James Bishop were fitted – most of us would prefer pipes to mechanism in a small organ and certainly there were none in any other English organ John Sutton had to do with.

Was it this "large scale Stopt Diap. for the Pedals" that gave Sutton his permanent dislike of heavy bass tone? There is an original set of unison pedal pipes of a very similar date in Northamptonshire and certainly they are not musical.

The organ was sold to the Cambridge church because, as we have seen, Sir Richard Sutton died in 1855 and, because of what his eldest son called his "most just" will leaving £40,000 each to his sons, the trustees sold the estate and house quite soon afterwards. The new Baronet (Sir John) must have realised that the organ itself would not add much to the value of the music-room and, with his extensive knowledge of Cambridge, may have suggested to the Vicar of St. Sepulchre's that the organ might well do for his church. Dr. Thistlethwaite observes that following the restoration of 1841-3 (the first work, incidentally, carried out under the supervision of the Camden Society) an organist was retained but "at a salary which suggests that the duties may have been restricted to turning the handle of a barrel organ".[64] Vicar Jameson would jump at the chance to obtain a 'proper' organ, especially if it was recommended by Sutton who must have had a good, if only restricted, reputation as an adviser on organs by 1855.

There are three chamber organs that have always been associated with the Suttons: two of them are claimed by Sir John in the *Short Account* as his (p. 54-55) and the third was certainly in the Sutton collection sold after the death of Canon A. F. Sutton in 1921. Mrs. Robina Clifton-Brown, Augustus Sutton's grand-daughter, told the writer that she remembered seeing all three organs in Brant Broughton Rectory up to 1920. Following John Sutton's claims they have all been attributed to Bernard Smith as their builder. The internal evidence will be dealt with in a later paragraph and for the moment we will follow what we can of their history.

The Northampton Organ

This, the largest and most elaborate of the three and the only one with two manuals, has its name because, for most or all of its life (except the eighty or so years when it belonged to the Suttons) it is believed to have been associated with either the town or the title: first in All Saints' church in the centre of the town, and then bought after Canon A. F. Sutton's death by the late Marquess of Northampton, himself an organist, and placed in the chapel of Compton Wynyates in Warwickshire.

As small organs go, this one has had a lot of ink used on it. Sutton himself wrote on it briefly in the *Short Account* as mentioned above; then his friend Canon W.E. Dickson had a descriptive paragraph on it in *Fifty Years of Church Music*. This was copied by the Revd. Andrew Freeman in *Father Smith*, p. 51, who added that "this instrument came under the notice of the Revd. August Sutton about 1840, when it stood in the gallery of All Saints' Northampton". This in its turn was used by F.W. Shaw (a Northampton organ-builder) in an article in *The Northampton County Magazine*, who himself added that it was placed in the gallery about 1725: its size, he continued, "would suggest that it was for minor services and choir practices as an auxiliary to the large organ, but it did duty for nearly a hundred years, after which it was stored away at the end of the gallery. In 1847 it was purchased by

The 'Northampton' organ now at Compton Wynyates

Sir John Sutton..." Freeman was a careful historian and we can be sure had evidence for what he wrote. His reputation in the organ world was such that it is only now that anyone has begun to question his statements and demand more evidence about items than he gave. The series of articles written by Shaw seem also to have been carefully researched and he could have known those whose fathers remembered the little organ in All Saints' gallery; but again, no references were given.

As indicated above, this organ is well documented as being in John Sutton's rooms at Jesus College in Cambridge; and when he lived abroad, it was in his sitting/music/drawing-room in the Gouden-Hand-Straat in Bruges – a sketch made of the room by his youngest sister shows it quite plainly. After John's death, his youngest brother, Frederick Heathcote Sutton, employed Messrs. Bishop to bring the organ back to England and they put it up again, after repair, in Brant Broughton Rectory.[65] The specification is:

Lower manual	Open Diapason	8	
	Stop Diapason	8	
	Principal	4	– all of oak
Upper manual	Stop Diapason from the lower manual		
	Flute	4	
	Fifteenth	2	
	Furniture	II	– all of metal

Mr. Mander's Organ

In the music-room at St. Peter's Organ Works in East London, the home of N. P. Mander Ltd., stands a small ancient organ with just one keyboard and no pedals or any accessories. The four stops are actuated by small upright wooden levers, two at each end of the keyboard which now runs from C to c^3, 49 notes. They are: Stop Diapason 8, Principal 4, Fifteenth 2, and Mixture of two ranks, twelfth and seventeenth throughout. A pair of solid doors enclose the front and the top is also hinged, and if you lift it, there appears the following note on a piece of paper glued to its inner surface:

> "This organ was built by Father Schmidt, and was used at New College Oxford for many years to teach the choristers to sing with. It had been disused for ten or fifteen years. And I found it in the brewhouse of the College, full of hops in June 1845. I purchased [it] of the Warden and Fellows of the College for 10 £. 0. 0. The Mixture stop had been lost and was renewed by Bishop.
>
> J. Sutton"

The organ now owned by N. P. Mander Ltd, formerly in New College, Oxford

O si sic omnes! If only everyone with an old organ, or indeed any historic piece of furniture, put down what he knew of its history and attached it to some relatively invisible portion of it! One is bound to add, *O, si sic* Sir John himself of other cases, but perhaps that is too much to expect. The organ is mentioned on pp. 54 and 55 of the *Short Account* and illustrated with a '*vignette*', as Sutton called it – recognisably the same instrument. New College Bursars' Accounts verify the sale in 1845 – "For the old organ, £10".[66] Tradition has it that this organ was used by Sutton, certainly in the Chapel at Jesus College, Cambridge, and possibly in the Hall as well before any of the chapel could be used, to accompany the choral services begun by the Chaplain and Dean until the Bishop organ was erected in 1849.

Freeman, in *Father Smith*, quotes a letter to *The Times* on 25 August, 1926, in which the writer stated that the late Dr. Harding

Newman, sometime Fellow of Magdalen College Oxford, who lived at Nelmes near Upminster in Essex, had "amongst other curiosities a fine chamber organ – by Father Smith, if I remember rightly – which had been discarded as worthless by one of the Oxford colleges".[67] J. C. Bishop's diary of 8 October, 1849, mentions that Sutton had a guest, a Mr. Newman from Oxford, that evening.[68] Was the organ given to him when Sutton left England and did it remain in the family until Dr. Harding Newman's death?

The organ appeared at Sotheby's in 1936, being bought by Capt. J. Lane of Snaresbrook in Essex, a noted collector of ancient organs, who in turn sold it to Mr. N. P. Mander.

Up to the last few years everyone has accepted Sutton's attribution of this and one or two more organs of similar size to Bernard Smith; but recently one or two voices have been raised to query it, notably Mr. Dominic Gwynn, organ-builder of the Tan Gallop, Welbeck Abbey, who prefers more proof of authorship than merely excellence of workmanship and similarities of case-work.

The New College archives reveal that there were no less than four small organs in the College by the end of the eighteenth century: they also reveal that the College itself never dealt with Bernard Smith, but with the Dallam family, and when they died out, with their successors in business, the Harrises. Small organs built either for the College or for individual members of it would be likely to be the work of the same men. Mr. Gwynn, after careful examination of both the 'Northampton' and 'Mander' organs and the marks on their pipes, writes to the author:

> "We cannot ascribe the Northampton organ to any known builder, though we do know that he built the organ formerly in Cheshunt House and now at Canons Ashby (Northants.) and probably the organ that used to be in New College and is now in St. Peter's Organ Works ... The most suggestive evidence is that on the Fifteenth AA key has been written Cart (and A re in two hands) ... 'Cart' (anglicisation of the French 'Quarte de Nazard') is unlikely to have been used by anyone but a Dallam or Harris after the return from Brittany."

The Dallams were Roman Catholics and left England between 1641 and November 1642 for Brittany, where they built organs right through the Commonwealth and picked up a good deal of French stop-nomenclature.

It seems likely, then, that Sutton's chamber-organs were built by a member of the Dallam/Harris school of English organ-builders; amusing, when he wrote of all organs being attributed to Smith by those unacquainted with his peculiarities!

King James II's Travelling Organ

To introduce this little organ, a quotation from the *Stowe Catalogue*, priced and annotated by Henry Rumsey Forster:[69]

> "2481   The travelling organ of James II., used in his camp on Hounslow Heath, with stop diapason, cornet, sesquialtra, principal, twelfth and fifteenth stops: after the Revolution, it was conveyed to Lord Wharton's seat at Winchendon, and from thence purchased by Mr. Grenville."

Stowe was sold to settle the debts of the second Duke of Buckingham (1797-1862) and the auction of the contents took forty days, beginning on 15 August, 1848, and realised £75,562.[70] The organ made £30 and was bought for Robert Sutton, Esq., of Rossway, Herts. It has not been possible to discover anything about him, but he must have been a member of the extensive Sutton family to which Sir John belonged (and which included the Manners-Suttons and the Sutton-Nelthorpes) for the organ was passed on to Canon F. H. Sutton at Brant Broughton Rectory.

In 1924 the organ was sold again, appearing at Sotheby's among other "important Jacobite relics" (which included the standard of Prince Charles Edward's bodyguard, and four glasses engraved with the Jacobite version of the National Anthem), the property of the Rev. Canon (A. F.) Sutton of Brant Broughton, Newark.[71] This sale must have been when Arthur Frederick Sutton left Lincolnshire for his short stay in Essex before his death in 1925. At this sale the organ was bought for £255 by H. & J. Simmons of Duke St, London W1. It was subsequently purchased by William Randolph Hearst, the American newspaper magnate, and taken to his palatial estate of San Simeon in California.[72] It is recorded somewhere that it went from there to St. David's School for Boys in New York.

The Revd. Andrew Freeman was able to see the organ and take notes, and wrote:

> "Soon after it came into the possession of the Sutton family, it was discovered that under the dull red paint with which the case was covered were some really beautiful pictures painted after the Chinese manner. These are not likely to be quite as old as the instrument, as this kind of enrichment seems to have been introduced into England subsequent to the reign of James II ... The front pipes, as in many old organs of this type, are wooden dummies.
>
> The instrument contains but one manual CC (no CC-sharp) to c, 48 notes, and the following stops:

The King James II organ

Left Hand:		*Right Hand*:
	Open Flute	Stop Diapason
	Twelfth bass	Twelfth treble
	Fifteenth bass	Fifteenth treble
	Sesquialtra bass	Sesquialtra treble

The stops, most of which draw in halves, are actuated by small iron levers, working to and fro in slots, at either end of the old black keyboard, the names being engraved on the ledge alongside. The accessories are a blowing pedal and a shifting movement. Another slot at the side suggests that there was formerly an additional pedal here for independent blowing."[73]

Without anyone in England having seen the organ since 1924, it may well belong to the group that includes the Mander and Northampton organs – in which case it may also have a Dallam or Harris origin.

Chollerton

In Chollerton church in Northumberland, where John Sutton worshipped when he was a private pupil at the Vicarage, is a small organ of undeniably ancient appearance. On the back of a chalk portrait of Sutton hanging in the vestry is the inscription: "Sir John Manners Sutton, Bart., Norwood Park, Notts., presented the Altar Madonna and the organ. 1850."

One must point out that in 1850 Sir Richard was the baronet and the Manners Suttons were another branch of the family altogether. The Altar Madonna was a picture, still in the church, and seeming to date from the late eighteenth century.

The organ was thoroughly rebuilt in 1903 by Harrison and Harrison Ltd. of Durham and is not, therefore, as Sutton discovered it and found it attractive. Internally it is a typical small single-manual organ of late nineteenth-century date with pleasing gentle tone. The case, apart from the straight toe-boards of the intermediate flats which must be a later replacement of original ogee ones, seems to be original and of the second half of the eighteenth century. There is no clue to its original builder but there are two other chamber-organs in England which resemble it closely enough for experts to believe that they came from the same workshop. Their cases are almost identical with Chollerton. They have keyboards with 'sandwich' black-and-white sharps and white naturals with carved fronts in arcades, and the one least altered has a sliding keyboard. There are slight similarities to some work by R. Gray, and Jonas Ley, who were both working in London in 1760-80, but nothing sufficient for a firm attribution.

The organ in Chollerton Church, Northumberland

A tradition has grown up that the Chollerton organ is by Father Smith: by a paragraph by the Revd. B. B. Edmonds in the British Institute of Organ Studies *Reporter*[74], it seems this was started by the late E. E. Adcock of Norwich, who wrote to *Musical Opinion* in March 1920 asking for confirmation of information he had been given. This seems to have been picked up by M. I. Wilson in *The English Chamber Organ*[75], and following him by Dr. John Rowntree in *Father Smith*[76]: Rowntree also cites the late Dr. W. L. Sumner in *The Organ* p. 144, a reference omitted from my copy of the book – though in any case, neither Wilson nor Sumner cite documentation themselves. The only reason to attribute this organ to Father Smith must be its Sutton connection, but we may suppose that when John found it, its tonal ensemble was sufficiently like what he felt was the ideal for him to buy it and present it to Chollerton. Harrisons' records are silent on any historical point and as the work they carried out in 1903 was very extensive (probably a new sound-board, as well as alterations to the tonal scheme, a swell-box, and pedals and their pipes), no label written by Sutton – as in Mr. Mander's organ – has survived.

Continental Organs

After John Sutton went to live on the Continent, his main interests were naturally centred upon the organs there rather than in England. Traditions there were different to those in England, of course, and Professor Williams has also shown how they differed from area to area in Europe.[77] Sutton respected this and while the work he commissioned at Kiedrich showed a remarkably sensitive blending of antiquarianism and utility for its date, the new organ he presented to Vijvekapelle in Belgium at the same time was more in keeping with that area's tonal tradition.

Kiedrich-im-Rheingau, Pfarrkirche, West End Organ

One of John Sutton's first works on the Continent was the restoration of the organ at Kiedrich. "The oldest playable organ in Germany"[78] has a little documentation from his own pen. The organ-case, minus the present doors, seems to date from the extensive re-building of the church in 1481-1493, when it was moved from the north wall of the nave to the west gallery. It probably had one manual then; a second was added about a century later, and major work was done in 1652. Local tradition says one or two pedal stops were added in the eighteenth century and their pipes were in two cases at the sides of the main one. Sutton's method of restoration deserves careful discussion: for technical description Franz Bösken's article in *Acta Organologica* vol. VIII should be consulted.[79]

Kiedrich Pfarrkirche – the organ, with Sutton's own work on the wall behind

The *Hauptwerk* (principal manual) windchest contains the signatures of Johann Wendelin Kirchner, a well-known Rhine-land organ-builder, and Nicholaus Nicholai (perhaps his foreman) and the date 1652: and although some considerably older pipes were re-used, it seems this is the date that the department took its present tonal shape. The second manual, the *Rückpositiv*, existed by 1710[80] but the stop-names suggest a date at least a hundred years earlier. A repair contract of 1710 sets out the specification thus:

Im Obern Orgel:
Principal acht Schue in Corpore	(8)
Hohlpfeif acht Schue in Corpore	(16)
Trompeth 8 Schue	(8)
Octav 4 Schue	(4)
Quint 3 Schue	(2 ⅔)
Superoctav 2 Schue	(2)
Mixtur 4fach	(IV)
Zimpel 2fach	(II)

Rückpositiv:
Principal 4 Schue	(4)
Hohlpfeif im Thon von 4 Schue	(4)
Octav 2 Schue	(2)
Quint 1½ Schue	(1 ⅓)
Zimpel	
Schnarrwerk 2 Schue	(8) – treble only.

5 Bälge, or bellows.

By the late eighteenth century the organ was unusable and various ideas for its replacement were mooted. Some repairs were carried out in 1839 and Sutton may well have seen it during this time on his first trip up the Rhine. However, by 1859 *Pfarrer* Zimmermann believed it to be worthless and allowed Sutton to have it taken down and transported to the Hooghuys' workshops in the Rue Nord du Sablon in Bruges. Work was done according to true principles in this order:

(1) The restoration of the stately fifteenth-century organ-case, of the highest artistic merit, had first priority: it must look as it did when first erected. It went to the Béthune workshops in Gand, perhaps then the only place in Europe where it could receive sympathetic treatment, and August Martin was commissioned to paint two new doors for it.

(2) The *Hauptwerk* windchest and pipes date as a unity from 1652, the time when Sutton's favourite English organ-builder, Bernard Smith, might have been setting out on his career. Apart from the replacement of the Trompeth – probably unusable by now – by a 4-foot Flute, they were restored as they stood.

(3) The *Rückpositiv*, though, was an intrusion in the original scheme of 1480-90. The pipework was restored and, as with the *Hauptwerk*, the *Schnarrwerk* treble reed was replaced, in this case by an 8-foot Gedact. A new sound-board was made and the whole department placed behind the main organ, under the tower.

(4) The Pedal department of one or two stops in a case of Baroque date, if not appearance, would not count for much beside the overwhelming claims of the *Hauptwerk*. However, here was an opportunity to test out Sutton's theory that a chorus upon the pedals of a west-end organ "might have a fine effect"[81]. So another new sound-board was constructed and the following stops planted on it:

C, D – e, 16 notes.	Subbass	16	
	Oktave	8	
	Doppelquinte	5 ⅓	
	Oktave	4	
	Quinte	2 ⅔	
	Superoktave	2	
	Mixtur	II	(⅓ & 1?)

This department also went into the tower, and a screen of the same heavy diagonal wooden slatting as appears at Great Walsingham and A. W. N. Pugin's most elaborate Roman Catholic church at St. Giles', Cheadle in Staffordshire, was placed in front. The most logical explanation of the strangely short pedal compass is that it was the original compass found when Sutton examined the organ: it is too short to be used for fugues[82] and such a chorus really can have no other justification. Hooghuys' conservatism might be another explanation, for the Belgian traditions he knew used hardly any pedal pipes at all.

The original *Hauptwerk* stop-handles remain, of iron and in two horizontal rows right and left of the music-desk. The whole of the Principal is in the speaking front (though for symmetry there are forty-seven pipes instead of forty-five). A new small gallery was made for the organist. It was designed by the Revd. John Gibson, the late Dean of Jesus College, Cambridge. This is evidenced by a letter from Sutton to Béthune: "7 November 1860 ... The Gibson gallery is now all you could wish ..."[83] It is quite small and is obviously meant to keep orchestral players out, and the choir in their *correct* place in the chancel. Martin's doors, with paintings of the Nativity and the Visit of the Magi, were fixed in 1861[84] and the whole composition is backed by a series of blue stencilled patterns on the tower wall. In the letter just quoted Sutton wrote: "... I finished the stone work of the church and coloured the plaster as far as the scaffold went for the organ ..." – thus showing us that he was well able to use his own hands in the work.

Since the restoration of 1986-7 by Th. Kuhn of Männedorf the

ORGAN LOVER

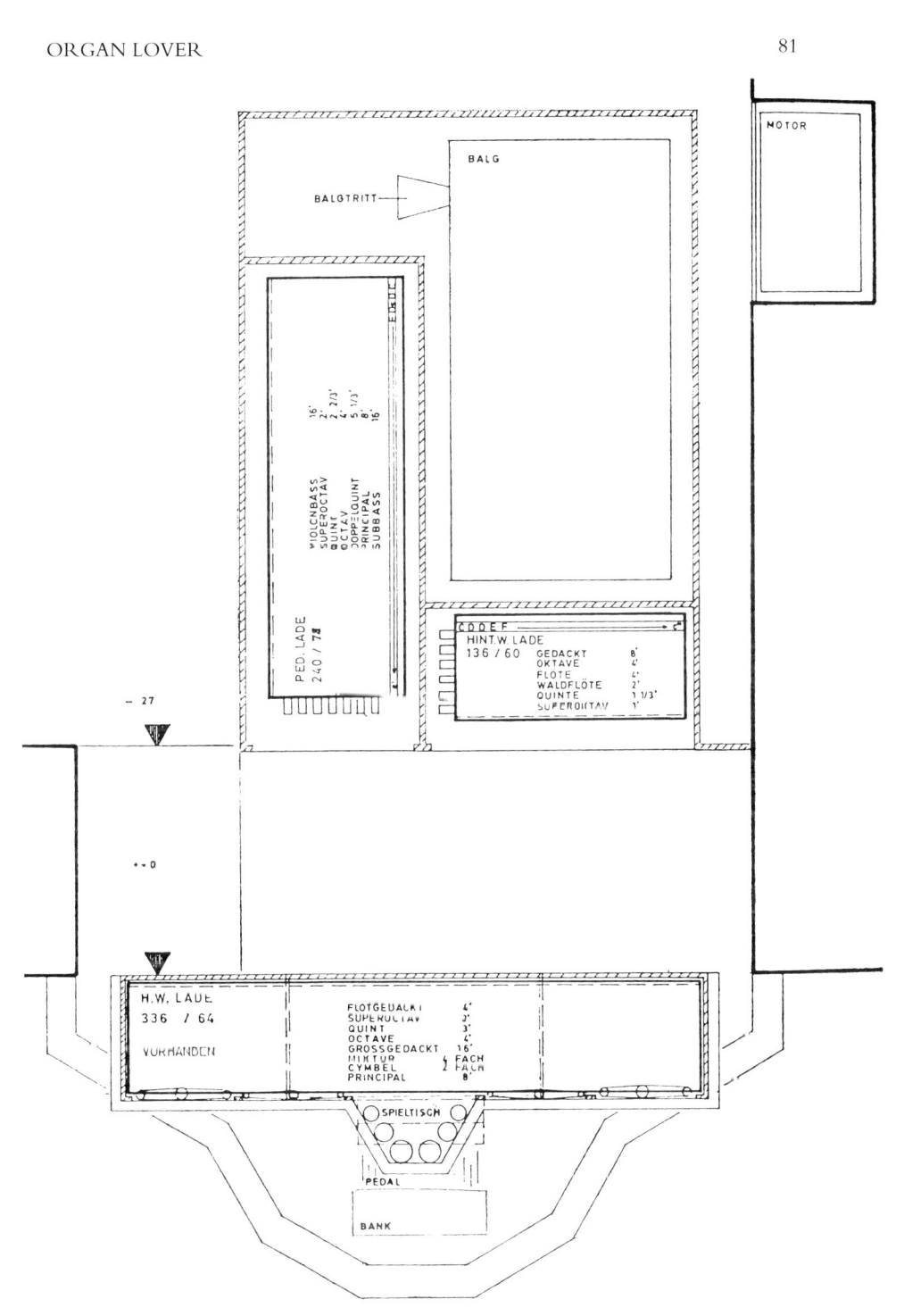

Plan of the Kiedrich organ showing the disposition of the sections as left by Sutton and Hooghuys in 1859

organ is disposed in one body and case and is not as Sutton left it. However, the really ancient parts are unaltered, as is its appearance from the floor of the church. It stands today as a most valuable monument from several points of view: as a medieval case, as a mid-seventeenth-century chorus, and as a tonal and visual restoration on true principles of the nineteenth century.

August Martin, 1837-1901, the painter who did most of Sutton's decorative work, especially the doors of this organ, was a pupil of Edward Steinle, 1810-1886, Professor at the Institut Städel from 1850 until his death. Steinle, in his turn, was taught by Johann Friedrich Overbeck, 1789-1869, who migrated from north Germany to Rome in 1809 and founded the Nazarene school of painting in 1810. This was based on the Italian Renaissance style and most of the artists of the school worked on religious subjects – as did Martin, dismissed by Bénézit in five words, "Il travailla pour les églises" (he worked for churches)[85]. Pugin, though, had called Overbeck "the prince of painters"[86] – so perhaps Sutton felt Martin was at least a princeling.

There are quite a number of letters in the Béthune Archives that are concerned with this organ; none are particularly technical, but they help to fill in the atmosphere in Kiedrich and elsewhere while this great work of restoration was going on.

The first one is dated 3 August 1858, and is from *Pfarrer* Zimmermann to Béthune:

> *"Es sind schon vierzehn Tage, dass ich Mr. Hooghuys erwarte, aber vergebens. Sorgen Sie doch, dass derselbe jetzt kommt. Am 15 August feiern wir das hohe Fest Maria Himmelfahrt, acht Tage darauf ist eine grosse Wallfahrt dahier, mit einer Oktave; dann ist Kirchweihfest. Es wäre doch sehr zu wünschen, wenn bis dahin die Orgel fertig wäre. Sollte Hooghuys nicht kommen, ich käme in die grösste Verlegenheit. Die Emporbühne muss nothwendig gereiniget werden, und die Pfeifen kämen dann durcheinander und zudem wüsste ich nicht einmal, wo ich die Pfeifen auflewahren sollte. Bitten Sie Herrn Sutton in meinem Namen, er möge doch sobald wie möglich den Orgelbauer schicken aus abgenannten Ursachen. Herr Sutton wird doch recht gesund sein, und sein liebgewannenes Kiedrich nicht vergessen haben. Wie lieb habe ich denselben gewannen, und wie freue ich mich denselben recht bald wieder bei mir zu sehen ...*
>
> P. Zimmermann,
> Pfarrer.

("It is already fourteen days since I expected Mr. Hooghuys, but in vain. Please see to it that he comes at once. On 15 August we celebrate the major feast of the Assumption, eight days after that there is to be a big pilgrimage here, with

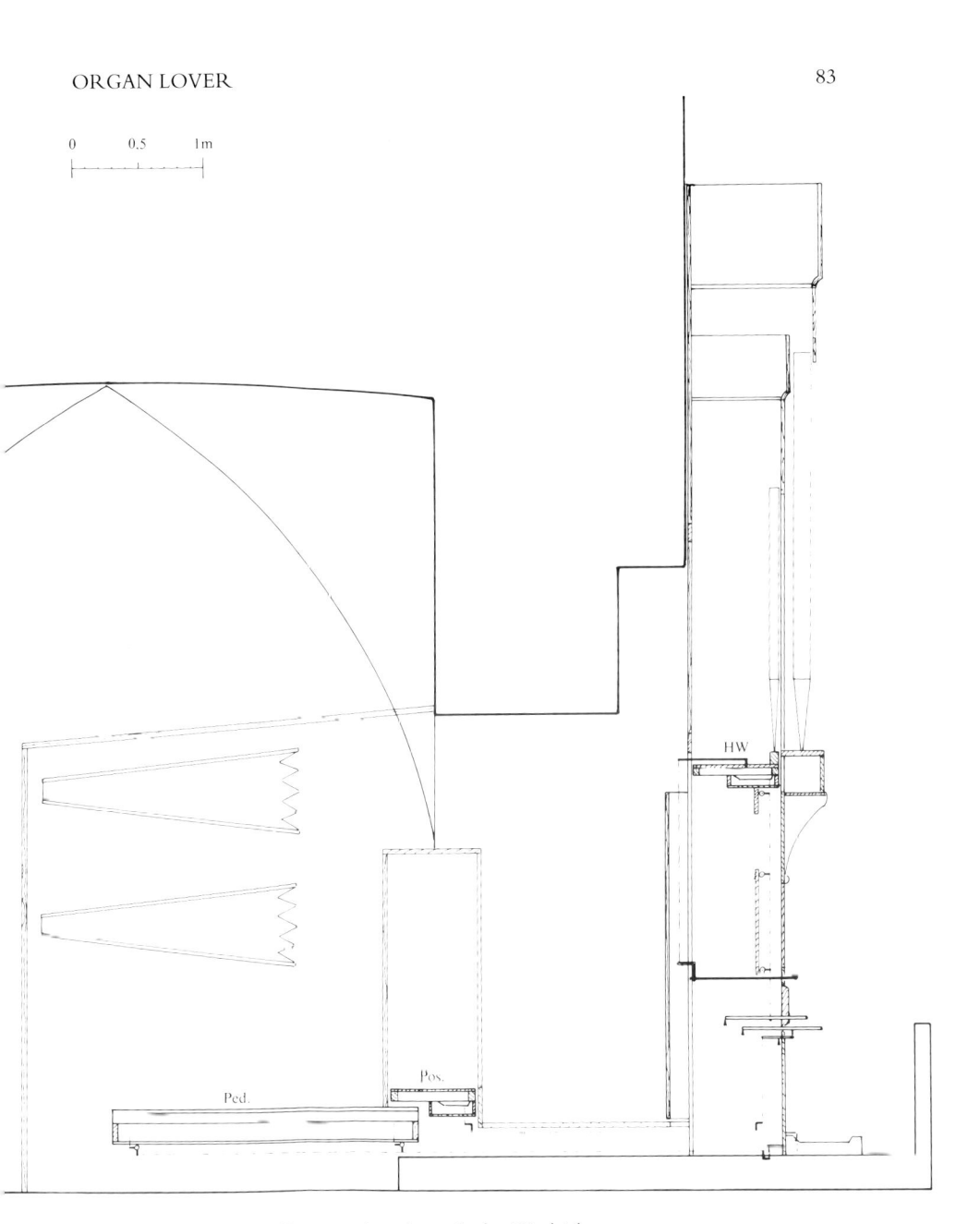

Cross section through the Kiedrich organ

an octave; and then there is the dedication festival. So it is much to be wished that the organ would be completed by then. If Hooghuys does not come, I shall be at an utter loss. The gallery is to be emptied, the pipes are all higgledy-piggledy and I have no idea where I can put them safely. Beg Mr. Sutton in my name, that he will send the organ-builder as soon as possible to deal with these matters. Mr. Sutton will be quite recovered now, and will not have forgotten his Kiedrich that has so gained his love. I am so glad to have his friendship, and how glad I would be to see him here with me very soon..."")

We seem to have read letters like this or heard of similar situations many times before! Obviously the *Pfarrer* did not realise the work on the organ was going to take so long and it seems pretty clear from this, and the next letters, that Hooghuys did not spend all his time on the Kiedrich organ. Be that as it may, Sutton soon went back to Kiedrich and on 11 August (no year, but it must be 1858) wrote:

"The *Pfarrer* is in a very bad way about the organ, what can we do to get Hooghuys here – I think the best way would be to get up a report that Mme. H. is going to be *confined again* immediately, and that she insists on his presence and *assistance* on the occasion, and further if he is not more at home she intends in future like a rabbit to be confined once a month – now if this succeeds and you get him to Bruges catch him and make Roboys pack him up in a case, and I will get permission from the minister to introduce him free of duty."

– which is the only example in the surviving correspondence of John Sutton being even gently improper!

By 30th. of the month Sutton was wishing himself elsewhere, but toe-nail trouble so that he could not bear a shoe, forced him to remain in the *Pfarrhaus*:

"(The *Pfarrer*) is wonderfully kind to me, but he makes too much of me, and bores me, so much that I shall be glad to get away, this *is not good of* me *but I cannot help it* ... I fear he must have seen some little impatience in my manner, however he is a very kind hearted creature and has been just as kind to me though he has been less in my room up stairs".

Things seem now to have quietened down somewhat and there is no more correspondence about the organ until 12 May, 1859, when Sutton wrote: "I am very much pleased with the Organ, it looks beautiful, so light with the metal pipes, red and gilding etc." However, there were soon little points that needed putting right and he wrote on 12 September, 1859, "... Gibson and I have been very busy with the Kiedrich organ gallery, and I think it will turn out a very satisfactory job." A year later John Gibson himself joined the correspondence:

"29 October 1860 ... Sir John Sutton is very busy making some good improvements in the organ, in form and in colour: the details he has given me display I think excellent judgment. He is determined to have a perfect work."

A week or two later, Sutton wrote,

"7 November 1860 ... The Gibson gallery is now all you could wish now it is coloured and has quite lost that heavy look we all disliked when it was first done and was in oak colour ... The Organ is finished and looks quite beautiful, I think I have got the blue a little too dark, however there is not much fault to be found with it. I finished the stone work of the church and coloured the plaster as far as the scaffold went for the organ..."

Oddly, in view of Sutton's words about the organ being finished, the great doors which are such a feature of it now were not completed until the following year. Sutton had been anxious about the colours to be used on them and once again a principle was at stake:

"Kiedrich, 11 October 1860. The young artist Martin has just left for Belgium. He wished to have a gold ground for the pictures on the organ shutters, and I agreed with him that it would look very well, but since he left it has struck me that it will not be possible to have a gold ground to pictures that are entirely without borders or frames of any kind, so will you be kind enough to make him understand that the idea of the gold ground must be given up and say [illegible – perhaps white or sky] introduced instead.

The shutters when open will have the appearance of two pictures without frames (diagram). I should like the pictures to be pale in tone as I think the organ looks rather dark and wants a little relief – Martin's plan for the outside pictures I think is very good in every respect, frames red with a little blue – figures grey on dull green ground with faces and hands in flesh colour – The decorator is painting the roof of St. Michael's Chapel beautifully. The *Pfarrer* is doing it at his own expense. I am sure you will be much pleased with this work ... With love to the children and kind regards to Mme. Béthune believe me yours very sincerely."

A further letter a month later made more suggestions, including a medieval example to be borne in mind:

"Kiedrich, 11 November 1860 ... Will you give my kind regards to Herr Martin, and tell him that I hope he will not

Kiedrich organ viewed from the side gallery

finish the shutters too much, they should not be done any finer than the Anna Altar at Gelnhausen. And above all things to keep them *pale in colour*, and introduce some white in costume, the Organ wants white about it very much, the white dress of the Angel under the gallery, is a great relief to the gallery, and by candle light has a very beautiful effect, the little gallery quite seems to hover in the air ... I should like to understand the arrangement with Herr Martin, I think it will be better to pay a *sufficient sum* for the shutters, and that he pay for his lodgings himself ... I wish to do what is liberal by him ..."

Eventually, the next year, the shutters were finished, transported to Kiedrich and placed in position; and Martin himself reported to Béthune in these words (we have to remember that this is a German writing in a French learnt in Belgium!). The letter is dated 6 September, 1861:

"Les volits de l'orgue sont bien arrivees et bien placees. L'effect n'est pas mal en general, mais monsiuer je ne me trompe pas, je sais maintenant seque manque. Le gens de Kiederich sont heureuses. "Nous avons la plus belle orgue de monde di faut ils, et notre monsiuer Anglais est un bonbrave home." Ils amaint avant quelques jours chez, leur peintre "Nous, voulons donner un cadeau au monsieur l'Anglais, qu'il peut aufai voir que nous lui aimons." Je di feait mes chers amis, "Donnez di votre caisse comunale une certaine somme a l'eglisse de Kiederich, elle est si pauvre, je vous savey cela mieux que mois, je pense, que votre mons. Anglais a plus di plaisir di ce cadeau, que d'une montre d'or on diem autre choses. "Eh bien ils sont prets a donner 2,000 florins pour le restaurations di leur eglise." Ce est tres jolie."

("The organ shutters have arrived safely and are safely in position. In general, the effect is not bad, but Sir, I am not mistaken, I know now what is lacking. The Kiedrich folk are happy. 'We have the most beautiful organ that could be wished for in the world, and our *Monsieur Anglais* is a most worthy man.' Here, they would like to paint them within a few days. 'We ourselves would like to give the English gentleman a present, so he can be assured that we love him.' I have told my dear friends what to do – 'Give a certain sum from your parish funds to Kiedrich church; it is so poor – you know that better than I: I think your *Monsieur Anglais* would gain more pleasure from this present than from a gold watch or any other things.' 'Good, they are prepared to give two thousand florins for the restoration of their church'. This is very nice.")

Kiedrich-im-Rheingau, Pfarrkirche, Chamber Organ

Tradition has it that Sir John Sutton provided this organ for use while the west-end organ was being rebuilt. This agrees with what we know he did at Jesus College in Cambridge, and believe he did at West Tofts, in neither of which places was there an organ before he came along. This particular chamber organ, or positive, is illustrated and noted in Rudolf Quoika, *Das Positiv in Geschichte und Gegenwart*[87] and we can understand at once why it caught John Sutton's fancy. In size and shape it is very similar to the chamber organs he had acquired in England. The stop-controls are hardly different and the tone has the same characteristics of sharpness and bite. The organ is thought to have been built by a Flemish master of the late seventeenth century and the specification (now in German) is:

Gedact	8
Flöte	4
Prinzipal	2
Quint	1⅓
Terz	⅘

Attention should be drawn to the most unusual octave tierce; Sutton was meticulous in preserving things as their makers arranged them, so it seems most likely that this is an original stop. Otherwise the design is normal for the size of the instrument, as is the case, although the marbled panelling gives the impression of unusual richness.

The organ has been used for the outdoor pilgrimage processions every August since it came to Kiedrich. One of the good things about the walled churchyard at Kiedrich is its favourable acoustic, so that this small instrument is well able to direct the singing of a large crowd of people. Besides this, the organ is used to accompany the boys' parts of the sung services in church all the year round, and for some of the interludes.

Vijvekapelle Church, near Bruges in Belgium

This church was built, with Jean de Béthune as its architect, between 1865 and 1867.[88] Sutton was certainly involved with the organ, though

The organ in Vijvekapelle Church

quite how far is not clear. A letter in the Béthune Archive from him inquires: "Have the shutters for Vijve Kapelle arrived from Hardmans yet?" We may think it rather strange for the shutters to be made in Birmingham while the rest of the case was being carved at Gand by Van Robaeys, one of Béthune's workmen. When they did arrive August Martin painted them with familiar scenes from the life of Our Lord and His Mother. Gaby Moortgat says that the case was made after an old Dutch model[89], and there are certainly features that can be paralleled in Holland, but there is none of the obvious copying that is evident at Eltville, for instance. One feels the design was probably Béthune's with suggestions (e.g. the doors) from Sutton. The gallery is of the usual Sutton polygonal shape, with linenfold panelling, and is quite small as at Kiedrich. Hooghuys built the musical part of the organ and the specification was as follows:

Manual, C (no C-sharp) to c^3, 48 notes.
Bourdon   8
Prestant   4
Flute   4
Nazard   2 ⅔
Doublette   2
Fourniture   IV
Cornet   III treble only, controlled by pedal
Trompett   8
Pulldown pedals, C-b, 11 notes.

It must be noted here that the cornice and spirettes of this organ-case are almost duplicated at St. Andrew-the-Less, Cambridge, an organ with several other Sutton characteristics but no incontrovertible proof that he was involved in its building.

Eltville-am-Rhein Church

This small organ was built in 1868 and cost 1,895 florins, excluding the shutters painted by August Martin, which were presented by John Sutton and cost 1,750 florins.[90] The case now faces down the south aisle from the east but was built originally in the first arch of the nave arcade, which was filled up with masonry to make it possible for this approximation of the "proper" position for an organ. The case is remarkable for the fact that it copies and combines features from the cases at Sion/Sitten in Canton Valais, Switzerland, and Kiedrich, a couple of kilometres away. The paintings on the shutters, for instance, copy those at Sion as exactly as a Nazarene artist could – that is, with deeper colours and slight modifications of head positions to show reverence and, incidentally, to fit a different shutter-shape. The photograph shows how the other features are dovetailed to make a

ORGAN LOVER

The organ in Eltville-am-Rhein (above) compared with the organ-case in Sion, Switzerland (right) drawn by A.G. Hill

Sutton's sketches of the proposed organ for Eltville-am-Rhein

very successful revival of a Gothic piece of church furniture.

The Sion influence at Eltville indicates that we certainly do not know about every journey that John Sutton undertook.

In addition, there were other organs in Germany that Sutton had to do with for, if he did not influence the work done on them, it is difficult to explain how they appear in the Hooghuys list of organs worked upon by the Belgian firm[91]. Many reasonable organ-builders were accessible in Germany without the added expense of transport to and from Bruges.

Freiburg-im-Breisgau, die Langschifforgel

The story of the work inspired and at least partly paid for by John Sutton at the Cathedral of Freiburg-im-Breisgau is long and complicated.[92] The original single organ-case, containing all the pipes and placed in the north triforium, dates from 1545, with a small gallery of five parts of an octagon. In 1867 Sutton offered 3,000 thaler for a new organ – or better, one rebuilt and using all the ancient pipes – and by 21 September, 1869, when John Norbury drew it[93] there was a sizeable *Positiv* case in position on the gallery rail, with cusped panels at the

John Norbury's drawing (1869) of the organ in Freiburg-im-Breisgau

sides. Shutters for both *Hauptwerk* and *Positiv* cases arrived in 1870 and Dr. Hill noted in 1883 that the paintings on them were "either modern or re-touched"[94]: they were probably the work of August Martin. Owing to John Sutton's early death in 1873 the organ was merely restored (perhaps with new action) as it stood and the new *Positiv* case remained empty until 1936, when, with another re-building, all the shutters were removed.

The Freiburg-im-Breisgau Langschifforgel today

When these organs in England, Germany and Belgium are viewed collectively they show an impressive adherence to the true principles laid down by John Sutton. Where the organs were new (clearly historic instruments had to be approached with different, though no less firm, rules) they had to be as small as possible whilst being adequate for their job. They must be raised off the floor and, ideally, in something that could be made to look like a triforium position, and they must be properly clothed in Gothic cases, with painted shutters to help devotion and symbolize the Holy Trinity. If the Bruges Seminary chapel had been completed, its organ too would have been built to these principles and the young, impressionable seminarians would, Sutton must have hoped, take the principles with them when they came to build and furnish their own churches in time to come.

Other Organs Associated with John Sutton

There are several other organs in England and Belgium with a strong likelihood of having Sutton connections or his influence behind them. They are listed below for the sake of completeness.

The Organ at St. Andrew-the-Less, Newmarket Road, Cambridge

In the minute-book of the Committee of the Cambridge Architectural Society[95] there is a short note under the date 14 November, 1853, of a discussion about the restoration of the church of Barnwell St. Andrew (another title for the church under discussion): "... the restoration of the Rood turret and staircase as a means of access to the organ ... if the proposed arrangements were carried out, there was great probability that an organ would be presented." No names are mentioned so there is no certainty that John Sutton was the likely donor, but the suggestion of restoring this sort of staircase in a church (and his sketch of his proposed arrangement in the Bruges Seminary Chapel on page 168 illustrates the idea well), the necessity of an organ-console approached in this way being high on a chancel wall – the West Tofts position – and the nature of the gift itself, all point to him.

This organ was described by the late Revd. Andrew Freeman in 1939[96] as having "a case of distinction", and he wrote that he was "convinced that Sir John Sutton had a hand in the provision of this pretty front, and likely enough Pugin designed it." The organ is placed on the north side of the chancel above the choir-stalls. As there is not enough height for a gallery the console is placed on the floor with about two feet of walling between its top and the beginning of the wooden coving that supports the overhanging impost of the case,

The organ in the church of St. Andrew-the-Less, Cambridge. Note the similarity of design to the organ-case in Vijvekapelle Church, Belgium (page 89)

giving a certain impression of detachment. "The front pipes (of plain metal, with the largest one embossed) are arranged as in the neighbouring Chapel of Jesus College, except that the tower is semi-circular instead of V-shaped. The carving is plentiful, elaborate and good. The woodwork of the case is painted dark green and dark brown, and the carving is partly red but mostly gilded. The upper part is slightly wider than the lower: the front overhang is more pronounced (than at Jesus College). The folding doors add to the effectiveness of the case, though they are plainer than the ones already described. The front pipes, like those at West Tofts, are unprovided with ears."[97] The architectural composition of the organ console, with a stone doorway on either side giving access to the vestry behind, and the organ-case above pulling the whole into unity, is dignified.

There is absolutely nothing in extant records about this case and organ, and the present situation of the church (not in Anglican hands) does not help investigation. Pevsner in *The Buildings of Britain — Cambridgeshire* says "organ case 1854 by Pugin" and it is true that a restoration did take place in that year — discussed, as we have already noted, by the Architectural Society of which Sutton was a member. Freeman himself noted in the article already quoted, that A. W. Pugin died on 14 September, 1852, so cannot be the designer. There is, though, an important clue in the case itself — the cornice and the mass of flat pinnacles above it is very similar to the same parts of the case at Vijvekapelle near Bruges in Belgium[98]. This church was designed throughout by Sutton's friend Jean de Béthune. The organ was built by Sutton's favoured Belgian craftsman Hooghuys and tradition says that Sutton gave at least some of the cost of it. If we accept John Sutton as the probable donor of the St. Andrew's organ, it begins to seem likely that the organ-case was designed by Béthune and made in his workshops at Gand.

The console bears the name-plate of A. T. Miller of Cambridge, a respected organ-builder of the last third of the nineteenth century. But he began to work on his own only in 1856[99], so someone else must have built the organ in 1854. The prime candidate seems to be George Dawson, who was certainly putting together organs from Belgium and England at this time, for West Tofts was made by him too. If, say thirty years later, the organ needed fairly extensive repair (Dawson cannot have been a very good workman for only one organ of his (Great Walsingham) remains in original condition) Miller was on hand to do the work, as he was at West Tofts. The fact that many of his earlier organs were provided with good cases[100] must have commended him to the Sutton brothers Augustus and Frederick, when looking for someone to carry out the West Tofts work.

It was impossible to carry out the plan suggested by John Sutton at St. Andrew-the-Less because the chancel walls were only about half the height needed for it; one wonders whether he had visited the church, or got it mixed up with another. But whether it was possible to fulfil his conditions or not, it is likely that he felt that as he had given his word to make a contribution to the organ, if not to provide it altogether, true principles demanded that he kept that word and the organ was built to what seems to be a possible Béthune design.

The Organ in Christ's College Chapel, Cambridge

This organ is included in the list, not because Sutton ever heard it, for in his time nobody did, but because he was instrumental in preserving the ancient pipework belonging to it for rebuilding when the time came.

An organ was supplied to the College by Charles Quarles (organist at the time at Trinity College, and Mus.B.) and opened in

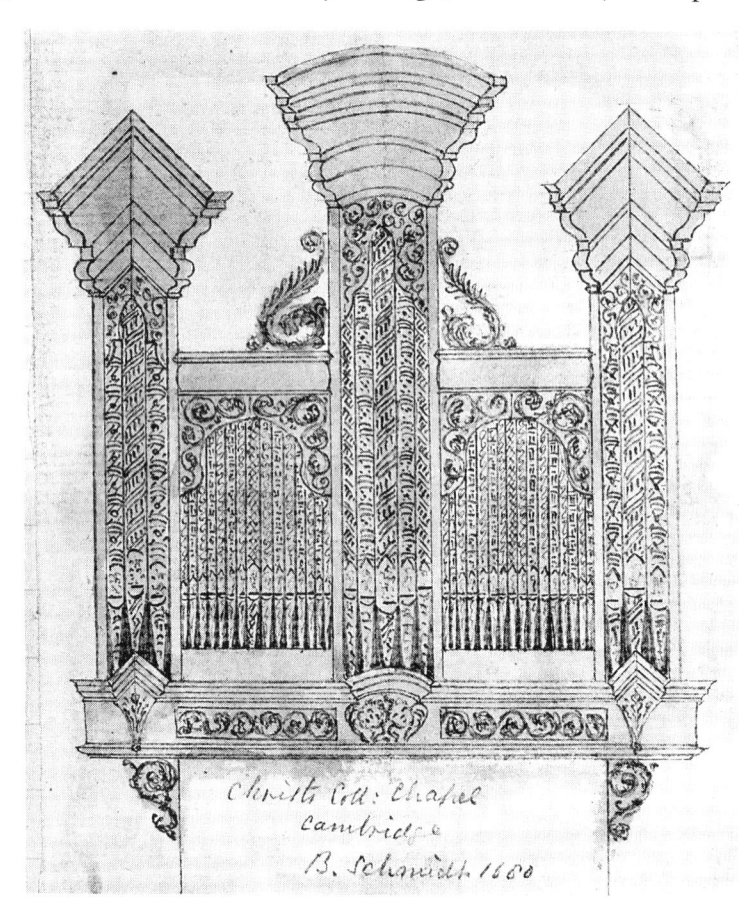

Drawing of the organ in Christ's College Chapel from the Sperling notebooks

April 1705[101]. Quarles' role is obscure – the surviving pipework may be by Bernard Smith and the style of the case certainly hints at the same builder. From about 1785 the organ was not used and was allowed to become ruinous.

The Revd. Andrew Freeman stated that Sutton "persuaded the college to allow the pipes to be stowed away in boxes to ensue preservation"[102]. There is an entry in J. C. Bishop's ledger dated 15 May, 1849: "Time and expenses examining the Organ at Christs College Cambridge preparatory to repairs – 1. 1.''."[103] As it is listed under "J. Sutton Esqr. Jesus College Cambridge" we must conclude that the visit was paid for by Sutton, but no further entry has been made for this college. The charge is remarkably small for a visit out of London; the normal cost of a tuning visit, admittedly for two people, was five pounds or five guineas even when "Mr. S. paid fare back"[104]. Perhaps Bishop supposed that the contract would be his and charged a nominal fee accordingly, for it would certainly not cover his train-fare.

If the pipes were stowed away in boxes by a professional organ-builder, Bishop did not do the work: did the elusive George Dawson? In the event, Bishop's were not employed to rebuild the Christ's College organ; this was done by Hill in 1865, long after John Sutton had left Cambridge permanently.[105] Possibly a judicious offer of money might have prompted the College to put the rebuilding in hand earlier but in 1849, with all the work at Jesus College unfinished and with the first stage of West Tofts church restoration under way[106], Sutton's finances must have been stretched to the uttermost.

Osmond Fisher's Organ

Another chamber-organ with John Sutton associations is now in private ownership in London and thanks are due to the present owner for sending this description of it, and for his comments. A photograph is to be found in Freeman & Rowntree, *Father Smith*, p. 184.

There are two notes glued inside the instrument:

(a) This organ was purchased in London by the Revd. William Lisle Bowles the poet. He placed it in the church of Bremhill, Wilts., of which he became Vicar in 1805. I bought the organ out of Bremhill Church, when Archdeacon Drury, the vicar, replaced it by a harmonium. The organ was repaired in the 18 fifties by Dawson of Cambridge, under the supervision of Mr., afterwards Sir John, Sutton, author of 'Organs built in England'. He was of opinion that this organ was of the date of Charles the first.

O. Fisher

(b) This organ was discovered in London by Canon Bowles of Salisbury (the poet) and placed by him in his Church at Bremhill, Wilts.; whence I bought it from Henry Drury (afterwards Archdeacon) and had it repaired at Cambridge by Dawson under the supervision of John (afterwards Sir John) Sutton. He considered it to be of the date of Charles I. There was formerly in the old organ in Exeter Cathedral, built by Loosemore, pipes diapered as the central pipe of this organ is.

O. Fisher

Fisher, as we have seen above, was Chaplain of Jesus College in Cambridge all the time Sutton was in residence there.

The organ has features in the windchest very similar to those found in the "Dean Bargrave" organ at Canterbury, which is dated 1629. On the other hand, the unusual number of half-stops suggests French influence of the second half of the seventeenth century, while some of the foliage carving on the case has a strong similarity to that on the Robert Dallam case at St. Mary Woolnoth in the City of London. The present owner, therefore, thinks it possible that Robert Dallam built the organ between the Restoration in 1660 and his death on 31 May 1665. Other possible builders might be Dallam's brothers, or Thomas or Renatus Harris.

The organ seems to have had the following tonal scheme when Fisher bought it:

GG (no GG-sharp) to c^3, 53 notes:
Stop Diapason   8
Open Diapason   8   treble only, metal, in front.
Principal   4   wood.
Two treble half-stops, and one bass half-stop.

We can assume that the three half-stop slides were empty, as the Open and Stop Diapasons and Principal obviously date from the seventeenth century. Fisher and Sutton may have decided to employ George Dawson to encourage him, or perhaps because more established organ-builders would not have done what they wanted. Possibly Fisher did not want to pay London prices and was impatient to have his new possession put in order as soon as possible!

Apart from plain restoration work, a new keyboard was fitted with short seventeenth-century style keys with hinges of parchment. The naturals are of plain wood and the sharps are black. The pin action was retained but the diagonal reservoir was replaced with a typical nineteenth-century horizontal one, with a feeder whose pedal is on the front-to-back axis of the organ, unlike most eighteenth-century examples where the pedal is parallel to the instrument's front. Folding doors were fitted to the front, or may have been replacements. The bass half-stop was joined to a treble one and a Mixture planted on them of 19 and 22 in the bass and then 15, 17 and 19 in the treble. The other treble half-stop was given a Fifteenth.

At some point in its history the stop-controls of this little organ were altered completely, the one original lever being that of the Stop Diapason on the bass key-block which is vertical with lateral movement. The other ranks of pipes are controlled by iron pedals, reading from the centre – Mixture, Principal, Open Diapason Treble and Fifteenth Treble. They are pressed down to put the stop 'on' and pushed upwards by the toes to silence it; the natural inertia of the action holds them in position.[107]

It is most unlikely to have been John Sutton who suggested these almost unique pedals, for such a radical departure from tradition is against all his respect for early organs – evidenced by all other restorations he carried out or advised upon. On the other hand, the treble half of the Mixture will produce just the sort of sharp, strong sound he liked, and is most likely to have been produced to his design. He was obviously aware of the unsociability of a tierce in the bass part of the compass, especially in the confined space of a domestic music-room.

The Prayer-Desk Organ

Two photographs with notes on their backs have been passed on to the author. The notes read:

> "Small Organ from St. Mary the Virgin, West Tofts, Norfolk, built by James Scott Organ Builder West Tofts Norfolk for Sir John Sutton who gave it to his brother who was Rector there. Was at 19 Moor Lane, Sculthorpe. Please return to G.W. Hole, 'Graywells', Sculthorpe, Norfolk."[108]

The Prayer-Desk Organ is not an impressive instrument: its compass is two octaves and a third, twenty nine notes, c to e² – tenor C to the E above treble C. Pipes of a single metal stop, no doubt Open Diapason, are disposed in various areas – some on a soundboard at floor level behind pierced doors, some small ones over the keyboard, and two towers at the sides. There is a flat pedal at the left side of the soundboard and from the right side, amazingly, projects a modern bicycle pedal – obviously a replacement for something less incongruous, perhaps connected with the winding arrangements of which there is no other trace in the photos.

What are we to make of this unusual little organ which must have been broken up when its owner of 19 Moor Lane in Sculthorpe either died or moved to smaller premises? Beside the organs of both

John and Frederick Sutton it is really rather uncouth and one cannot see it installed in the lovely chancel at West Tofts, with all its colour and artistry. If in fact it was there once, what would it be wanted for? An old friend, the late Canon Gordon Paget, who was still at 93 a mine of Norfolk and organ lore, wrote:

> "I think that the probable explanation of the Prayer Desk Organ is that Augustus Sutton wanted a little organ next to his stall, which he could play in an emergency, or for a funeral, to save him going into the vestry and climbing up a staircase into the loft to play the larger one."

But he continued, and this may be important:

> "I never saw anything like it in West Tofts church when I visited it many times – the only extra instrument was a little 4-octave harmonium keyboard immediately under his prayer-desk in the returned chancel stalls, to give the intonation, I suppose, for a hymn or plainsong tone."[109]

It looks as though there may have been a mix-up in someone's mind between the West Tofts people's memory of Augustus Sutton playing some sort of organ in his stall (and whether pipes, reeds or electronics, all are lumped together under the word 'Organ') and the vague idea that as the probable builder of the little organ was James Scott of West Tofts, there must be a connection with the Suttons somewhere.

A tentative suggestion is that this organ was not made for John Sutton at all (few people outside the family have realised that he left England semi-permanently in 1855) but for Augustus Sutton for use in the workhouse chapel at Thetford which he designed and to which he certainly took his choir a time or two[110]. He had not much money to spare, but would have scorned the use of a cheap substitute for an organ so possibly a small product of his village organ-builder, which would support the singing of aged men and women and could be played by the chaplain from his desk, was presented to the workhouse chapel. When this chapel was closed someone remembered that the organ had West Tofts connections and drew their own conclusions.

Bruges, St. Gillis

This church, which is where Sutton worshipped when living in the city, has a very long organ-history. The first mention of organs in the records comes in 1408: "*singhende messe met orghele en met beyeerdene*" (sung Mass with organ and glockenspiel). Up to 1850 the church owned a large one-manual organ originally built by Andries Jacob Berger in 1743. It must have been a brilliant-sounding instrument for by 1842 its abbreviated specification was as follows: 8 (Bourdon), 4,4,3,2,1⅗, II,III,II, Cornet, 8 (halved), 4.[111] However, in 1850 an organ was obtained from the former Jesuit Church in Turnhout for which no details remain except that it was often in organ-builders' hands during its comparatively short stay in St. Gillis. In 1878 Louis-Benoit Hooghuys built a two-manual organ for the church in his own style, but it was the ex-Turnhout organ that Sutton must always have known (though it does not appear in any of his remaining letters) while he was in Bruges.

Bruges, Cathedral of St. Salvator

It seems that Sutton's reputation as a knowledgable organ-lover soon got around in Bruges: the minute-book of the church committee of the Cathedral (*"het bureau van de kerkmeesters"*) records under date 5 June, 1856:

> "Furthermore, Mr. de Stoop informed the committee that Sir John Sutton, the English artist, would make a gift of a new stop for the *Positif*, to the fabric. This stop would serve to reinforce (the effect of) the small organ and would be made after the fashion and style of the ancient stops of the *Grand-orgue*, to the point where it would chime in with the general character of the whole instrument."

On 24 November of the same year the restored organ was inspected by the said Sir John Sutton, the Englishman then living in Bruges –

Interior of St. Salvator's Cathedral, Bruges, c.1910

"*organiste-amateur de distinction*", who wrote the following report:

> "This is to certify that I have examined the organ in the cathedral and find al[l] in perfect order. I believe the organ at this present time to be in as good condition, as when first placed in the church."[112]

The stop Sutton presented seems to be the Holpijp 8ft which still exists in the present organ.

Bruges, The Seminary Chapels

There is no evidence at all about what instruments John Sutton provided for the chapels of his seminary in Bruges, whether in the students' original house or in the Schippers' Capel that he cleared and arranged himself. It is most unlikely that there was no organ at all, for that would be against all his instincts; and equally unlikely that it would be a large instrument because it was going to be only temporary.

In the Béthune family home at Kasteel Marke there are two little nineteenth-century organs, one of which is in the chapel. Both look rather like small upright pianos with a piece of fabric stretched inside a plain rectangular framework in front to let the sound out, and no visible pipes. Blowing is by means of harmonium-style pedals. Family tradition says that one came from a relative's house in Bruges: might it not have been made by Hooghuys? – and might not the other one, so similar in appearance, have been made by him too? The ex-Bruges example is almost portable, with two stops only; the other has a third rank. Neither can have been expensive and either would have supported the singing of up to thirty young men quite adequately, without any of the frills or unnecessary power Sutton disliked. If indeed Hooghuys produced this sort of tiny organ, such an instrument might well have been provided for the temporary chapels of the Anglo-Belgian Seminary.

Organ-builders Associated with John Sutton

John Sutton is only known to have used two organ-builders in England, Bishop and Dawson, but others have tenuous connections with him, notably James Scott. In Belgium and Germany he entrusted all the work for which he paid to Hooghuys of Bruges.

James Scott of West Tofts

Norfolk could boast of several small organ-builders in the mid-nineteenth century. Two of them had their workshops in Norwich the county town – Mark Noble who had been apprenticed to the London organ-builder G. M. Holdich, who had himself learned his craft with J.C. Bishop, and James Corps. Both these men built quite a number of instruments, Noble very much in the style of his master Holdich. There were also several craftsmen who had been trained in other trades altogether but turned to organ-building with greater or less success – such as J. Bullen of Pulham Market who built an organ for Diss Corn Hall in 1855 and who was really a blacksmith and engineer. Then there was Benjamin Collins of Lammas who, although White's *Directory of Norfolk 1864* calls him an organ-builder, was actually a shoe-maker. He built a large two-manual organ at Scottow church with help from some of the estate craftsmen from Scottow Hall. Two of the turned stop-knobs, with most attractive ornament on the fronts, are in the author's possession and they were obviously made by an estate cabinet-maker with plenty of time for detail. Samuels and Twyford, who built an organ for New Buckenham church, were respectively a hair-dresser and a paper-bag maker! And finally there were Mack of Great Yarmouth and James Scott of West Tofts who is the subject of this section.[113]

It is inevitable that an organ-builder who lived in the village where the church was restored and provided with an organ by John Sutton should be associated with him in people's minds, as he has frequently been; but in fact no liaison between the two men has yet been evidenced, let alone proved. The dates are wrong. We have seen that Sutton left England virtually for good in 1855 and James Scott of West Tofts appears for the first time in Harrod's *Directory* of 1863 as a carpenter, then in White's *Norfolk* as an organ-builder in 1864, and in *Kelly's Directory* of 1865 also as an organ-builder but with the name John. There is no mention of him in the 1875 *Kelly's Directory*. He built organs at Marham, Tittleshall (which went to Mileham and is now at Beeston), Weeting, East Walton and Boughton in Norfolk, and perhaps at Fakenham Magna in Suffolk[114]. They are all small, of four or five stops on the manual and perhaps an octave of pedals and pedal pipes, and some have a short compass. None of the instruments have ornamental case-work. Internal evidence shows that Scott made all the wooden parts for his organs, only the metal pipes being bought in from outside. One of the instruments, at East Walton, has a signature on the back of the roller-board, and the Beeston example is the only one with a name-plate on the console. Perhaps Scott was influenced by Augustus Sutton, his rector, not to put name-plates on his organs, in true Camden Society anonymity. He may have read John Sutton's book and noted his dislike of organs too big for their job, but almost certainly he had read John Baron's book *Scudamore Organs*, in which both short compass and caselessness were advocated[115]. But no firm evidence that James Scott and John Sutton were associated in the provision and building of any one organ has ever appeared.

Hooghuys of Bruges

The Hooghuys family had come to Bruges in 1806[116]. They had spent some time in Middelburg but originated in the province of Holland in the Netherlands. Gerrit-Simon Hooghuys (or Simon-Gerrit, according to which source one follows) worked on the organ at St. Gillis in Bruges before his death in 1813[117]. His son Simon-Gerard continued the business until he died in 1853 and it is with Simon-Gerard's son Louis-Benoit (1822-1885) that we are concerned. Two of his brothers were dead by the time John Sutton came to live in Bruges and while Francois-Bernard (1830-1888) was probably associated with him, Louis-Benoit was the dominant partner in the firm.

"Hooghuys war ein Orgelbauer, der sich von den neuen Richtungen im Kunstgewerbe des 19 Jahrhunderts inspirieren liess. Die frühere pauschale Ablehnung dieser Neo-Stile ist heute als nicht gerechtfertigt erkannt; dies trifft auch für das Schaffen von Hooghuys zu. Seine viele Instruments zeigen, dass er in der spätklassischen Orgelbau-tradition Flanderns verblieb."[118]

(Hooghuys was an organ-builder, who allowed himself to be influenced by the new directions in the decorative arts of the nineteenth century. The exaggerated lack of appreciation of this new-style Gothic current earlier in this century, is now recognised as being wrongly inspired: we meet it in the work of Hooghuys. His many instruments demonstrate that he remained firmly in the late classical tradition of Flanders organ-building.)

After Louis-Benoit Hooghuys' death his son Aime-Jean, a much lesser figure, published a list of his father's organs by way of announcing that he had taken over the business[119]. In it, new instruments were not distinguished in any way from those that were only restored or repaired, so the picture is not an entirely honest one. However, we learn that Louis-Benoit built an organ in Norway – quite a small instrument of one manual and eight stops in Tvedestrand – as well as a couple in the Netherlands, and carried out quite a lot of work in Germany, we may suppose all under Sutton's influence. The organs built in Holland we can understand as the family came from there and perhaps repairs were carried out on grandfather Gerrit-Simon's instruments – but Norway? Anyhow, there it is in the list, and we must take Aime-Jean's word for it.

It is obvious from reading the specifications of his organs that survive that Louis-Benoit Hooghuys was a firm follower of the Belgian or south Netherlands organ tradition[120]. The first manual had to have at least a dozen stops before a second manual was contemplated: The '*Temple Anglais*' in Bruges, for instance, had fourteen stops for only one manual, and there are several others with similar arrangements. In contrast to English organs in this third quarter of the nineteenth century there was hardly ever an independent pedal stop – the 16' Bourdon normally being placed on the principal manual. Where an independent pedal department was provided Aime-Jean has written '*ped. separe*' in every case in his list – and there are not many Belgian ones. Even the organ built for Louis-Benoit's own parish church of St. Jacques in Bruges in 1869, though with no less than twenty-eight stops on its two manuals, had no pedal stops at all.

However, the fact that Sutton employed Hooghuys to restore the Kiedrich organ – arguably the most ancient he knew and so of tremendous importance to him – proves that this relatively minor Belgian craftsman was prepared to take a great deal of trouble over restoration work, and that Sutton regarded him as being very capable. The preservation of the Kiedrich organ alone is enough to write his name in an organic roll-of-honour.

REFERENCES

1. *Stones and Story*, p. 295.
2. pub. Aldersgate Street, London: J. Masters 1847. (New edition: Positif Press, Oxford, 1979.)
3. *The Library of the Fathers*, ed. E. B. Pusey (Oxford, from 1838).
4. James F. White, *The Cambridge Movement* (Cambridge University Press, 1962), p. 20.
5. J.M. Neale and F. Webb, *The Symbolism of Churches and Church Ornaments: a Translation of the First Book of the Rationale Divinorum Officiorum, Written by William Durandus, sometime Bishop of Mende* (Leeds, 1848).
6. Cross, *The Oxford Dictionary of the Christian Church* (Oxford University Press, 1957).
7. Hopkins and Rimbault, p. 52.
8. Hopkins and Rimbault, p. 69.
9. John Baron, *Scudamore Organs, or Practical Hints respecting Organs for Village Churches and Small Chancels, on Improved Principles* (London: Bell & Daldy, 1862) p. vi.
10. W. E. Dickson, *Fifty Years of Church Music* (Ely: Hills, 1894) p. 22.
11. Paragraph suggested to the author by Mr. Austin Niland.
12. *Dictionary of National Biography*.
13. In the possession of Mr. Michael Gillingham.
14. *Short Account* p. 5.
15. *Ecclesiologist*, 1843, p. 60.
16. *Letters of John Mason Neale* (London: Longmans, Green & Co., 1910) p. 14.
17. A copy of the seventh edition in *The Cambridge Movement*, James F. White, *op. cit.* p. 231.
18. *A Few Hints on the Practical Study of Ecclesiastical Antiquities for the Use of the Cambridge Camden Society*, third edition, (Cambridge: 1842) p. 16.
19. *Short Account*, p. 27.
20. Camden Society: *A Few Words to Church Builders* (Cambridge University Press, 1844) pp. 5-6.
21. *Ecclesiologist*, 1843, p. 4.
22. *Ecclesiologist*, January 1845, p. 6.
23. *ibid.* p. 7.
24. William Hill, 1789-1870: in business 1825-1870.
25. Dr. Henry John Gauntlett, 1805-1870.
26. Hopkins and Rimbault, p. 443 *seqq.*

27 Visits in 1837, 1840, 1842: Thistlethwaite, *BIOS Journal* VII, 45.
28 Clutton and Niland, *The British Organ* (London: Batsford, 1963) p. 89
29 James Chapman Bishop, 1783-1854.
30 Specification – see Elvin, pp. 142-3
31 *Musical World*, 15 September 1855, quoted Elvin, p. 157.
32 Dugdale, *Monasticon Anglicanum* (London, 1655), quoted *Short Account*, p. 102.
33 Sandford, *The History of the Coronation of King James II* (London, 1687), quoted *Short Account*, p. 53, footnote.
34 John Baron, *Scudamore Organs* (London: Bell & Daldy, 1862) pp. 30-31.
35 *Short Account*, p. 100.
36 *ibid*. p. 8.
37 *ibid*. p. 108.
38 *ibid*. p. 97.
39 *BIOS Journal* VII, 90.
40 J. C. Bishop's Estimate Book, 1845-51.
41 "Organo-Historica: or the History of Cathedral and Parochial Organs", *The Christian Remembrancer* or *The Churchman's Biblical, Ecclesiastical and Literary Miscellany* XXII (London: 1819-1840) – quoted N. Thistlethwaite in *BIOS Reporter* VII *et seqq*.
42 Elvin, p. 174.
43 Elvin, p. 174.
44 Letter to the author.
45 Letter and list, giving dating of the pipes, in the author's possession.
46 Suggestion by Stephen Bicknell, *BIOS Reporter* VI, no. 4 (Oct. 1982) 8.
47 Elvin, p. 173.
48 *BIOS Reporter, ut sup*. 8.
49 e.g. St. Paul's in 1849 – entirely new Swell and two other stops replaced: Elvin, p. 163.
50 Elvin, many estimates pp. 95 *seqq*.
51 Elvin, p. 148.
52 Bishop & Son's Ledger.
53 Diary in Bishop Archives
54 Thistlethwaite, p. 47.
55 Stanton, p. 11.
56 Letter to the author from Mr. R. A. J. Bower, organ-builder.
57 Diary in the possession of the Revd. B. B. Edmonds.
58 Enclosure with letter to the author from Mr. R. A. J. Bower, organ-builder.
59 Hardman.
60 In a manuscript diary of organs visited, in the possession of the Revd. B. B. Edmonds.
61 Bishop.
62 Bishop.
63 Bishop.
64 Thistlethwaite, p. 41.
65 Bill in Bishop Archives.
66 Quoted, *Father Smith*, p. 166.
67 Quoted, *Father Smith*, p. 75.
68 Bishop.
69 *The Stowe Catalogue* (Fleet Street, London: David Bogue, 1848) p. 245. Courtesy V. & A. Museum.
70 *The Stowe Catalogue*, p. 245.
71 *Sotheby's Catalogue* (London, 1924) including Freeman's photograph of the organ. Courtesy V. & A. Museum.
72 *Father Smith*, p. 148. There is some doubt as to whether W. R. Hearst purchased a second organ in England in 1922 (information from the late Dr. W.L. Sumner, quoted Wilson, *The English Chamber Organ*, p. 136): but might even an American millionaire find two seventeenth-century organs for sale in two years?
73 *Father Smith*, pp. 46-47.
74 *BIOS Reporter* V, no. 2 (May 1981) 10.
75 Michael Wilson, *The English Chamber Organ* (London: Cassirer) p. 93.
76 *Father Smith*, p. 187.
77 P. Williams, *The European Organ 1450-1850* (London: Batsford, 1966).

78 Kiedrich Tourist Book.
79 Franz Bösken's article is the only subject of this volume.
80 As in the following repair contract, quoted Zaun, pp. 113-114.
81 *Short Account*, p. 11.
82 *ibid.*
83 Béthune.
84 Letter from August Martin to Béthune, 6 September 1861; Béthune.
85 Bénézit, *Dictionnaire des Peintres, Sculpteurs, Dessinateurs et Graveurs* (Paris, 1976).
86 Stanton, p. 87.
87 Rudolf Quoika, *Das Positif in Geschichte und Gegenwart* (Kassel: Bärenreiter, 1957) p. 35.
88 Letter from M. G. Potvlieghe to the author, 18 August 1966. Nearly all information in this paragraph from it.
89 Gaby Moortgat, *Oude Orgels in Vlaanderen II* (Brussels: B.R.T. Publications, 1965) Photo's of the organ-case and keyboard, pp. 136-7.
90 Eltville parish records.
91 Patrick Roose, "Werklijst anno 1885 van L. B. Hooghuys", Brussels: *Orgelkunst*, December 1983, p. 5.
92 Carl Winter, *Das Orgelwerk des Freiburger Münsters*, (Christophorus-Verlag, Freiburg-im-Breisgau, 1967).
93 John Norbury, *The Box of Whistles*, (London, 1887).
94 A.G. Hill, *The Organs and Organ Cases of the Middle Ages and Renaissance* (London, 1883 and 1891).
95 Cambridge University Library.
96 *The Organ*, vol. XVIII, p. 144.
97 *ibid.*, p. 145

98 Photograph of Vijvekapelle in Moortgat, *Oude Orgels in Vlaanderen*, II, B.R.T. Brussels, 1965, p. 137.
99 *The Organ*, vol. LXV, p. 127.
100 *ibid.*, the whole article.
101 Thistlethwaite, *The Organs of Cambridge*, Oxford, Positif Press 1983, p. 22.
102 Freeman, *Father Smith*, London, 1926, p. 43.
103 Bishop Archives.
104 Bishop Archives.
105 *The Organs of Cambridge, ut sup..*
106 see p. 9.
107 Description of this organ from letters to the Author from the present owner.
108 Photos in the author's possession.
109 Letter from Canon Paget to the author.
110 Notes in the West Tofts registers in Norfolk County Record Office.
111 Lannoo/Peeters, *Orgeln in der alten Grafschaft Flandern*, Berlin, Merseburger, 1985, p. 9.
112 A. Fauconnier & P. Roose, *Het Historisch Orgal in Vlaanderen IVa*, Brussels 1986, p. 145.
113 The facts in this paragraph from art. in *The Organ* vol. LXII, pp. 112 - 120.
114 Letter to the author from Mr. Robin Wilson.
115 John Baron, *Scudamore Organs*, London, Bell & Daldy, second edition 1862.
116 Lannoo/Peeters, *op. cit.*, p. 10.
117 *ibid.*, p. 9.
118 *ibid.*, pp. 10 and 12.
119 P. Roose, art, Werklijst anno 1885 van L. B. Hooghuys, in *Orgelkunst VI*, no. 4.
120 *cf.* Williams, *The European Organ 1450-1850, ut sup*.

CHAPTER III

Sir John Sutton – Restorer of Churches

The nineteenth century, as most people know, was a great time for the building and repairing of churches. In England, the Oxford Movement had a tremendous influence on the clergy and the moneyed classes (wages were low, so that the great majority of people had little or no chance to help) and the system of church rates gave the impression that the repair of churches was indeed the responsibility of the better-off. On the Continent, both the problems and the methods of dealing with them were different but, whether in or out of England, John Sutton's money, enthusiasm and knowledge were welcome. We know nothing, sadly, about which buildings he contributed money to in the diocese of Plymouth after he went to live in Europe, for no records have survived. The same is broadly true of his work in Germany and Belgium, except that Zaun gives some of the Kiedrich work, and a recently-discovered transcript of a lecture given two months after Sutton's death gives us what must be nearly a complete list of it. The over-riding impression, though, is that he was determined that nobody should know exactly what he spent on his building projects; what mattered was the architectural result, and the restoration of the old builders' concepts, all offered to God.

In the present chapter, the buildings are dealt with as far as possible in order as the work was begun, and a note is added on Sutton's houses in Bruges and Kiedrich, which also have marked characteristics.

Lady Sutton's Chantry

Lady Mary Elizabeth Sutton, Sir John's mother, died on 1 January, 1842, in London. She left a large family, and her husband did not marry again. Quite soon afterwards there was a move to keep her memory green, as is shown by this entry in the Painting Daybook in the Hardman Archives:

> "Painting at Chantry and Tomb at Sir Richard Sutton's,
> Lynford Hall, near Brandon, Suffolk. 25 days,   £59 - 10 - 0.
>
> A. W. Pugin, Esq., for drawings for above painting   £10.
>
>   5 December 1846."[1]

We might take this to mean that the first Chantry was at Lynford Hall itself and not as at present in West Tofts church, which figures in a later entry in the same book. However, in 1846 Sir Richard had applied for a faculty to sink a vault on the south side of the chancel for himself and his family, above which was to be erected a family mausoleum and a memorial of his late wife.[2] And when his fifth son Augustus arrived as Rector in 1849, he made a sketch of the church from the south-east which shows the gable-end of a building to the south of the chancel.

A. W. N. Pugin visited Lynford, according to his diary, on 4 October, 1844, and on this date only.[3] Did he then take away with him all the information he needed for providing full working drawings not only of the Chantry that was to be, but also for the parish church at West Tofts? So far no plans of the Chantry have been found, which is a pity because it was the first of Pugin's designs in this field, ante-dating the Rolle Chantry at Bicton by at least four years.

If the entry in the Hardman Painting Daybook is followed up, there is another possible site for this Chantry – at Lynford Hall itself: for the site of the medieval parish church at Lynford, St. Helen's, formed the south-west corner of the courtyard when the new Hall was built in 1720. In fact, a section of flint walling and two piers dividing the chancel from a north or south chapel remain to this day, and one of the unexpected things Sir Richard Sutton did was to have them faced with white bricks.[4] It would have been possible to incorporate these fragments in a new building, but in that case all would have been destroyed in 1863, when the Lynford Hall the Sutton family knew as home was pulled down. It seems then, that the 1846 Chantry and tomb were at West Tofts church, and the Chantry was re-built and re-decorated during the building of the new chancel in 1856. The tomb itself, of course, remains and some drawings for it still exist, together with Pugin's notes on them:[5] "early vine leaf from

Drawings by A.W.N. Pugin for Lady Sutton's tomb

Southwell" and "early foliage from the Lincoln casts" illustrate his well-known habit of using existing medieval designs for new works – and in this case the sources were appropriate as Lincoln was well-known to Lady Sutton, and Southwell was the home town of her daughter-in-law Helena (John's wife). Over the tomb-chest is a canopy with heavily crocketed gables on trefoil arches, resting on marble pillars. In the centre of the chest is a brass cross inlaid, at the foot of which is the inscription, "Blessed are the dead which die in the Lord. Rev. 14, 13." Round the side edge of the slab is inscribed:

> "Here lieth the body of Dame Mary Elizabeth Sutton, daughter of Benjamin Burton Esquire County Carlow and wife of Sir Richard Sutton Baronet of Norwood Park county of Nottingham and Lynford Hall Norfolk, who departed this life the first day of January in the year of our Lord MDCCCXLII, aged 44, also William Sutton, infant son of the aforesaid who departed this life in the year of our Lord MDCCCXXVIII."

The tiles on the floor are by Minton whose firm was used by Pugin for many of his largest and most prestigious buildings;[6] the tomb was made by Myers' sculptors.

When did John Sutton and Pugin meet? Professor Stanton suggests it was in "the early and friendly phase of (Pugin's) contact with the Cambridge Camden Society".[7] This may be, but the earlier date of 1837 is possible. In the notes prepared by Mr. Clive Wainwright of the Victoria and Albert Museum for the Victorian Society's tour of Norfolk in 1977, and the section on Oxburgh Hall, occurs the sentence, "the Chapel is certainly a very important early work by Pugin, dating from 1837". Now Oxburgh is only about a dozen miles from Lynford as the crow flies and, if as is perfectly possible, John Sutton's interest in architecture was dawning at this date (he was seventeen, an age of many romantic notions!) it is more than likely that he would ride or drive over to see what was going on; and if the young (25) architect was visiting the site at the same time, a friendship could easily have sprung up.

West Tofts, Parish Church of St. Mary the Virgin

It is not possible to visit West Tofts church now except with special permission, for since late in the 1939-45 war the district in which it stands has been a Battle Area and de-populated. This is a great sadness; as Professor Stanton rightly says,

> "On a number of occasions (A.W.) Pugin was called upon to rebuild, or rebuild and redecorate, medieval churches in Anglican hands ... the first five were serious, respectful and

evocative performances. His achievement at West Tofts was more — it was brilliant; he not only rebuilt the church extensively but added a family chantry and a new chancel and decorated the interior in a style richly reminiscent of the Norfolk churches he so much admired ... These churches and other projects of his last years show with what assurance Pugin strode from one commission to another, leaving on each the impression of his personal taste and giving to each the benefit of some of the inventiveness, freedom and competence he achieved, sadly enough, just as his life was ending."[8]

St. Mary's is a most impressive building by any standards, and even in its present bare interior condition, is full of atmosphere. Outside there is a fine fifteenth-century tower at the west end — and a very rare example of a carved list of donors' names dates it as between 1451 and 1486 — which from the Pugin restoration until 1930 had a leaden spire as well. Continuing slightly to our right there is the four bay nave, whose windows were renewed by Pugin, and the south porch which is entirely his work. Then comes what appears to be a short south transept from the first bay of the chancel, and the fine lofty chancel itself continues on for three more bays to the east. The small vestry on the north side has a turret with a timber-framed top, and finally we come to the Pugin north aisle, which, says Tricker,

"... has its own gabled roof. The dignity of this aisle is enhanced by sturdy buttresses and windows in a later development of the Decorated style ... the east window is a handsome nineteenth-century reproduction of a *c.*1330 window with reticulated tracery".[9]

Before all the work of rebuilding and restoration began, Ladbrooke had sketched the church in the eighteen-twenties. His picture shows the present nave and tower (without any tower pinnacles) with the space occupied by the present porch filled with a fourth window the main entrance to the church at this time was at the base of the tower. There is a short, low chancel with a triple east window, and one window and a small door on the south side. The nave seems to be roofed with pantiles (though at one time it was thatched, as is not uncommon in East Anglia) and to have a small finial on its eastern gable.[10]

Augustus Sutton, fifth son of Sir Richard Sutton and Rector of West Tofts from 1849 to 1885 when he died, kept a diary of the re-building work in the parish Burial Register (kept now in the Norfolk County Record Office in Norwich). This reveals, in the margin, that "the Architect for the undertaking was August Welby Pugin", and dates the first part of the work firmly — "On Thursday

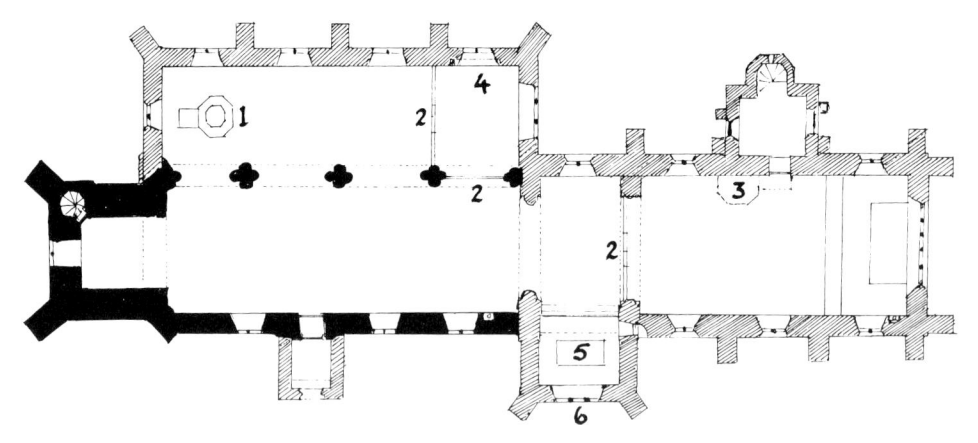

■ Mediaeval Fabric.   ▨ Pugin's 1850s Fabric.

1. Font.
2. Screens remaining.
3. Organ loft.
4. Tomb of Emma Helena Sutton.
5. Tomb of Mary Elizabeth Sutton.
6. Tomb of Sir Richard Sutton.

Plan of St. Mary's Church, West Tofts

the 26th. of April 1849 the foundations for the new north aisle etc. were commenced." This work was completed on 18 July, and the blocked arches into the nave were re-opened the following year. Only on 1 September, 1849, was the Faculty granted: "for a new north aisle, with a screened place for sittings for the family, at a cost of £1,320, to be provided by John Sutton Esq., as a memorial to his mother, the late Lady Mary Elizabeth Sutton. Architect Mr. A.W. Pugin." The document goes on to explain, "New chancel etc. to be carried into effect as the said John Sutton may from time to time be able to raise the funds".[11] Was an "etc." ever intended to cover quite so many additions? It seems that the south porch was built in 1850 and in the same year the wooden font ("the present thing of wood") was burnt at the Rectory, and replaced by an ancient stone one from Swaffham. A new bell-frame and new bells to make up a ring of six had been installed in 1849, and two more were added in 1852. There was then a gap in the work when nothing structural was done, although no doubt the business of furnishing the interior of the nave and north aisle went on.

Augustus Sutton's notes begin again in 1855: "On Wednesday June 27th. the first sod was turned for the foundations of the new chancel", and a marginal note observes, "E. Welby Pugin, Architect" – for Augustus Pugin had died in 1852. However, all the drawings of the chancel and the Sutton Chantry are dated 1850, so this must mean that Edward Pugin merely supervised the work according to his father's plans. Building went on quietly for eighteen months, for in 1856 "on Wednesday Decr. 10th. the gable of the Chantery on the south side of the Chancel was finished thus completing the exterior of the new chancel". We may suppose that about ten days were needed for the removal of scaffolding and builders' rubbish from the interior, and then "On Tuesday Decr. 23rd. the boarding was removed between the church and Chancel thus shewing its fine proportions for the first time to my great dilight [sic]. A.S." This is parallelled by an entry in the Sunday Book, as Augustus Sutton called his services register:

> "On Xmas Eve the boarding between the church and the new Chancel was removed to present a grand effect on the day of the nativity of our Blefsed Lord, and *grand indeed it was*. I shall never forget the taking down of board after board the grand prospect increasing as it did each minute".

This part of the church, unusually, is not only higher but slightly wider than the nave: it is in the Decorated style and has its own western bell-turret with two bells, perhaps in imitation of some Flemish churches. Perhaps they were used for week-day services, or early-morning ones on a Sunday.

> "The architecture of this chancel is uniform and by no means fussy, although it is a noble structure and great dignity is given by the gabled buttresses and large two-light windows, with their elegant tracery and corbel heads, as well as the handsome five-light east window".[12]

The Sutton Chantry is not quite as tall as the chancel: it has its own south window beneath which, well hidden now by sand, is Sir Richard Sutton's memorial, imitating a medieval coffin-lid with a floriated cross.

Eventually all was furnished and complete, and "1857 Thursday 13th. August dedicated the new chancel the archdeacon preached, 32 clergy present, about 130 present". Mr. Tricker says the robed clergy went in procession from the rectory to the church singing the Benedicite.[13] The Rector himself read the prayers of dedication, for it seems the Bishop, the Hon. and Right Revd. Frederick Pelham of Norwich, was not invited – it might have been anticipated that he would disapprove of some Tractarian features of the building, though in fact a good deal of its enrichment, such as stained glass and altar hangings, was not yet there. On the other hand, the whole ethos of the place, with the carved reredos and its statuettes of saints, the coloured screens and the altar raised on three steps, spoke loudly already of the Oxford Movement. It is not known whether Sir John Sutton, as he was by then (for his father Sir Richard had died in 1855),

Interior of West Tofts Church, looking east, c.1900

attended the service or not – probably not, as he had only been received into the Church of Rome a couple of years before and was really living on the Continent.

It is difficult now to recapture the atmosphere of West Tofts church in what we might call its heyday, about 1885, just before Augustus Sutton's death; but some features of its interior arrangements and furnishing call for comment. The first thing that would catch the eye of the visitor then was the trio of carved wooden screens, coloured and gilded; two of them separated the eastern bay of the north aisle from the rest of the church, and the third was the chancel screen, standing in the eastern arch (for there were two) leading into the chancel and sanctuary. Later in his life John Sutton was to write to Jean Béthune of how difficult he found it to relate to a church without screens and, as we shall see, he reinstated the stone chancel screen at Kiedrich:in this he was a true disciple of Augustus Pugin, one of whose last publications as *A Treatise on Chancel Screens and Rood Lofts, their antiquity, use and symbolic signification* (London, 1851). At West Tofts, the upper decorated beam of the chancel screen (the bressummer, as the ancient writers would have called it) was carried across to the north aisle wall on the west side, and to the outer walls of the chancel on the east, thus giving an even greater impression of spaciousness.

In later years, a figure of Christ crucified was placed on top of it, together with six candlesticks, thus cutting off the eastern limb of the church even more effectively from the nave where the congregation sat – for cut off it was indeed, and this is one of the strange features of the place. The double chancel arch, with an empty bay between them serving only as an entrance to Lady Sutton's Chantry on its south side, and the screen together ensure that the church is acoustically and visually divided into two; and this effect was underlined by the fact that the Hall pew faced the pulpit, which itself was placed some little way down the south wall of the nave between the first two windows, and had two pews to the east of it. It was underlined too by the returned clergy-stalls against the eastern face of the screen, which meant that anyone sitting in them had their backs to the congregation; and Pugin's plan for the pulpit reveals that it was originally a two-decker, combining the priest's desk facing north, another desk on the same level for the Bible lessons, and the pulpit itself[14]. There was a stool provided in case of a visiting preacher so that whoever conducted the service could sit down during the sermon, and holes were bored in its base – "these quatrefoils pierced for ventilation, and zinck perforated behind to prevent vermin"[15].

The chancel screen at West Tofts, designed by Pugin

Is this a remarkably late survival of the seventeenth and eighteenth century division of the English churches into two liturgical areas – one for the Offices of Morning and Evening Prayer, and one for the Holy Communion? A survival, moreover, in the teeth of the Camden Society's writings and beliefs about the proper arrangement of a parish church?[16] We shall never know just how the church was used in Augustus Sutton's time as Rector, but it would have been perfectly possible for him in his first years of using the complete church (say 1867-1870) to have used the chancel stalls for his Holy Communion congregation to sit in, for about twenty people could be accommodated there. An "early service" congregation in those days would not often number many more than this. Would it be right to assume that Sir Richard Sutton, brought up in the early years of the century, had a great influence on the arrangement of the nave of the church? – and was only prevented by his early death from having as great an influence on the chancel as well? All these things are possibilities, but once the organ was built in its swallows'-nest gallery on the north side of the chancel, the only place for the choir must have been the chancel stalls, for in any other position in the church they would have received no support from the organ at all.

Other features of the church we have not mentioned so far are the set of oak pews whose poppy-heads were 'all to be cut from old poppy heads in churches near Tofts", and a note from another drawing by Pugin reads, "the carving must be very *rough simple*. The old seats are rough worked but they look very well. You must not work them up too fine."[17] By contrast, the "seat for Sir Richard Sutton" had no note of simpleness about it: it was not elaborate, but the end of the kneeler (as Pugin called it) that faced the congregation had a space left on it for the family's arms to be painted, and the finials of the seat had on them "pheasants at one end, partridges at the other", and of the kneeler "hare at one end, rabbit at the other, out of the solid. These should be modelled for me to see."[18] Apparently the seats within the screens at the east end of the north aisle were relatively plain; no drawing of them has survived. It was only well after the Sutton era that an altar was placed in this enclosure, for the ecclesiologists believed that there should only be one altar in every church. There is a letter from Frederick Heathcote Sutton dated 16 October, 1872, which observes about St. Mary Magdalene church in Oxford, "It was designed for a number of side altars, and does not and never will suit our liturgy."[19]

The tomb of John Sutton's wife is on the north side of the family area in an elaborate arched recess, whose canopy is a mass of tracery, crockets and pinnacles, in the centre of which is the coat of arms flanked by angels with inscribed scrolls. It is a masterpiece of design, and a faithful reproduction of mid-fourteenth-century workmanship.

The inscription reads: "Here lieth the body of Emma Helena, wife of John Sutton Esq., daughter of Col. Francis Sherlock R. H. She died 26th. of January 1845 aged 24, on whose soul sweet Jesus have mercy." Perhaps it was as well that the Faculty system was not as strict in those days as it is today, and that the Bishop of Norwich did not visit the church at that time, for such an ending to an epitaph would be regarded as very Roman Catholic, and therefore inadmissible, in the eighteen-fifties.

The font and cover, a copy of that at Mundford nearby, was made in 1857 and occupies the whole of the western bay of the north aisle; it has thus a really dignified open setting, unlike those of similar date that seem to have been put anywhere that was not needed for pews. Not that the pews at West Tofts were empty during the rest of Augustus Sutton's life; regularly in the Sunday Book he noted congregations of over a hundred from a parish of only about 240-250 souls. Returning to the furnishings of the church – the two candelabra of about eight lights each hung, rather strangely, before the chancel screen: one would have expected them to be near the sanctuary, to enrich the place where the Holy Communion was celebrated – but there is no doubt they they took away some of the bareness of the area where they were. On Easter Day 1868, Augustus noted that he "used lights on the Altar for the first time"; this was in defiance of a recent judgement by the Privy Council, so the candle-ends were kept as a triumphant bit of evidence of his High Church sympathies – they are still in the Record Office in Norwich now!

As time went on, the church was further enriched; an altar-frontal was made in 1862, and for some time the work of replacing plain windows with coloured ones went on. Both Augustus and his youngest brother, Frederick Heathcote Sutton, were skilled designers and firers of stained glass, being responsible for quite a number of windows in Lincoln Cathedral, as well as for a few at West Tofts. But in connection with stained glass, there is a strange little tale revealed in the Béthune letters:

"West Tofts Rectory, Brandon, 12 March 1860.

My dear John,

Several letters have passed between the Bishop and myself on the subject of the removal of the remains of poor Helena from this church, and I am afraid you will be much annoyed to hear that it can not be done: the fact of her having died in communion with the church of England the Bishop says prevents his being able to grant a faculty for the removal of her remains to a Roman Catholic burial ground ...

Augustus Sutton."[20]

On Sunday, 27 March, John Sutton wrote from Bruges to Béthune:

> "... I wrote to Hardman the other day to ask him whether he had begun the glass for the Cho^r windows at Tofts and he answered that they were not yet in hand, so I have asked him not to make them at all."[21]

(Then follows a suggested list of furnishings for the Schippers' Chapel in Bruges to the same value). It would not be strange at that date for someone who had embraced the Roman Catholic faith, and whose wife's body lay in what to him was unconsecrated ground, to wish to have the body exhumed and buried elsewhere; nor would it be strange for an English bishop to refuse the request. In any event, by this time Sir John Sutton was finding many things to spend his money on in Europe, and there is evidence in the Hardman Archives that he was doing his best to stop supplying the enrichments for West Tofts without hurting his brother's feelings too much – a letter from John Hardman, 6 April, 1859, to Revd. Augustus Sutton:

> "... I wrote to (Sir John's) agent in London and have now received their reply which simply instructs me to alter and complete the North Transept window and not anything more at Sir John's expense..."[22]

In fact, there is a note elsewhere in the West Tofts registers that Augustus Sutton went to visit his eldest brother at Kiedrich in the

Postcard showing West Tofts Church, c.1910

Rheingau, so although the end of financial support of West Tofts church must have hurt, there was no estrangement because of it.

An intriguing entry in the Hardman letters is dated 25 September, 1858:

> "Mr. Powell and I have made enquiries respecting a Fresco painting ... but hitherto without success. We do not know anyone who could carry out the work in the ancient style. Possibly Mr. Pugin might find someone in London."[23]

Augustus Sutton had been enquiring about a Doom painting on the chancel arch. Surely anything less than this could have been tackled with complete assurance by Hardman's as they had certainly by now done plenty of painting on walls.[24] Foiled of this, Augustus Sutton was able to buy some of the ancient choir stalls from old St. John's Chapel in Cambridge for the chancel at West Tofts, for his boys to sit in. F.H. Sutton found them at Rattee's the builders in 1871, for sale at three shillings a panel.[25]

One further point is raised by the original furnishings of this church: the question is sometimes asked whether Pugin, convinced as he was of the rightness of his designs and ideas, ever designed objects that were not foreshadowed by Gothic work of the thirteenth and fourteenth centuries. This pulpit proves that he did, possibly consoling himself with the thought that in those centuries, Protestantism did not exist.

The final word must come from the Revd. Benjamin Armstrong, Vicar of East Dereham 1850-1888, who wrote in his diary on 23 October, 1871:

> "Drove to West Tofts to see the lovely church restored and decorated by Sir J. Sutton and family. The reredos of alabaster, with statues, tinted and under canopies, was designed by Pugin and carried out by Italian artists. Everything is in the most perfect taste imaginable."[26]

Jesus College Chapel, Cambridge

The history of many of the colleges that make up the ancient Universities of Oxford and Cambridge is a long one. Jesus College was founded by Bishop Alcock of Ely in 1497, using the buildings and endowments of the suppressed Priory of St. Radegunde. Naturally the priory church became the college chapel, losing a good part of the nave, and the north aisle, in the process. College chapels, though, stood rather outside the eighteenth-century indifferentism which resulted in the decay and slovenliness of furnishing of many of the parish churches; and whether to keep up their own dignity as clergymen, or to impress undergraduates who had to be at Morning Prayer daily, the Fellows often kept them in good repair, and furnished them at some expense. Jesus College chapel was a case in point. Dr. Percy Dearmer published in *The Parson's Handbook* a print of the east end of the chapel produced in 1835, showing an altar and surroundings of much dignity and indeed elaboration for that date.[27] However, ten years later the stone fabric of the chapel obviously needed repair, for in the college's Conclusion Book (the record of the Fellows' Meetings) is the entry under 20 December, 1844: "That Mr. Salvin, architect, be employed in the restoration of the Chapel."[28] Appeals were sent out to former and present members of the college to subscribe to the work, though as the accounts show, a high proportion of the cost was borne by the college itself. John Sutton, whose young wife had died recently, sent a hundred pounds to the restoration fund the following year. Restoration actually began in 1846, with the building of the new north aisle.[29]

Meanwhile the Dean, John Gibson, was busy designing the new Gothic stalls for Fellows and undergraduates (and perhaps it should be noted here that the Conclusion Book certainly does not record even half the decisions that must have been taken: many of them must have been verbal, and we have to piece together what happened from some letters, coupled with a good deal of conjecture), and he wrote to his colleague, Osmond Fisher the Chaplain, on 21 August, 1846: "The bookboard ends are actually working and some finished and in excellent style, even Sutton was disarmed and could find nothing distasteful."[30] It seems that even at this early stage in his life, John Sutton had acquired a reputation for demanding correctness in Gothic details. It was becoming increasingly obvious, however, that the north-eastern corner of the tower of the chapel was unsafe: "11 May 1847. Agreed that the Dean be authorized to take some competent opinion as to the Stability or possible strengthening of the Walls and Piers of the Chapel."[31] And in *Stones and Story of Jesus College Chapel*, Fisher is quoted as having been near the chapel when some stones fell and "I set to work to shore up the tower [with some removed beams] with my own hands. While I was at work, Mr. Sutton and Pugin appeared. Sutton had brought him from London to take measurements for the organ he was going to give. The result was that Pugin was employed by the college for some strenthening work."[32] It seems that the College then dismissed Salvin and accepted Pugin's ideas for dealing with the tower corner:

> "29 October 1847. Agreed also that it is expedient to take steps without delay for strengthening the North East angle of the Tower of the Chapel, and that the Plans for effecting this object, now submitted to the College, be adopted."[33]

Naturally this emergency work took time, and the whole energies of the building team. Gibson and Fisher obviously had hoped that the choir would have been restored in 1847, but this was proved vain. Gibson to Fisher, 16 September, 1847:

> "... All this delay puts us in a very awkward position. I am engaged to go away, and there will be no one to look after the men, or to give any further order of any kind. If I were to stay I have no authority to do more than will be finished in a week or two. Sutton is very fidgetty and I think very naturally: the organ is down and Bishop wants to get rid of it – it must be put somewhere and he has hurried it under the impression that the choir would have been ready this year. – then again his [Sutton's boys'] choir will have to be conducted thro' another unsatisfactory year – and though it is impossible to do as we intended I think for Sutton's sake, if for no more cogent reasons, the work should proceed..."[34]

Work now seems to have continued fairly steadily to its completion. Meanwhile, at Sutton's request and expense, Pugin produced designs for the altar and its frontal, the screen, lectern, pavement and decoration of the roof. The Master of the college, Dr. William French (1786-1849), was not altogether happy about the way things were going: a canny man, he foresaw that if any one member of the college were allowed to give a great deal of money, it would be difficult to resist his ideas. The *Dictionary of National Biography* speaks of him as "urbane" and this quality shines through this letter to Gibson:

> "Dear Sir, I am ready to offer Mr. Sutton my best thanks for his intended liberality, more especially as I think the outlay will not be great. For I would not have the College draw too deeply upon his kindness..."[35]

Though undated, this note must be put at about this point in the restoration work. Certainly it does seem that Sutton's liberality influenced things to a certain extent: there is a letter from William Brougham, a former Fellow of the College and now a Master in Chancery, offering a lectern "taken from a most excellent example in my Brother's Chapel at Brougham" with a competent sketch, and dated 26 January, 1849.[36] This offer was not accepted; the lectern now in the chapel is one copied from that in St. Mark's Venice, and paid for by Sutton. The choir and sanctuary of St. Radegunde are not wide – with the seats facing each other, as is the custom in English college chapels, you can nearly shake hands with someone in the opposite front row – and this lectern, with its pivoted candle-holders, could be thought to be too large for the building (incidentally, the Venice model is now thought to be English work). What the Master had foreseen was not altogether acceptable to the Fellows, as can be seen from this letter written by Fisher half a century later: Dr. Arthur Gray had written a history of the college incorporating a description of the Chapel's restoration, and sent a copy to Fisher as a compliment to a former Fellow who had done so much in the work, and the old man puts things right in the gentlest way — 1 Dec. 1902.

> "There is one statement about the restoration of the chapel which is not quite correct. The college did not call in Pugin to their assistance. Salvin was called in and the north aisle built to his plans. Then he was dismissed. We worked for a long time without any architect upon the *fabric* and the *stalls*. Then Sutton got designs for the roof pavement rose window screen and organ from Pugin and paid for the *designs* himself and also bodily for the screen and organ. The only work in which Pugin was *employed* by the College was the stone work fixed to strengthen the NE piers of the tower. Sutton employed the power of the purse to get some things his own way which we did not quite wish for ..."[37]

There are one or two letters and bills which throw a little light on the details: a bill submitted by Pugin to Sutton in 1849 reveals that £5 was paid for the design for the Communion table, and £5 for patterns for the ceiling, and a guinea for the design for the altar cloth.[38] A letter from Pugin to Crace, who made all the fabric furnishings Pugin designed, dated 12 Novr. 1848 reads:

> "... 2. I am anxious about Mr. Sutton's work for Cambridge as though it is a small thing yet he is such a glorious man that I wish to take any pains and I told him you would be sure to make a good job. — I should like therefore to see a further [illegible, but must mean pattern] for the cushions ... and the fringe ... — and especially about the decoration of the green velvet altar covering ..."[39]

Another letter quoted in *Stones and Story of Jesus College Chapel* says, about the altar, "... the top three inches thick, as I know you like solid tops." There are letters from John Hardman of Birmingham from December 1848 onwards, about stained glass for the windows, and one of these reveals that during the severe weather in January 1850 there were only calico blinds to some of the windows to keep the cold out. Finally, a note in the accounts reveals that John Sutton paid £120 for the screen.[40]

On All Saints' Day, 1 November 1849, the chapel was reopened with a full choral service, "said and sung", as a contemporary account says, "in the manner of our cathedral churches, as was the case originally in all college chapels in the University".[41]

The work received general approval. *The Guardian* gives a description of the decoration of the roof, which was overpainted later in the century by G.F. Bodley:

> "The whole of the roof is varnished, and the ribs and bosses decorated in vermilion and gold; but the portion above the sacrarium is still further enriched with sacred devices on the panels in green, vermilion, white and gold. The aisle roof is blue with stars in white, and the rafters oak colour, the principals being relieved with vermilion."[42]

Interior of Jesus College Chapel, looking west

The report went on to describe the organ in glowing terms.

The Ecclesiologist, the organ of the Camden Society, was never distinguished for praising contemporary work, and these reports must have made the readers flock to see the chapel: the report of the Annual Meeting of the Cambridge Architectural Society –

> "Your Committee view with satisfaction the ecclesiastical restorations completed or in progress in the university and town: and they most earnestly hope that such as are proposed for the parish churches of Cambridge, may be carried out in the same 'Spirit of sacrifice' that has been so nobly manifested in Jesus College Chapel."[43]

In 1851, in a section entitled "Ecclesiology in Cambridge", the editors declared, "Jesus College Chapel deserves to be mentioned first." – and went on with a series of superlatives:

> "The interior effect of this eastern limb of the cross is most striking ... a noble sanctuary ... the floor is unusually rich in effect, its former black and white marble being used in patterns with encaustic tiles ... the organ in a very beautiful and appropriate case ... we have seldom seen anything more graceful and suitable than the treatment of this organ: which is due mainly, to Mr. Pugin, next to the unselfish zeal of the generous member of the college who has done so much for this restoration ... it remains to add that the old tradition of reredos-hangings in Jesus Chapel is continued; there being a rich woven stuff suspended, as a dossal, behind the altar. The altar candles are coloured in patterns: and in addition to the altar candlesticks, there are two fine standard do., of brass, at the angles of the footpace. The frontal, when we saw it, was of green, handsomely embroidered in a cross with the evangelistic symbols ... It will be acknowledged that, whether ritually or architecturally, few restorations are more complete or correct than that of Jesus College Chapel."[44]

The final sentence must have given everyone great satisfaction.

Kiedrich

The parish church of St. Valentin and St. Dionysius in Kiedrich is an impressive building by any standard. This part of Germany was Christianised early in the Dark Ages, and the nearby church at Eltville boasts an eighth-century tombstone. We may suppose that the Romans brought vini-culture with them, and the *Königsterassen* (royal terraces) on these southern slopes of the Taunus hills are known all over Germany as some of the finest vineyards of the country. Small wonder, then, that by about 1480 when the church received its present shape (possibly as a result of the gift of an important relic, part of the skull of St. Valentin, from a Prior of Eberbach nearby), there was enough devotion and enough money about for it to be a really thorough-going work. And to a great extent the church has kept its fifteenth-century shape and atmosphere; the whole building seems to draw itself up to point the worshipper heavenwards. It consists of a stately nave and side-aisles of three bays, a chancel with an apse (three

The parish church of St. Valentin & St. Dionysius in Kiedrich

sides of an octagon) at the east end, and a lofty and massive tower with spire at the west end of the nave. There are stone galleries to both north and south aisles, and these seem to have been built more to provide sites for additional altars than to make convenient space for more worshippers, for the spiral stairs to them are not really inviting. The fact that the aisles are two-storied has resulted in the arcades being two-storied as well, so that instead of the tall, narrow arches to be found in England of that period, there are two rather wide and hence rather flatter ones, one over the other with the gallery dividing them. As both aisles and galleries have stone vaults, one can well understand the weight these arches have to carry. In fact, the whole church is vaulted in stone, with the usual Continental increase of elaboration over the chancel and sanctuary; and the whole is under one immense, steeply-pitched roof, whose western apex actually cuts into the east window of the belfry. There is a flèche over the western part of the chancel.

The church retains a great many, if not all of its ancient furnishings, in spite of the Napoleonic wars which raged around the district: for instance, the original *Sakramenthaus*, the stone-spired aumbry of the German lands for reservation of the Sacrament; rather incongruously, a small baroque reredos to the high altar; some Gothic *Flügelältere* (winged altars); a really lovely Madonna and Child of about 1330; and some carved pews of the sixteenth century, of truly Düreresque elaboration. In John Sutton's time, all the altars were provided with frontals and, as now, there was a definite atmosphere of homeliness, of the villagers' own place of worship enriched by succeeding generations.

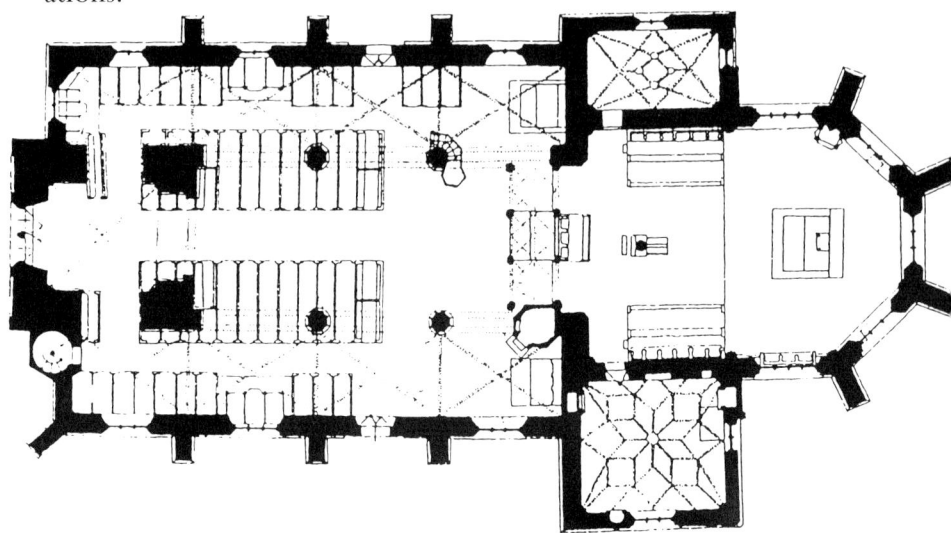

Plan of Kiedrich Church

View of the high altar at Kiedrich as Sutton would have known it

subject relating either to the Life of our L^d. or the Blessed Virgin - Now I think you may find some of these very useful for the E. Windows by encreasing them into larger Pictures and bringing the stone work through them, they are well coloured and some have several figures in them. When you are at Bruges you can ask Mgr. Boone and he will show them to you, and you will soon see which pieces will be best adapted for encreasing in size. I am very anxious

One of the characteristics of some nineteenth-century church-restorers was that nothing was written down about their spending on the church concerned, for it was a matter between them and God. At Kiedrich, then, there are no accounts preserved, and it seems unlikely that Sutton allowed any note of the amounts he spent to be recorded. We have only what Canon Zaun wrote, and the occasional mention of what went on, in the Béthune letters. Zaun says:

> "At the *Pfarrer's* request he arranged for a number of painters and artists to come here, who restored the pews and the St. John altar, and carried the re-building of the rood-screen and the decoration of the church nearly to their conclusion. The restoration of the exterior, and the repair or very nearly renewal of the aisle windows and their glazing with stained glass was completed a few years later."[45]

This is underlined by the recently-discovered lecture by *Chorregent* Georg Hilpisch:

> "Our parish church has to thank him for the restoration of the magnificent gothic sacrament house, the two new beautiful winged altars, the building of the sandstone chancel screen with its figures, the provision of professionally embroidered vestments partly obtained in old convents and monasteries, and partly made new by the Sisters of the Poor Child Jesus here and in Cologne; and the complete restoration of the church and chapel to the glory of gothic."[46]

Much of the work was done around 1866-71: there is a letter to Béthune from Cöln [*sic*] (Cologne) dated 16 November, 1869:

> "You will be very glad to hear that the works have progressed famously this year, the whole north side and the Chor part the E. Window the stone work is entirely repaired and well done and what is more extraordinary in that *Volcanic* district without Earthquakes which have confined themselves to the other side of the R. (Rhine), Mainz Darmstadt etc., etc. The fact I mean that we have orderly workpeople, and no difficulties of any kind have occurred of late. I hope you will soon have the glass ready for the north side, I have got new round glass from Venice for the upper and late part of the Church, this is just arrived in Mainz and will soon be leaded there. Now I want to talk about the great windows at the East End – Do you remember being with me many years ago at Nürnberg at the old Jews, and seeing some very nice late glass to be sold, well I bought 12 pieces small but complete little Pictures, each

to get the K. church finished and off my hands, for it has been a great anxiety to me for many years and both you and I are getting on in life and I become *less energetic* than formerly. I hope ... that we may *yet get* some *fine glass made*, though we are both now nearly 50 years old ..."[47]

The glass for the north window seems to have come quickly after this letter, for there is another dated 30 December, 1869:

"... to thank you again for the windows, the more I examine them the more I am pleased with them, they really leave nothing to be desired and I hear all who have seen them, are as much pleased as I am. They produce a great effect in the Church and every thing is improved by the tone of light they produce. (He goes on to say that he had insisted on the iron guards being replaced outside) ... They are rather shocked at a shade being thrown over the face of one saint by an iron crossing, but this in no way injures the general effect, and church windows always had irons to keep out thieves."[48]

Another supply arrived nearly two years later:

"Kiedrich, 28 November 1871. The glass is all in its place and will be quite finished this evening. I am very much pleased with it indeed, it goes so well with the old glass on the other side. I have asked Blumer to send some little red bits in place of the blue for the window over the door that all these little points may be the same, I thought blue preponderated a little too much and think this slight change will improve the general effect ... I am anxious to get the 3 East windows in the Cho^r. finished as soon as I can, but I think we shall have to make a journey to Munich together, to consult the windows in the same style in the Dom. (then there is a water-colour picture with a note – "*arms* for the Church but treated with supporters, crest etc. in the late German style a little *arogant* [sic] and *swaggering* looking – I have a great idea this *receipt* will answer.")[49]

What would a present-day artist think if his work was altered in this way? But apparently Béthune was ready to bear it, and the friendship seems to have continued unruffled.

Finally, Sutton had the fifteenth-century chancel screen (in German "*Lettner*") rebuilt but to a different design. It had been originally of four bays, but was removed in 1682 and two altars (the Marienaltar and the St. John Nepomuk altar) put in its place. When Sutton had it re-built, he arranged for it to have three bays only; it is

The Johannesaltar (c. 1500) restored by Sir John Sutton

not easy to find any divine truth for four to signify, but three has always represented the Trinity! – and this is no doubt what he had in mind. Kiedrich tradition has it that he removed the two altars himself at dead of night so that his plans could go forward, but it is a little difficult to imagine him behaving in quite such an English-Lord-of-the-manor way – and, in fact, if the approval of the diocesan authorities had been obtained, there would be no need. There is a hint in one of his letters that all did not go smoothly over the operation – "the Lettner affair" – and quite likely there were some grumbles in the parish about the changes. But as will be seen below in connection with St. Gillis in Bruges, Sutton was never happy unless a church possessed a chancel screen.

In recent years with the changes in liturgical fashion, the Marienaltar has come into its own once again, and is now placed under the central arch of the screen with the beautiful fourteenth-century Madonna and Child statue behind it.

This screen has a strange affinity with that projected for the chapel of Ushaw College near Durham, by A.W. Pugin.[50] When the drawing was shown to the Kiedrich people some years ago, there was an immediate cry of "*Unser Lettner* (our screen)!" All sorts of speculations arise in the mind, but it would not be sensible to follow them up.

At Bruges, Sutton actually did nothing architectural at his parish church of St. Gillis; this was not because he was not feeling generous, but because the church was not provided with a chancel screen. He wrote to Béthune about the church on 6 August 1859:

> "That church so distresses me from having no screens, that I can never make up my mind to do anything there on that account. I feel more and more every day, how impossible it is to attain *anything like a Gothic effect*, when all is thrown *open into one space* ..."

This gives the clue for his feeling about screens – they were to add to the general feeling of mystery and other-worldliness which a church building should have. Sutton gives examples of screens being removed, always with (for him) pretty violent language: the canons of Munster, for instance, took down a "most beautiful" screen "out of compliment to the new Bishop – how stupid Priests are always about screens." And when the Canons of Mainz proposed a similar operation in 1859, they too came under the lash – "they are going to play the fool next in the Cathedral". In this same letter Sutton observed, "The modern Germans are wonderfully ignorant of the old Church arrangements, this is the more wonderful as they have these things on every side". – obviously meaning that if the Germans had been taught the Camden Society's inductive method, they would very soon have found out how to furnish and arrange a church of any size. By contrast, the parish priest of the next-door village of Eltville proved an apt pupil:

> "The *Pfarrer* of Eltville is a very good and active man, and very anxious to have his church made what it should be – he *promises* to have the *Sacrament House restored* and to have the New Altar without Tab¹. [= tabernacle] upon it".[51]

The angriest letter of all that still exists was written to Béthune from Bruges on 13 February, 1859, and is worth quoting because it shows how influential he was already with the Bishop and other diocesan authorities, only two years after his reception into the Roman Catholic church:

> "... They have done such an *abominable* thing in the Cathedral, and I only saw it to day at Mass – Close to the Skreen I repaired, I am in such a rage, and have vented it to day upon – Felix, Mr. Fait, Mr. Boone and every body I have seen since including the Van Heuls – They have destroyed that nice bit of arcading by the side of the skreen and put plain brick work in its place and *inserted* a *trumpery Gothic* Nitch in *Oak* (only fancy) for that *stupid* plaster Cast of Gerty

(?) of the blessed S(acrament?). The arcade used to look so nice broken through for the late chapel, I am vexed more than I can tell you, and have offered to pay the expence if they will only put it back as it was before. [Here a couple of sketches, before and after, and a note along the side of the paper: an Oak nitch made to look like a stone one fixed in a plain brick wall.] It is such a pity they could not let the old wall alone by the Boot Makers Chapel, it was so curious to see how the old men made their additions, and now it is *almost unintelligible* beside the corner has lost all its picturesqueness *I am furious*, and I am sure I shall not enter the church again *for months* – I am so fond of the Cathedral I cannot bear to see it so bullied by these stupid asses – Pray write a line to the Bishop and tell him what a bad job it is. I do not think he knows any thing about it – only fancy in the place of this arcade, Gertys stupid figure in a late ill designed oak nitch all cross trussed as if made of stone can you imagine any think more perfectly beastly and detestable.

...[Then across the margin] I have just been in the Cathl. with the Bishop and Felix, and his Lordship has *stopped* the work and asked me to send him a sketch."[52]

When Sutton turned to re-building and re-arranging houses, the same sort of system seems to have been followed: we have only one side of the correspondence, and obviously when the two men were together a great deal of work was agreed on without documentation. Sutton had found a possible dwelling in Bruges by 1858 –

"Soden by Frankfurt, Sepr. 10th. 1858 ... Mr. Boone thinks he will be able to buy the house for me at a reasonable rate."[53]

He then sketched out a plan for altering the house on the ground floor, which included moving the cellar into the next house (!) and "destroying the present high room", perhaps by putting in another floor. In true medieval style, the kitchen was to be as far as possible from the dining room.

Evidently the house was bought and at least to some extent rearranged at this time, as by November of the same year a detailed letter about furnishing was sent to Béthune:

"... Now I will answer your questions about my own house –

1. Will you if you please gild the little flowers, and the hair and beard of the man's head, and the Hair and head dress of the Woman's on the Pink chimney Piece, also paint

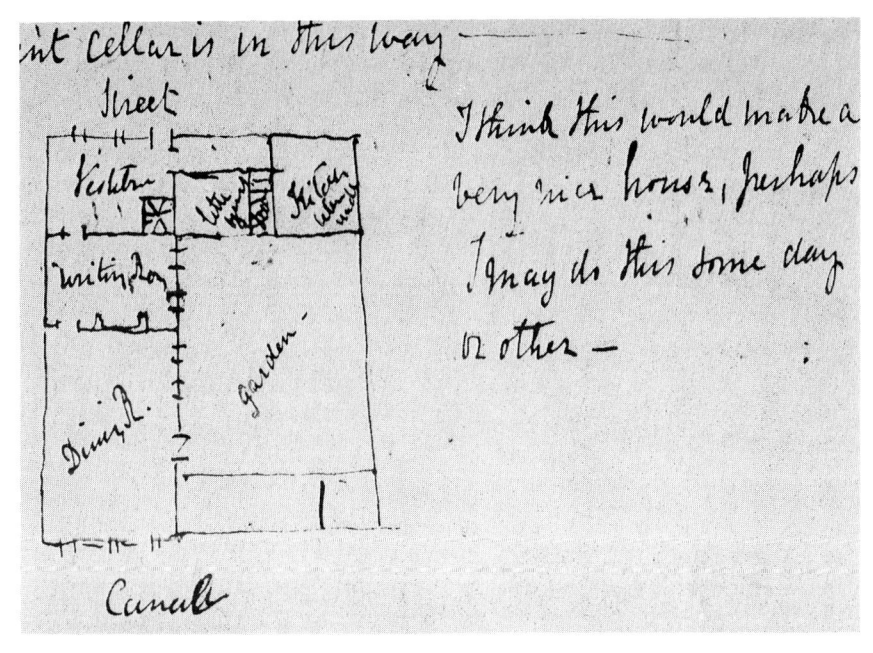

Sutton's sketch of the plan of his house in Bruges; letter to Béthune, 1858

the bricks pink, the same colour as the chimney, in the arch leading into the tribune.

2. I think the moulding turning round the windows will improve the wainscote, I think it is the usual Flemish way – when I have seen it in England the other way it has been in framed panelling (small sketch).

3. I do not much like the idea of casing the beam in my bed room, could it not be patched up, and the rotten part covered with *lead paper* as the lining of a tea chest and then painted, will you *consider* this if you please, the beams look to me always more or less shams when they are cased.

4. I think there is stone for the Kitchen chimney (*all except the feet*) *in the house* if I remember right the only part wanting is the 2 little feet (sketch of an open fire-place – if this was all his cooks had to work with ...)."[54]

The house on the Gouden Handrei still remains, though now used as warehouses. There is a wooden loggia projecting over the canal at the back and it is possible to trace parts of the Latin text, "*Ave Maria, gratia plena ...*" painted on it.

At Kiedrich, Sutton bought three smallish houses and had them converted into one[55]. The house has been greatly enlarged since his time (it is the centre of a large "*Weingut*"), but the main downstairs room is much as he arranged it, facing north with a long window filled with circular opaque leaded lights of heavy glass. Was this perhaps to discourage the Kiedrich locals from looking in to see whether he was at home? – for he often resorted to strange little subterfuges to keep them in ignorance, like having his correspondence addressed to Herr Schmidt at another house in the village. If it was, they had their revenge, for twenty years ago there were still tales going about of the spiral staircase in his house, built to stop ladies in crinolines getting upstairs, and of how they suspected him of keeping a woman in his grand piano!

Drawing of Sir John Sutton's house in Kiedrich (now much extended). His downstairs room was the one with the very broad window

As with his musical life and work, it is Kiedrich that can boast the most enduring remains of John Sutton's absorbing interest in church architecture and restoration. No doubt others would have carried out the work in later years, if he had not done it, but all would have been without his enthusiasm and tremendous attention to detail, and quite possibly valuable medieval features would have been lost.

REFERENCES

1 Hardman.
2 T. W. Tricker, *St. Mary's, West Tofts, Norfolk: History and Guide 1981*, p. 4.
3 Alexandra Wedgwood, *A. W. N. Pugin and the Pugin Family* (London: The V. and A. Museum 1985) p. 22.
4 Mr Rand, the present owner of Lynford Hall, in *letter* to author.
5 In private ownership.
6 Stanton, p. 140.
7 Stanton, p. 138.
8 *ibid.*
9 R.W. Tricker, *op. cit.* p. 10.
10 R.W. Tricker, *op. cit.* back cover.
11 Norwich Diocesan Faculties Register.
12 R.W. Tricker, *op. cit.* p. 11.
13 R.W. Tricker, *op. cit.* p. 7.
14 Book of drawings in private hands.
15 Pugin's notes in book of drawings.
16 See G. W. O. Addleshaw & Frederick Etchells, *The Architectural Setting of Anglican Worship* (Faber & Faber 1948) for a complete discussion.
17 Pugin's notes, *ut supra*.
18 Pugin's notes, *ut supra*.
19 Magdalen College, Oxford.
20 Béthune.
21 Béthune.
22 Hardman.
23 Hardman.
24 Hardman.
25 Letter from F. H. Sutton to the Revd. R. O. Assheton, Rector of Old Bilton, in possession of the author.
26 Diary of the Revd. Benjamin Armstrong, ed. A. C. T. Armstrong, *op. cit.*
27 Twelfth Edition (Oxford 1932) facing p. 1.
28 Jesus College Archives.
29 A History of Jesus College.
30 Jesus College Archives.
31 Conclusion Book.
32 Stones and Story, p. 300.
33 Conclusion Book.
34 Jesus College Archives.
35 Jesus College Archives.
36 Jesus College Archives.
37 Jesus College Archives.
38 Jesus College Archives.
39 Crace Papers (R.I.B.A.).
40 Jesus College Archives.
41 History of Jesus College, p. 189.
42 The cutting from *The Guardian* is in Jesus College Archives.
43 No. 86, October 1851, pp. 323-325.
44 No. 81, April 1850, p. 21.
45 Zaun, p. 169.
46 Copy in *Tausendjahrige Kiedrich*.
47 Béthune.
48 Béthune.
49 Béthune.
50 V. and A. Museum.
51 Béthune.
52 Béthune.
53 Béthune.
54 Béthune.
55 Zaun, p. 169.

CHAPTER IV

Sir John Sutton – Musician

Argument from silence is always a dangerous game, but there has to be a little of it when we come to John Sutton's musicianship, for there is hardly any direct evidence about it at all. We know nothing of his training, of who taught him to play the piano and organ, of who introduced him to the study of harmony or guided his first attempts at improvization. The probability is that this teacher was someone in the cathedral tradition, where improvization, knowledge of harmony and of figured bass were a necessity – which is why the suggestion was made in the introduction to the *Short Account*, that he could have been George Skelton, Organist of Lincoln Cathedral (1794-1850). We know from Zaun that Sutton spent a good deal of time with his grandparents in Lincoln, and moneyed people like the Suttons would expect to use a professional musician of cathedral-organist calibre to instruct any of their children who chose keyboard instruments for their music.[1] Sutton's father ordered an organ for him when he was at Eton

Chollerton Vicarage

College, and this seems to show that he was playing well enough for this to be a reasonable gift, and a reasonable way for his father to spend money.

It is pointless to guess any more until he arrived at Chollerton at the age of sixteen, to stay for five years as the private pupil of the Vicar, not too far from Durham and its Cathedral. He admired, and became friendly with, the organist there, William Henshaw (Organist of Durham 1813-62), and it is quite possible that he continued his musical studies under him. Henshaw was a strict disciplinarian and in order to achieve the highest standards of singing, he worked his choir-boys very hard.[2] If *mutatis mutandis* he worked Sutton as hard, here lies the explanation for the way the latter's playing was occasionally admired in Europe; for a first-class English cathedral organist's training, then as now, prepared a young musician for almost anything. Sutton went on to Cambridge where, after a few years, he was able to recruit and train a choir with *élan*, and when he left England and went on to Bruges and Kiedrich, in both of which places important work was done, he had excellent principles to guide him.

At Jesus College, Cambridge

> "18 December 1846. Agreed also that the best thanks of the College are due, and the Master be requested to convey the same to John Sutton Esq. Fellow Commoner for his kind and unwearied exertions in training, and that with so great success, six Boys for the performance of Choral Service; and that he be requested to continue the direction of that part of divine Worship in the College Chapel, so long as may be convenient and agreeable to himself, in the same manner and as entirely as if he were appointed to the office of organist."[3]

This is the first evidence of John Sutton's successful musicianship; the boys were drawn from the city of Cambridge, says Zaun[4] – and having arranged for them to sing in the chapel, Sutton repaid them by teaching them the normal elementary school subjects of the time himself:

> "He instituted a choir-school within the College, and there for ten years he taught the boys himself, not only in singing but in general subjects and rather than desert them, ungrudgingly remained in Cambridge through the vacations."[5]

As we have seen elsewhere, restoration of the Chapel began in 1846, and Gray also says that "intoned services were first introduced by Osmond Fisher in the Hall while the Chapel was under restoration"[6] – so it seems that the thanks of the College were offered to John

Sutton after the first term of choral music at Jesus College. Gray goes on to say that

> "... the introduction of an organ, a trained choir of boys, and Gregorian chanting, was then a singularity in college Chapels, unknown except at King's and Trinity and, on Sundays and saints' days, at St. John's ... gave the College a distinctly High Anglican impress – moderate indeed, but conspicuously contrasted with the indifferentism which then characterised Cambridge in religious matters."[7]

Gregorian chanting means plainsong, then becoming quite popular on the parish church side of the choral revival; and with the social atmosphere of the time, it is likely that the boys sang it on their own – for the undergraduates would be unusual indeed if they had used their voices themselves. Over the singing of the Psalms, the authorities differ: there is the immediately preceding extract, while the *Parish Choir*, quoted by Dr. Rainbow, says that "the psalms and canticles were sung antiphonally to Anglican chants"[8]. Either seems equally possible; Sutton had been in the Camden Society for about six years by 1847 and, given his medieval outlook, plainsong was very reasonable. Having once taken part in it he was the more ready, years later, to devote a great deal of his money and attention to the revival and preservation of the Kurmainzer plainsong at Kiedrich. It should be noted too that Fisher, the chaplain of Jesus College, in the letter quoted previously at p.124, mentions only the one mistake in Gray's *History*. As he was intimately concerned with the revival of choral music in Jesus College Chapel, and a musician, he would surely have noticed and commented upon such an important error.

On the other hand, Rainbow points out that, broadly speaking, plainsong was a feature of the parish side of the choral revival rather than the cathedral and collegiate side[9]. Sutton would have been thoroughly used to Anglican chants from his cathedral experience and, while we may be sure that the 1840's habit of each singer getting in the words as well as he could would be abhorrent, quite a small amount of work would be enough to "point" a Psalter for six or even eight boys.

There is a third possibility: quite a number of Anglican chants based on plainsong exist – for instance, no. 196 in the Cathedral Psalter Chant Book[10], named merely "Old Melody", and a version of the "*Tonus Peregrinus*" at 249. If, when drawing up his list of chants, Sutton was feeling very medieval, he might well have had only this sort of chant, and as was common at the time, one chant only would have been used for all the psalms for any one service. The boys would have sung the psalms in unison, and Sutton was a fine improvisor – so it would have been easy for Dr. Gray and others unversed in music to believe that plainsong was being used. The *Parish Choir* correspondent would know better, and Sutton could be satisfied that early music, adapted into the collegiate tradition, was being heard by the undergraduates.

There were by now two plainsong Psalters printed in England that might have been used, Oakley's *Laudes Diurnae* and Dyce's *Order of Daily Service*, both published in 1843 (was a book with the title *Oxford Psalter* likely to be used in Cambridge? – though this, the work of W.B. Heathcote, was produced in 1845): *Laudes Diurnae*, even though the psalms were written out and pointed in full, "had proved demonstrably faulty"[11]: *The Order of Daily Service* did not print out the words coupled with the music, but provided a full and reasoned Appendix giving a complete set of rules on how to sing the psalms to plainsong. Dyce did observe, though, that "no degree of facility of performance will be arrived at without almost daily practise [sic]"[12] – which no doubt the Jesus College boys had.

What does survive from Sutton's time as organist of Jesus College is the book of words of anthems he published in 1850. Naturally, the college has a whole set of them, for the Commemoration of Founders and Benefactors is bound up with them and is used every December; but the copy examined is in the University Library, and was in the collection of Dr. A. H. Mann, Organist and Fellow of King's College[13]. The first pages are transcribed here in full (and obviously page 1 should come after pages 2 and 3).

Page 1:   The Full Anthems

Page 2:   A Collection of Anthems,
               used in Divine Service upon Sundays,
                    Holy-days and their Eves,
                              in
                      Jesus College Chapel
                          Cambridge

                      To which is added
                The Form of the Commemoration
                       of Benefactors

                         ****

                          Chiswick
                Printed by Charles Whittingham
                            1850

Page 3:   This collection of Anthems was made by John Sutton,
              Soc. Comm. and Organist. 1850.

On p. 4 and seqq., the words of the anthems are written out in full. Here are the titles and composers, with dates and details by the author:

Full Anthems:

The proud have digged pits　　　　　　　　　　　　　　Dr. Tye
　(*Christopher Tye, 1497-1572, Master of the Choristers at Ely Cathedral
　and Gentleman of the Chapel Royal.*)
Our God ascendeth up on high　　　　　　　　　　　　Dr. Tye
　(*metrical Psalm XLVII*)
If ye love Me　　　　　　　　　　　　　　　　　　　　Tallis
　(*1505-10 – 1585, Waltham Abbey and Gentleman of the Chapel Royal.*)
Hide not Thy face　　　　　　　　　　　　　　　　　Farrant
　(*died 1550 as Organist of St. George's Chapel, Windsor.*)
Lord, for Thy tender mercy's sake　　　　　　　　　　Farrant
Call to remembrance　　　　　　　　　　　　　　　Farrant
Teach me, O Lord　　　　　　　　　　　　　　　Dr. Rogers
　(*1614-1698, organist successively of Christ Church Dublin, Eton College,
　and Magdalen College, Oxford.*)
Lord, who shall dwell.　　　　　　　　　　　　　　Dr. Rogers
Behold now, praise the Lord　　　　　　　　　　　Dr. Rogers
Praise the Lord, O my soul　　　　　　　　　　　　Dr. Rogers
O give thanks　　　　　　　　　　　　　　　　　Dr. Rogers
Behold, how good and joyful　　　　　　　　　　Dr. Rogers
O pray for the peace of Jerusalem　　　　　　　　Dr. Rogers
How long wilt Thou forget me　　　　　　　　　Dr. Rogers
Praise the Lord, O my soul　　　　　　　　　　　Dr. Childe
　(*1606-1697, organist to Kings Charles I and Charles II at Windsor.*)
O Lord, grant the King　　　　　　　　　　　　　Dr. Childe
Deliver us, O Lord　　　　　　　　　　　　　　　　Batten
　(*1585-90 – 1637, an organist of St. Paul's Cathedral.*)
O praise the Lord, all ye heathen,　　　　　　　　　　Batten
The Lord hear thee　　　　　　　　　　　　　　　Dr. Blow
　(*1648-9 – 1708, organist of the Chapel Royal and Westminster Abbey.*)
Save, Lord, and hear us　　　　　　　　　　　　　Dr. Blow
Consider mine enemies　　　　　　　　　　　　　Dr. Blow
The voice of the Lord　　　　　　　　　　　　　　Dr. Blow
O how amiable　　　　　　　　　　　　　　　　Richardson
Behold now, praise the Lord　　　　　　　　　　　　Aldrich
　(*1647-1710, Dean of Christ Church, Oxford.*)
O give thanks　　　　　　　　　　　　　　　　　　Tucker
　(*died 1690, Precentor of Westminster Abbey.*)
Lift up your heads　　　　　　　　　　　　　　　Dr. Turner
　(*1651-1740, Chorister of Westminster Abbey, the Chapel Royal and St.
　Paul's.*)
O Israel, trust in the Lord　　　　　　　　　　　　　Dr. Croft
　(*1678-1727, Organist of the Chapel Royal and Westminster Abbey.*)
Veni Creator　　　　　　　　　　　　　　　　　　　Handel
　(*Cosin's translation, four verses.*) (*1685-1759*)

MUSICIAN

There is sprung up a light	Handel
O praise God in His holiness	Weldon
(1676-1736, Organist of the Chapel Royal.)	
I give you a new commandment	Shephard
(early in the sixteenth century: his services and anthems were published 1565.)	
Thous visitest the earth	Dr. Greene
(1694-1755, Organist of St. Paul's and the Chapel Royal.)	
Blessing and glory	Dr. Boyce
(1710-1779, London organist: published a standard collection of cathedral music.)	
Try me, O God	Dr. Nares
(1715-1783, Organist of York Minster and the Chapel Royal.)	
Blessed is he that considereth	Dr. Nares
The Lord descended from above	Dr. Hayes
(either William, 1707-1777, or his son Philip, 1738-1797: both were Professors of Music at Oxford, and Organists of Magdalen College.)	
Lord, hear the voice	Jackson
(1730-1803, Organist of Exeter Cathedral.)	
Through all the changing scenes	Jackson
How num'rous, Lord	Jackson
Come unto Me, all that labour	Jackson
Lord of all power and might	Mason
(1724-1797: poet, and Precentor of York.)	
O Lord, we beseech Thee	Pratt
(Organist of King's College, Cambridge, in Sutton's time.)	

The Verse Anthems

Awake up, my glory	Wide
(1648-1687, Organist of Salisbury.)	
Prepare ye the way	Wise
Blessed is he that considereth	Wise
Sing unto the Lord	Dr. Christopher Gibbons
(1615-1676, Organist of Westminster Abbey.)	
How long wilt Thou forget me	Jer. Clarke
(1659-1707, Organist of St. Paul's.)	
We wait for Thy loving kindness	Dr. Croft
Lord, what love have I	Dr. Croft
The Lord is my light	Dr. Croft
O hold Thou me up	Marcello
(1686-1739, a Venetian: the English version of his psalm paraphrases was published by Garth and Avison at Newcastle 1757.)	
Give ear unto me	Marcello
O sing praises	Pergolesi
(1710-1736, a Neapolitan.)	

O Lord, have mercy	Pergolesi and Marcello
Bow down Thine ear	Leonardo Leo

(*1694-1744, a Neapolitan.*)

I know that my Redeemer liveth	Handel

(*a section of 'Messiah' as far as the chorus, 'Even so in Christ'.*)

Holy, holy, Lord God Almighty	Handel
O sing unto the Lord	Handel
O come, let us sing unto the Lord	Handel
As pants the hart	Handel
My song shall be alway	Handel
Blessed is the people, O Lord	Handel
Blessed are those that are undefiled	Greene
The Lord is my shepherd	Greene
Like as the hart	Greene
Behold, I bring you glad tidings	Greene
The souls of the righteous	Nares
God is our hope and strength	Nares
O come hither, and hearken	Nares
Wherewithal shall a young man	Nares
Hear my prayer	Kent

(*1700-1776, Organist of Trinity College, Cambridge, and Winchester Cathedral.*)

My God, my God, look upon me	Reynolds

(*died 1770, Gentleman of the Chapel Royal.*)

Ponder my words	Corfe

(*died 1820, Organist of Salisbury Cathedral.*)

I will sing of mercy and judgment	Novello

(*1781-1861, Organist of the Portugese Embassy Chapel.*)

Turn Thy face	Attwood

(*1765-1838, Organist of St Paul's, pupil of Mozart, teacher of Walmisley.*)

Lift Thine eyes	F. Mendelssohn Bartholdy

(*1809-1847.*)

O praise the Lord, all ye His hosts	F. Mendelssohn Bartholdy
O Lord, Thou has searched me out	F. Mendelssohn Bartholdy
Ponder my words	Dr. Thomas Attwood Walmisley

(*formerly of Jesus College and Professor of Music in the University.*)

"This anthem was composed for, and first used at, the service on All Saints Day 1849: being the day of the opening of the choir of Jesus College Chapel, after its restoration."

Haste Thee, O God, to deliver me	J. Sutton
O God, Thou art my God	Wise
I will arise and go to my Father	Wise
The Lord is my shepherd	Wise
I was glad when they said	Tucker
The Lord is King	Aldrich

The Commemoration of Benefactors follows, and then twenty-six hymns. These must have been bound in later, as J. B. Dykes' tune *Nicaea* was only written for the first edition of *Hymns Ancient and Modern* which was published in 1861.

The words of Sutton's own anthem run like this:

"Haste Thee, O God, to deliver me:
    make haste to help me, O God. Cho.
As for me, I am poor and needy:
    but the Lord careth for me. Solus.
Thou art my Helper, and Redeemer:
    make no long tarrying, O my God. 2 Voc.
Thou are my helper, etc. Cho."

Other indications of the forces used in the various sections of the anthems appear in the text – 3 voc., 4 voc., vers and recit. They were directed towards helping the undergraduates to listen to the music intelligently.

There is nothing very exceptional about the choice of composers, considering the date of the anthem book, and Sutton's own conservative tastes at the time (evident all through the *Short Account*). Music of the seventeenth and early eighteenth centuries predominates, but the most striking omission in the list of composers is Purcell – were some of his harmonies too rich for John Sutton, whose own liking for Bach, Handel and Mozart would mean a fairly severe harmonic grounding? The little collection of Italian composers should be noted; it was quite the fashion at one time to re-set the church music of Italian and other composers to English words. There is a large section of this sort in the *Brougham Anthem Book*, which Sutton's resembles in other respects, and was published in the eighteen-forties: it includes seventy-five titles by twenty-seven composers, forty-five of them by Palestrina, a later love of Sutton's in Bruges. Occasionally *Brougham* adds the name of the arranger – "adapted by Dr. Aldrich", or "Arr. J. Pratt.". It's reasonable enough when the great popularity of Italian opera in Handel's time is remembered, to expect that Italian church music would enjoy something of a similar vogue. John Pratt, organist of King's College in Sutton's time, had done quite a lot of this work, but not everybody approved of it. W. E. Dickson, Sutton's friend and Precentor of Ely, wrote, in his autobiography, *Fifty Years of Church Music*:

"Another very favourite anthem was an adaptation of the first Mass of Mozart – 'Praise the Lord, O my soul' – introducing the exquisite melody to which the illustrious composer has set the words of the Agnus Dei. Pratt's adaptations were made without the slightest regard to the original words present in the mind of the composer; even the order of sequence of the movements was not respected; but no matter – these anthems were highly popular, and the number was small indeed of critics bold enough to question the propriety of the selection, or the style of its performance."

It is not clear who provided the alto, tenor and bass parts for all this music when it was sung. The professional singers in Cambridge at this time were few, and College Sunday services were timed so that most or all of them could sing in two or more chapels, just as the organists doubled up on their duties. Perhaps Sutton found others who could sing in the city, but on the other hand, the choir that sang on All Saints' Day 1849 was of four boys' voices only, as the anthem *Ponder my Words* written specially for the service, attests,[14] and a full choir would certainly have been expected on the day of the re-opening of the restored chapel. So *The Parish Choir*, reporting that there were eight boys by now, probably was correct; it also mentioned that the boys wore buckled shoes, and surplices that were rather in vogue at the time – in shape like a circular poncho with no separate arms, and just a hole for the head.[15] Was the Jesus College Anthem Book only a splendid hope, if men were not found to sing the lower parts?

The most succinct account of John Sutton's musical work in Bruges is to be found in Rembry: *De Bekende Pastoors van St.-Gillis te Brugge*:

"*M. van Coillie was geen muzikant, maar hij was innig overtuigd dat het muziek, op behoorlijke wijze en volgens den geest der H. Kerk, uitgevoerd, grootelijks bijdraagt tot het verheffen der goddelijke diensten. Ook aanveerdde hij met gretigheid, den voorstel, in 1858, gedaan door heer baron John Sutton, van het orkestmuziek, in voege tot dan toe in St.-Gillis, te vervangen door het zoogezeide muziek van Palestrina, dat, edel en statig, het huis Gods alleszins weerdig is, en allerbest, overeenstemt met de verhevenheid der kerkceremoniën. Baron Sutton verplichtte zich het uitvoeren van dit muziek to bekostigen, en heirtoe eene jaarlijksche somme aan de kerkfabriek te betalen, op voorwaarde nogtans dat een geestelijke met het vormen en het bestier der muzikanten zou belast wezen. Deze voorstel droeg eenieders goedkeurig weg, en, den 26 Feb. 1858. wierd M. Adolf Fraeys, student op het groot seminarie, en bijzonder ervaren in het vak van muziek, door Mgr. Malou tot kapelmeester benoemd van St.-Gillis. Ruim veir jaar, vervulde M. Fraeys dit ambt; zooveel iever en kunde wist hij aan den daag te leggen, dat St.-Gillis welhaast al de andere kerken van Brugge, onder opzicht van kerkmuziek, overtrof. Onder-pastor benoemd van Sint-Andries, bij Brugge, den 25 Juni 1862, kreeg M. Fraeys voor opvolger M. Amandus Leun, den bekwaamsten zijner leerlingen, die elf jaar, en met den besten uitslag, het moeielijk ambt van kapeelmeester waarnam. Spijtig genoeg, het Palestrina's muziek is onderbleven sedert den 12 Juni 1873, ten gevolge van het overlijden van baron Sutton, voorgevallen den 5 derzelfde maand."*[16]

(M. van Coillie [P.P. of St. Gillis] was no musician, but he was deeply convinced that music, if performed in a proper way and according to the spirit of Holy Church, could contribute greatly to the offering of divine worship. So he accepted with alacrity the suggestion made by Baron Sutton, in 1858, that the orchestral music used up to that year at St. Gillis be replaced by the music of Palestrina, which noble and stately as it is, is in every way worthy of the house of God – and agrees in every way with the offering of church offices. Baron Sutton pledged himself to pay for the singing of this music in addition to the annual sum he was to pay to the church fabric, on the firm understanding that a priest would be given the title and the daily duty of director of music. This suggestion did not receive much approval; so on 26 February 1858 M. Adolf Fraeys, a student at the senior seminary specially experienced in musical matters, was appointed choirmaster of St. Gillis by Mgr. Malou. M. Fraeys carried out this duty for more than four years, and brought so much enthusiasm and ability to his duties that St. Gillis soon surpassed all the other churches of Bruges with its music. When he was appointed curate of Sint Andries near Bruges on 25 June 1862, M. Fraeys had as successor M. Aime Leun, the most capable of his pupils, who occupied the difficult post of choirmaster for eleven years with excellent results. The more was the pity, then, that Palestrina's music was stopped after 12 June 1873, as a result of the death of Baron Sutton, which occurred on the fifth of the same month.)

Hilpisch says that the choir was "virtually the same" as that founded by Sutton in Kiedrich church – so nine men and sixteen boys.[17]

In Kiedrich

To worship at a Sunday or red-letter-day *Hochamt* in the parish church of Sts. Valentin and Dionysius in Kiedrich seems to take one a long way back in time. Not only is Latin used in the service, but the ancient Propers (Introit, Gradual, Offertory, Communion and Post-Communion sentences) are sung by the choir only to the Kurmainzer plainsong. Dressed in very English-looking surplices, the choir of men and boys occupies stalls facing north and south beyond a stone chancel screen; when they sing Propers or anthems, they group themselves on the high altar steps, and use a single large volume of music resting on a special desk. How does this all come about?

In medieval times, and indeed up to the Thirty Years' War (1618-48), many of the Rhineland churches seem to have been collegiate in all but name. Each altar in a parish church was an individual foundation supplying a frugal living to the priest who served it; and he, in addition to the Mass offered daily at "his" altar, was bound to attend, and sing at, the parish Mass offered by the parish priest at the high altar, as well as certain of the Offices – sometimes all of them, or at any rate Vespers and Compline of great feasts.[18] A typical extract from the Kiedrich archives is this foundation document of the altar to St. Katharine dating from 12 January 1382: "...*auch sal der furgenant prister deme perner gehorsam sin mit syne Ruckelin zu chore zu gen zu metten zu messen zu vespern zu vigilie* ..."[19] (the aforementioned priest shall also be in attendance on the parish priest with his surplice to go into the choir for mattins, for mass, for vespers and for vigils). At Kiedrich, there are six altars besides the high altar and so when they were at full strength six *altaristen*, as these priests were called; a very respectable choir indeed if they were all musical.

In the seventeenth century, the number of priests available for service as *altaristen* decreased drastically, and has never recovered enough for the system to be re-introduced (even if Germany had not suffered as much as she has from inflation, so that the original altar-bequests are now worthless), and to make sure that the Mass at least was still offered with music, laymen were drafted in to sing.

It could not have been long after John Sutton's arrival in Kiedrich, that he would find out that the parish school was also extremely ancient. The custom of the Electorate of Mainz, and the Rheingau, was that the parish schools should be responsible for teaching Latin and music, and that masters and boys should assist at daily worship in the parish church as well. It is said that this tradition goes back to the Emperor Charlemagne (*c*.742-814):

> "*Das ist Aufgabe und pädagogisches Ziel der 'Volksschule' seit dem Jahre 800 und ist es bist fast zum Jahre 1800 geblieben. Auch die humanistischen Einflüsse der Reformationszeit änderten daran nichts. Wesentliche Aufgabe der Schule blieb die vorbereitung der Jugend auf die würdige Gestaltung des Gottesdienstes.*"[20] (This is the theme and teaching aim of the "People's School" ever since the year 800 and stayed so until nearly 1800. Even the humanistic influences at the time of the Reformation did

not alter it at all. The preparation of young people for the worthy offering of the service of God remained the essential theme of the schools.)

Kiedrich was established as a parish in 1277; schoolmasters are mentioned in the fifteenth century, and are named from 1540. The *Capitelstatuten* (ruridecanal chapter statutes) of 1420 for the Rheingau deanery laid down that the schoolmasters should give instruction in reading, writing and singing, and worship in church and at processions "*veste chorali*", or surpliced.[21] These instructions were echoed in years and indeed centuries to come, and in 1721 the deanery schoolmasters were told to lead both spoken and sung parts of the Mass ("*vorangehe*"); and were instructed to use the last hour of the mornings in "*Figuralgesang*" or music in parts, and the first hour in the afternoons for plainsong – and Latin was still enthusiastically encouraged.[22] All this rich worship went on more or less unaltered until 1760, when the singers migrated to the west gallery in the church, which was enlarged to accommodate them. "*Die Musik entfernte sich nicht nur räumlich, sondern auch geistig vom Altar, wobei es offen bleibt, was hier Ursache und Wirkung ist.*"[23] (The music took itself away from the altar not only spatially but also spiritually, so that both motive and results of it were no longer obvious.) But worse was to come: there was a movement of thought in eighteenth-century Germany which regarded both Catholicism and Protestant orthodoxy as powers of spiritual darkness depriving humanity of the use of its rational faculties. Most of its representatives believed passionately in the goodness of human nature, and this blinded them to the fact of sin, and produced an easy optimism and absolute faith in the progress and perfectibility of human society once the principles of enlightened reason had been recognised.[24] The German Emperor Joseph II (reigned 1765-1790) instituted many "reforms" following these principles, most of which were directed against the rule and directions of Rome; and he had a number of followers among the higher clergy of the German lands. For our purposes, it is enough to say that in the Electorate of Mainz the schoolmasters were no longer required to take their pupils to church every day, and both music and Latin were removed from the curriculum as being of no practical use. In church, the pressure was for at least the congregation's part of the services to be in German, and the last Archbishop-Elector of Mainz, Friedrich von Erthal, decreed on 11 March, 1787, that only German hymns should be sung during Mass, and issued a hymn-book for the purpose in the same year.[25] Staab says severely, "*Nicht mehr die 'gloria Dei' erschien dieser Zeit Hauptzweck des Gottesdienstes, sondern Belehrung und Erbauung der Gläubigen (mit Hilfe von oft trockenen, flachen und moralisierenden Liedern.)*"[26] (At this time, God's glory was no longer the chief aim of the services, but the informing and building up of the believers – with the help of songs that were frequently sugary, superficial and moralising). It was not only in the Electorate of Mainz that such hymns became the norm: in Austria the Vienna Masses, as they came to be called, were sung everywhere on Sundays and took the form of an almost continuous series of vernacular hymns, sung by the congregation while Mass went on at the altar seemingly divorced from the people in whose name it was offered. Franz Schubert, Michael Haydn and, of course, other lesser composers, wrote sets of these hymn-masses; in England, the hymn corresponding to the *Sanctus* in Schubert's "German Mass" is quite well-known.

Kiedrich and the villagers around resisted these changes stoutly. At Rüdesheim troops had to be used to quell them, which says a great deal about the people's attachment to their traditions. In the end, many of Joseph II's ideas and reforms died with him, and after 1792, Kiedrich and the other villages of the region took up the ancient plainsong once again. The Napoleonic wars followed, and English people have little idea of the devastation that could result from having one's village fought over, invaded, evacuated and then the whole process beginning again with a second set of soldiers demanding food and perhaps looting the homes of the villagers. It is amazing that so many of the church's treasures remain in Kiedrich. After the Congress of Vienna in 1813, church life revived under a Bishop of Mainz (nominated by Napoleon in 1802) who was no longer an Elector of the Holy Roman Empire, nor a German aristocrat. It is believed that this Bishop of Mainz, Josef Ludwig Colmar (1760-1818), very nearly gave the Kurmainzer Choral its death-blow, and this point is dealt with in the commentary on Sutton's letter of 18 January, 1862, to Jean de Béthune.[27]

When John Sutton arrived in Kiedrich in 1857 the memory would still be quite fresh about the old plainsong, and grandfathers would be quoted as telling of how they had attended Mass every day. This daily attendance of the schoolmaster, the boys versed in music and Latin and, when still available, the *altaristen*, is very like the English cathedral and collegiate tradition – and must have been attractive indeed to someone like Sutton, a lover of history, Latin and music (and any true Camden Society man would have revelled in it too). It is not in any way surprising that he determined to restore as much of the traditional way of worship as he possibly could. By the time of his death it was not as complete as he would have wished because it is believed that he intended to found a small college of perhaps four priests as well, but what he accomplished has not only survived to this day, but has been made the foundation for much more.

(right) A page from the new Kiedrich Graduale *(1961) showing the ancient neum notation of about 1260*

uer natus est no-
bis et filius datus
est nobis cuius im-
pe rium super hu-
merum e ius et uoca bitur nomen
e ius magni consili i an gelus.
Cantate domino canticu nouum quia
mirabilia fecit. E u o u a e. idenit omnes fines ter re saluta-
re de i nostri Iubilate de o

Kiedrich Chorschule

The document in which John Sutton expressed his wishes and promised the endowment for the choir-school of Kiedrich and its officials, was drawn up with a great deal of care, in Latin, and was matched by an equally careful answer from the Bishop of Limburg-on-the-Lahn, as Ordinary and diocesan.[28]

After the religious preamble setting out his aims –

> "... *ad laudem et gloriam Dei Omnipotentis, in honorem B. Mariae semper Virginis sine labe originale conceptae, sanctorum Martyrum SS. Valetini et Dionysii atque omnium Sanctorum, necnon in augmentum divini cultus praesertim in parochia et ecclesia parochiali Kideracensi peragendi...*"

(... to the praise and glory of Almighty God, in honour of Blessed Mary ever Virgin conceived without original sin, of the holy Martyrs Sts. Valentine and Dionysius and all saints, as well to enrich divine service especially in the parish and parish church of Kiedrich...)

the first article laid down the number of choristers, nine men and sixteen boys, led by a choirmaster who must be a priest, and an organist who was also to be regarded as a member of the foundation.

The second article laid down that the whole choir, vested in cassock and surplice – *talari et superpelliceo* – should sing the Kurmainzer plainsong – *Cantus Moguntini* – at a considerable list of services every year:

– On St. Valentine's Day and during the octave (as in the English Prayer Book "and seven days after"), during the eight-day August pilgrimage period and on every Saturday of the year, Vespers and Compline.
– At Prime on all principal feasts which have their own Vespers.
– On all Sundays and red-letter days, Vespers and Compline.
– At Christmas, Easter, Pentecost and All Saints' Day, Lauds at 6 a.m., Prime and Terce before Solemn Mass, and in the evening Vespers and Compline.
– On Wednesday, Thursday and Friday of Holy Week, Mattins and Lauds.
– On all Sundays and red-letter days throughout the year, St. Valentine's Day and the octave, the eight-day August pilgrimage period, the feast of the church's consecration, the Visitation of the Blessed Virgin Mary and St. Dionysius' Day, to sing at Mass.
– To attend all Processions laid down in the Mass-book, especially at the Purification of the Blessed Virgin Mary, Palm Sunday, Maundy Thursday and Good Friday.

- At the wish of the *Pfarrer*, to be at Mass on Palm Sunday, Good Friday especially at the Singing of the Passion, and on Easter Even at the Blessing of the New Fire, of the Easter Candle, of the Baptismal Water and at Mass.
- At the special offices on Ember Days, St. Valentine's Day, the Visitation of the Blessed Virgin Mary and St. Dionysius' Day.
- Finally, to be at all festal functions ordered by the Bishop, at which the *Pfarrer* wishes for choral music.
  To this was added in 1868 an order that Mass should be sung during the whole of St. Valentine's octave (sc. February 14-21).

It was a heavy programme for a village choir, and it must be right to assume that Sutton was trying to recapture some of the richness of Rhineland worship in medieval times.

A school for the boys was also endowed, where special attention was to be paid to Latin and singing – and to the normal subjects of the German curriculum, so that the choirboys' progress should not be hindered by their membership of the choir.

Article 6 sets out the financial base of the foundation:

- The Bishopric of Limburg for the administration costs, was to receive annually 200 Gulden. (at 7 to the pound, just under £30)
- The *Pfarrer* of Kiedrich, 360 (£51).
- The Curate of Kiedrich, 200.
- The *Chorregent* or Choirmaster, 720 (£73). He was allowed freedom in the intentions with which his daily Mass was offered, as long as he remembered Sutton himself, and prayed that the Sutton family would be converted to Roman Catholicism. He was to receive an additional 100 gulden for heat and light in the choir-school.
- The Organist of Kiedrich, unless the Bishop provided another organist for the choir's music, 250 (£35).
- Every adult singer, for the practices as well as services, 48 (£7).
- Every boy, 12 (£1.50).
- The organ-blower, 10.
- The verger, 25.
- and 200 was provided yearly for the Chorrgent's mass, robes, the choir-robes and other smaller things.

The complete endowment was 67,225 gulden (£9,603), which Sutton paid over as a lump sum.

One item in this document that immediately catches the eye is that the *Chorregent* and the *Kaplan* (the curate) are quite definitely regarded as two different individuals. Sutton was, in effect, restoring as much as he could of the collegiate character of the clerical staff of

In nomine Sanctissimae & individuae Trinitatis. Amen.

Ego Joannes Sutton, Liber Baronetus Norwicae sive Notts, hoc tempore habitans Kiederaci, quod est vicus in praefectura Alda-villensi, Ducatus Nassoviae, quam in animo habeam ad laudem et gloriam Dei Omnipotentis, in honorem B. Mariae semper Virginis sine labe originali conceptae, Sanctorum Martyrum SS. Valentini et Dionysii atque omnium Sanctorum, necnon in augmentum divini cultus praesertim in parochia et ecclesia parochiali Kiederacensi peragendi, in dicto loco Kiederich chorum cantorum ecclesiasticum simulque scholam choralem erigere et dotare, in qua cantus planus sive Gregorianus atque artes liberales tradantur, optimum judicavi has dare literas testimoniales, in quibus eas stipulationes, quas si Reverendissimo

First page of the document of the re-founding of the Kiedrich Choir-school, 1865

Petrus Josephus

Miseratione Divina et Sanctae Sedis Apostolicae gratia

Episcopus Limburgensis

Sanctitatis Suae Praelatus Domesticus, Solio Pontificio Assistens, Comes Sacri Palatii et Aulae Lateranensis etc.

Notum testatumque facimus:

Postquam devotus in Christo Nobis dilectus filius ac Dominus Joannes Sutton, Liber Baronetus a Norwood Park Notts, hoc tempore habitans Kideraci vico Dioecesis Nostrae in Rhingavia sito, sua sponte et re perbene consulta, statuit, in laudem et gloriam Dei omnipotentis, in honorem Beatae Mariae Virginis sine labe originali conceptae, Sanctorum Martyrum Pontificum Valentini et Dionysii et omnium Sanctorum, nec non in augmentum cultus divini, praesertim in parochia et ecclesia parochiali Kideracensi peragendi, in dicto loco Kiderich chorum cantorum ecclesiasticum simulque scholam choralem ea ratione erigere et dotare quae in afigisis litteris fundationis manu propria laudati Domini Baroneti subscriptis ejusque sigillo consueto munitis

First page of the Bishop of Limburg's Decree setting up the Choir-school

the parish, and with three priests, High Mass could be offered on Sundays and feast-days with the proper number of ministers as priest, deacon and sub-deacon. It might well not have been possible for him to endow a further priest's place at Kiedrich without special permission that might not be forthcoming. But what he could do, he did; and it must have been a disappointment for him to find that the diocese of Limburg immediately disregarded his wishes by appointing the *Kaplans* of Kiedrich as *Chorregents*, apparently oblivious to their suitability or otherwise for the post. Apart from the possible damage to the choir's musical performance, there were personality difficulties during the early years, which made Sutton refer to it several times in the Schneider letters as "our poor Choral Stift", and express his thanks when it was remembered by Mgr. Schneider at Mass.

Minor points are that the choir has always occupied the chancel of Kiedrich church to sing in – another return to medieval ways advocated by the Camden Society, and that English surplices with round necks have always been worn rather than the square-necked Continental variety. It has always been a tradition that the singers lived in the village, or at the very least were born in it, and certainly up to recent years, every boy who could sing in Kiedrich was expected to spend a year or two as a member of the choir.

The money given by Sutton as the endowment fund was invested in a comb factory: this failed at some point, and what with that and the astronomic inflation of the German currency after the 1914 war, all was lost.[29] But with great devotion to Sutton's memory, the nine adult members of the choir went to the Bishop of Limburg and asked that they might continue to sing for nothing, so that the *Chorstift* might be saved. Permission was granted and gradually the diocese took over the financial responsibility for the foundation. From about 1930 onwards, increased scholarship, and enthusiasm for something unique, has resulted in a great raising of the standard of the choir's singing; and a widening of the repertoire which now embraces fifteenth, sixteenth and seventeenth century music. The choir makes records, and came to England, by invitation, for the Aldeburgh Festival in 1973, when apart from their official appearances – one of them a Sung Mass according to their own tradition – they sang a Requiem at West Tofts for the Sutton family, with the present author as celebrant.

It is a wonderful thing that this choir, with the *Kurmainzer* plainsong, has survived its initial difficulties, the urge for uniformity in the Roman Catholic church in the hundred years from 1870, and the atmosphere of the nineteen-thirties and nineteen-forties in Germany. It stands today as John Sutton's most enduring monument – and with his devotion to his boys, to history and to music, it may well be the one he would himself prefer.

As there had been a set of anthem-books produced for Jesus

College in Cambridge, John Sutton decided that the Kiedrich choir must have a new set of books too. This was not going to be easy, for anyone who reads about Kiedrich or visits the village and its church soon finds out that the music is unique. In fact, it was sung throughout the Rheingau and the archdiocese of Mainz until the eighteenth century, and hence comes its title – the *Kurmainzer* plainsong, or plainsong of the Electorate of Mainz. (Incidentally, the German word for plainsong, used by Sutton too, is *Choral*, which is puzzling to English people who use the word to mean a hymn-tune from the Reformation period.) Church musicians who sing and accompany plainsong in England are used enough to the idea of regional or national variations, for all that was popularised in the Anglican church during the nineteenth and early twentieth centuries was the Sarum variant. By the end of the fifteenth century nearly all English churches used the music sung at Salisbury, and naturally the manuscripts available to the nineteenth-century revivers were of the Sarum books. The *Kurmainzer* plainsong was equally the national German variant:

> "*Die Unterschiede zur römischen Choralnotation lassen sich in der Erhöhung des Spitzentones um einen Halb- oder Ganzton, in der Erweiterung von Intervallen, etwa der Terz sur Quart, und in der Auflösung Starker, unbeweglicher Tonfolgen zu bewegten Melodien auf dem gleichen Vokal auch für den Nichtmusiker erkennen.*"

> (The differences from the Roman editions of plainsong are in the raising of the peak-notes by a semitone or a tone, in the widening of intervals – as a third to a fourth – and in the loosening of stiff, awkward series of notes into flexible tunes for straightforward singing, that even unmusical folk can attempt.)

It was, and is now, written and printed in neumes, and anyone wishing to study it must learn this notation.

It is something of a surprise to an Englishman, whose countrymen lost all interest in plainsong after the sixteenth century as being popish, to find that an edition of the *Kurmainzer* Gradual (a book containing the proper music sung by the choir at Mass) was printed in 1671 on the orders of the Elector-Archbishop Johann Philipp von Schönborn of Mainz.[31] Lord Clark has written,

> "... many of these rulers of small German principalities – bishops, dukes, electors – were in fact remarkably cultivated and intelligent men. Their competitive ambitions benefited architecture and music in a way that the democratic obscurity of the Hanoverians in England did not. The Schönborn family ... were really great patrons whose name should be remembered with the Medici."[32]

It seems that the people of the Rheingau were very much attached to this music: the parish priest of Östrich wrote in a new music-book he was forced to use in 1788, "*Nur der Choral, weil er sonst war, und den Rheingauern eine ganz eigene Lieblingssache ist, hat ihr ganzes Herz*". [33] (Only plainsong has the Rheingauers' complete affection, because it was special, and was their own beloved thing.) In a previous century, then, there would be no question of substituting other church music for the plainsong, but as the *Kurmainzer* liturgy and calendar were altered to fit in with the Roman use, so the plainsong was put onto five lines instead of four, some texts were re-set to music already existing with other words, and other music was drastically shortened

Interior of Kiedrich Church, looking east

and altered. Naturally, some of its character was lost in the process – the Germans say that it was "*barockisiert*" (baroquised), which is certainly as accurate a word as one can find.

Sadly, when John Sutton decided to have his new edition of the plainsong printed, it was the von Schönborn books that his advisers recommended him to copy. There was little scientific knowledge of plainsong in Europe at the time, for the work of the Benedictine monks of Solesmes, who specialised in it, only bore fruit in their *Editio Vaticana* of 1908; and certainly to have undertaken a comparison and correction of the seventeenth-century work with the surviving medieval books would have taken years and years. It took five years for the Sutton books to be produced merely by a copying process, and he had not the time to make a scholarly job of it. Throughout the Schneider letters there are requests to thank Herr Weber and others for their work in the production of the new edition, and certainly advisers, binders and printers worked extremely hard on it. The cost was immense, for new founts had to be made for the neum notation, and the vast volumes for the choir-desks (40 × 55 cm.) would surely not fit into any normal machine of that time, so would have to be put together by hand.

Sutton also had a *Manuale* produced – this time in much more manageable size – for the choir-offices in which the Kiedrich choir took part: this does not figure in the extant correspondence. There was, however, what he calls "the little book" which apparently contained hymn-tunes – and to increase our confusion of language, he calls them Chorals!

> "Triercher Hof in Coblenz, Xmas Day 1869 ... I enclose one of the Chorals from the little book, I have been trying to put harmony to from the bass – I feel there are some mistakes, and the original bass not very nice – will you ask the Cho.ʳ Regent to correct the mistakes on another piece of paper, and then I think I shall succeed better with the next try – ..."[34]

With no delay at all, Mgr. Schneider got the priest (Herr Weber) who had supervised the new plainsong books – and who lived, like him, in Mainz – to look over this work, and another letter was written from Coblenz on 27 December:

> "Will you give Mr. Weber my best thanks for his corrections, I must learn a little thorough Bass (General B) I harmonize too much by ear – I am surprised to find I have made a mistake in one note in the *melody*, and I have looked at the little Book again and find I have read it wrong, but the Book is very badly printed, some of the Chorals are

quite wrong, the Bass and melody cannot be played together – but I think they could be made out by comparing one Choral with another – The *Durdrei Klang* was a *fancy* of my own and not indicated by the Bass – It is what was called the *Terz de Picardy* and is often found in old music ..."[35]

The impression is that the friends were preparing to re-publish a small book of hymn-tunes for use at Kiedrich and that Sutton was intending to write four-part harmony from the original figured bass, to make it possible for future organists at the church to play it, but found himself rather rusty. But it was just like his gentle spirit to have his efforts examined by somebody else. The *Tierce de Picardie* is when a major chord ends a tune set in a minor key. The book turns up again right at the end of the period, for there is a letter headed "Amelie les Bains, Monday." (Sutton spent the winter of 1872-3 in the south of France looking after his consumptive Irish servant.) The letter has several sketches of books to illustrate Sutton's meaning, which was that the printing took up too little of the pages, and in any case began too near the middle of the book when open.

> "I have just now received the little Book, I like it very much with one exception, and this exception is perhaps an advantage in a practicle [*sic*] sense, as it opens so well. But the shape of it takes off from its old fashioned look, it is too wide this way --- and inside the printing comes too far from the middle. [Sketch] It ought to look so [Sketch].
> Will you please get one or 2 bound for me in this manner, and never mind whether it opens well or not, and have the margin cut a little more off outside also, to give it the proper stingy old fashioned look – ... [then in a postscript] Will you please send 3 copies of the little Book, to Francis Randolph, one for himself another for his brother Wilfred & one for his father, addressed to Francis at Bruges – the Boys are both learning German."[36]

It seems that this book must have been in German, so was most likely a collection of hymns. Edmund Randolph, Francis' and Wilfred's father, was a lifelong friend of Sutton and had married his wife's sister. But how typical of Sutton to be perfectly happy with a book that didn't open well, as long as it had the "proper stingy old fashioned look"!

Finally, there is in the Schneider papers one page in a completely different hand – English, cultivated and obviously used both to Latin and to liturgical texts: might it be written by Edmund Randolph, who, after his own conversion to the Roman Catholic faith, seems to have had no employment, but visited Kiedrich from time to time? It reads like this:-

General Content
of
the *Processionale*.

I

Matutin and *Laudes* for Christmas
Easter
Whitsuntide
All Saints
three last days of the *Charwoche*
horae minores for the latter days.
(then in John Sutton's hand) I think the *matutin* for the 3 days in the
Charwoche sh.ᵈ be added (the office with the candles)
(sketch of candlestick)
if you like the office of ascension day
and assumptio B. Mar. Virg.

II

The *Processionale* as it is in the *Manuale*.

III

Te Deum.
Antiphons Stella coeli
Tota pulchra
Inviolata from the *Manuale*
Responsorium of S. Valentin particularly for Kiedrich in the 8ᵛᵒ.
Processionale.
Please to tell me, what size 4°. as the (here the ms. ends)."

There is little to be said about this except in the way of conjecture, as it does not seem to have been brought into being in any way. Obviously, though, the work of providing the Kiedrich choir with a full set of liturgical books was to go on; and like many other projects, was halted by Sutton's early death. The *Charwoche*, or *Karwoche*, is Holy-Week, and "the office with the candles" must have been *Tenebrae*.

John Sutton's own musical efforts, comments and taste

"*In der Musik, besonders dem Clavier – und Orgelspiel, brachte er es soweit, dass es für ihm nicht nur keine technischen Schwierigkeiten mehr gab, sondern auch alles gefühlvoll und mit feinster Phrasierung von ihm vorgetragen wurde. Seine Lieblinge waren Händel, Beethoven, Mozart und Sebast. Bach, deren Eigenthümlichkeiten er in prachtvollen Extempore-Stücken wiederzugeben verstand.*[37]
(He brought his music to such a pitch that, especially in piano and organ playing, there were no more technical

difficulties for him. and he played it all with feeling and with exact phrasing. His best-loved composers were Handel, Beethoven, Mozart and Sebastian Bach, whose musical styles he understood how to reproduce in fine extempore pieces very well.)

So Canon Zaun writes shortly: not because he knew no more about Sutton's musical tastes, but simply because he seems to wish to move on to other more concrete examples of his generosity to the church at Kiedrich. It does, however, give some valuable pointers: technical accomplishment, the ability to improvise in the style of his favourite composers, and as we might expect with the gentle John Sutton, a considerable amount of feeling for the music's inner meaning. Perhaps in the last years, the little concerts that once took place in his rooms at Cambridge were resumed when he was at Kiedrich, to the delight of a few guests.

In general, Sutton's letters are extremely practical; he deals with the business of the moment, sends his compliments to the family or friends of the addressee, and that is that. There is not, then, much to read about his musical activities; the one fact that does come over is that he would undertake no regular playing for a choir once he was living on the Continent, probably because he knew anything of that sort would keep him from the architectural journeys and studies that he felt were his particular calling. But there are few notes in his letters, and one or two points that we can glean from elsewhere.

During his stay at Freiburg-im-Breisgau soon after he left England, he wrote in a letter to Jean de Béthune, "they have got a very respectable Piano which is a great comfort to me".[38]

Then there exists, among a portfolio of drawings by one of his sisters, Judith, who was profoundly deaf (and who merits no mention by name in Burke's *Peerage, Baronetage and Knightage* because she died unmarried!), a little drawing of his room in the Gouden-Hand-Straat in Bruges:[39] in twentieth or even nineteenth-century terms, there is no real comfort there – a table, a couple of high-backed chairs and the two main articles of furniture – a grand piano and the "Northampton" chamber-organ described in the chapter about organs. It must have been there that the practice took place described in a letter to Mme. de Béthune dated 25 Janury, 1860: the letter is really about the lining for a projected set of green velvet vestments, but at the end John wrote:

"I played over the piece of Mozart again for about two hours, & the two boys came again the evening before last and we succeeded in making the movement that you heard *attempted only*, go very well indeed, & hope we shall succeed as well with the other two movements, & that next time

Judith Sutton's drawing of the living-room in her brother's house in Bruges

you come to Bruges you will be able to hear the whole Quatuor complete."[40]

This must have been one of Mozart's trios, but for what instruments we are left ignorant; perhaps the boys were seminary students lent to Sutton occasionally for a bit of music-making, or they might have been the sons of St. Gillis' people. In any case, the fact that he practised on his own for two hours is enough to show us that, if he found no technical difficulties in the work of Mozart, John's standards must have been high indeed.

A little before this, on Christmas Day 1859, he had written to Béthune: "They sang one of Palestrina's masses exceedingly well at St. Giles's today, and I was much pleased."[41] But like any other choir, this one had its off days "Bruges, Sunday 27 March 1860 ... they have just sung the Misere [sic] so badly in St. Giles's that I do not doubt, but that all the beer in the immediate neighbourhood of the Church has turned sour..."[42]

Three weeks later John Sutton was in Rome:

20 April 1860 ... "I have liked Rome pretty well, but have seen very little that pleases me – However the Grand Mass in St. Peter's on Easter Sunday with the Pope etc., etc. and beautiful Plain Chant and Palestrina, was so magnificent as to make me forget all about St. Peters..."[43]

which reminds us that, like Augustus Pugin, Sutton was unable to appreciate the baroque splendours of Rome in any way unless brought to life in worship with what they felt to be true catholic music.

In June, he was back in the Rheingau:

> "Kiedrich, 25 June 1860 (about a Mass he had attended in the St. Hildegard-Kapelle in Rüdesheim) ... the Plain Chant most beautifully sung in Latin in the real old chant, entirely by the country people taught by the Priest, they sung also during the latter part of the Mass several hymns very beautifully. The Priest is a very extraordinary person, very learned and very musical ... yesterday being a great feast he took the Organ himself and a Cap^n. (a *Kaplan* – in English, a curate) from Mainz sung Mass & preached. I believe this is his custom, he gets a friend to help him on great feasts & conducts the choral part of the Mass himself..."[44]

Did Sutton mean that the Rüdesheim people were singing the *Kurmainzer* plainsong still, nearly two years before he was able to re-introduce it to Kiedrich? – for the phrase, "the real old chant" does seem to point that way.

A most important letter is dated 18 January, 1862:

> "... At present I am bound here, as we have begun Plain Chant for High Mass, Vespers on high Feasts and Comp^n. (Compline) on Saturday evening, & as yet without me they cannot manage the Organ, the School Master and Organist is not worth much, though a clever man and a good organist, he is not on terms with the Pfarrer and Kiedrich people & the Pfarrer will ask no favour of him: he is soon to be removed & then I shall no longer be *indispensable* here ... The Comp^n. they can sing very well without the organ. The old people are delighted to hear the old Latin song again they remember having heard in their youth, this was given up here in 1817."[45]

And just over a year later, to complete this reference, he was still in Kiedrich –

> "24 February 1863: ... The Pfarrer wants me to go & says the singing is of no consequence & that the Plain chant can be given up till *I return*. I cannot bear the idea of the church singing being made a plaything for my amusement."[46]

There is no trace in the records of how or why "the old Latin song" was "given up here in 1817", but the late *Pfarrer* Wilhelm Klippel used to say that Bishop Colmar, the Alsatian Bishop of Mainz appointed by Napoleon, sent to Paris for plainsong books and thus dealt the *Mainzer Choral* (or Mainz plainsong) its deathblow except for its present survival in Kiedrich. This is in fact very probable, and it is right to exonerate the Bishop from behaving too much like a victor; for one thing that can be picked up from present-day historians is that at the end of the eighteenth century the Elector-Archbishop of Mainz was trying very hard to replace Latin with German in the services — an effort resisted stoutly by the Rheinlanders, who could see no good reason for giving up their Roman Catholic traditions and unity. After all the traumas and troubles of the Napoleonic Wars, and the collapse of the German-Austrian Empire in 1806, including the disappearance of the episcopal states, it is easy to understand that church life and church music had suffered some severe blows. A simple way to bind at least the musical life of the diocese together, would be to provide one plainsong use for all the churches; and with the amount of knowledge of plainsong available at that particular point in history, it might as well be Parisian plainsong as any other — at least the Bishop would know it!

There is another letter, headed merely "Cöln – Saturday Night", but probably to be dated in the middle or late 1860's because that is when the main work of re-printing the plainsong books for the Kiedrich choir was going on. It reads:

> "I have just received your letter, and thank you very much for sending the proofs —, I have written on each what I think of them, the lines on which the notes are placed, must be much thicker and in disjointed bits --- The books were thickly printed to be seen at a distance, these letters & lines can hardly be seen far off and hurt the eyes — I feel convinced that the ground for Cho.r Pults [Pult=desk] & great Books, is to keep the body in a good posture, for no one can sing in a *grand voice*, and *breathe well*, *poking* over a little Book close to the eyes — The old people were always *practical*, and choral must be *sung out*, 3 men standing in a good position with good voices, make more effect than 50 Seminarists, with their voices not quite settled, and poking over little books — There is only one of the old set left here in Cölner Dom (Cologne Cathedral), but I remember the effect 3 or 4 of these fellows made 20 years ago, and you have the same effect in the Popes Chapel at Rome still, but formerly in Cöln the effect was still better from the greatness of the cho.r You see in old picture the Position the Cho.r singers held themselves at the Ch.r Pults — I think we shall get the book easily in order, with the exception of the initial Letters, and in these days, where a little bit of common good art is required the difficulty is very great. What you have sent are

very bad, and remind me of Pustels (?) Books, these w*ll* spoil the whole Book, we can make another attempt but if this fails too, I think we had better give up the little pictures and have plain Red great Letters instead – ... (then a postscript) I think would be easier to print the Book in *wood cut*, instead of copper – I think the original must have been printed so – ?"[47]

The letter demands some consideration and explanation. The Kiedrich choir has at least from the days of Sutton, sung from very large books, with both text and music printed so as to be seen easily by the whole choir. A photo' of the choir in the nineteen-thirties shows two groups of three men, and two groups of five boys, each sharing one of these large books on a stand attached to the choir-stalls, so that the choir was then in two groups facing each other, one on either side of the chancel.[48] Now, in the nineteen-eighties, there is a single desk in the middle of the chancel and the choir group themselves on the altar steps to sing from the single large book. This, as Sutton himself points out, is obviously taken from many medieval representations of singers grouped round one book; today we recognise that this could have been the result of the crippling expense of hand-written books – but to a romantic like Sutton, the reason for a single book was to make sure the singers would stand upright and produce their voices properly. It is certainly an arguable position to take, but what of the tradition that we seem almost to have lost now, that plainsong must be sung out? For someone brought up in the Anglican Church it must have gone back to Sir Walter Scott, for instance, *Ivanhoe*, where Friar Tuck was surprised by some visitors in the middle of a carousal, and removed the traces of his intemperate eating and drinking while "he struck up a thundering *De profundis clamavi*"[49] to make sure the sounds of pots and cups clashing against each other were drowned. More importantly because it is a record of fact and not fiction, is a report in the *Ecclesiologist* of the consecration of St. Ninian's Cathedral, Perth, on 11 December, 1850.[50] Here Frederick Helmore, one of two brothers closely connected with the revival of church music in Britain and both extremely enthusiastic for plainsong, had spent some time in residence, training the choir for the new cathedral: and the magazine told its readers that "had they been present on that occasion to witness the singers clustered round the great brass lectern in the choir, and to hear them thunder out the *Urbs Beata Jerusalem*, as arranged in our *Hymnal Noted*, they would have some idea how glorious a thing is Gregorian Hymnody."[51] In Scotland, where the Episcopal Church is not established, there was a certain amount more freedom from political and other influences than prevailed in England at the time, and so the authorities of the new cathedral were able to arrange the building, the services and the singers practically as they wanted. Reading this report, and in later years adding to it from his experiences in Cologne Cathedral and the Sistine Chapel in Rome, Sutton was obviously determined that Kiedrich's choir should be arranged on the best ancient principles.

The final few sentences, about the initial letters, illustrate the difficulties everyone who tries to reproduce the art of a former age must encounter: for fashions, personal ability and technical know-how all change, and there was apparently nobody in Mainz at the time who could reproduce medieval illuminations for initial letters in the spirit, and with the standard Sutton required. From our more distant viewpoint in the late twentieth century, it hardly seems likely that woodcut could have improved things; it must have been another of the idealising dreams.

In a letter of 15 February, 1870, Sutton described the festivities of the previous day – St. Valentine's Day and so Kiedrich's Patronal Festival. It seems there were six Masses on the day (more than one of them sung, as "I was not at High Mass as poor Willy, was quite knocked up with the cold, and I did not much regret it, as the Sermon lasted nearly an Hour") but at the Mass he did attend:

> "... we had a Priest from Marienthal, who was formerly at Ober Wezel, who is very musical he sung the Mass with Mainz – Pater Noster & Preface ... There was Piano Forte from the Cho.ʳ R. and Organist 4 handisch, and solo from the Marienthaler and *myself of course*. All was very *quiet* and *decent*, and *I don't believe* they drunk 84 bottles of wine – as on a former occasion – However if they did, the effects were not to be observed ... St. Valentine's Lied from the people has lost none of its force ..."[52]

It does seem that Sutton's seclusion was broken now and then on a great day, and some guests went into someone's house for a little musical celebration: was it his own house, perhaps? The only other houses that seem likely to have had gatherings were the parish priest's residence, where in fact the letter makes clear Sutton dined, and the von Ritter's house, which in England would be the manor house; but the family is never mentioned elsewhere in the letters, and it must be assumed that Sutton did not come into contact with them very much.

Two extracts from a lecture delivered by Georg Hilpisch, the third Chorregent of the Kiedrich Choir School (he was appointed on 1 October 1871), describe Sutton's devoutness and musical ability:

> "I had the opportunity over many months to observe how devoutly (Sutton) prayed, with what devotion he attended daily Mass, which the Chorregent is bound to offer daily at

8am all the year round for the convenience of the elderly and infirm, how edifyingly he appeared at the communion rail, how humbly he accompanied the Most Holy Sacrament at processions, and what a wonderful example he gave in every way without a trace of ostentation. In his own person, he dressed so simply that anyone who didn't know him would have found it easy on their first meeting to do as (*Pfarrer* Zimmermann's) housekeeper did, and offer him alms; so moderate in his eating that his own needs for any day would be covered by ten groschen, Mr. Sutton had a sympathetic heart and open purse for all in need."

"... and when Sutton took his seat at the organ, the beautiful instrument came alive under his expert hands, and sang with the glorious improvisations of that gifted man."

This chapter ought to end with the testimony of a devoted friend – George Aloysius Mann, an attorney who seems to have led a rather shadowy existence divided between Bruges and London.[53] It seems, reading between the lines of his letters, that Sutton gave him a good deal of help of one kind and another: phrases like "so good and kind a friend" and "our well beloved kind friend and benefactor" appear pretty often in his notes to Jean de Béthune: but even though it is not the witness of a disinterested critic, this letter dated 23 January, 1867, when the *Kurmainzer* plainsong had just been begun once more, is valuable in that it shows Sutton's skill as a choir-trainer:

"On Xmas morning I went with Sir John to the High Mass at 5 o/c... I am really enraptured with the Choral music here at Kiedrich, what pains and labour dear Sir John must have taken to organize so perfect & satisfactory a choir of devotional & real ecclesiastical music ... when you listen to this beautiful music you fancy that the glorious Choir of Angels are pouring forth the praises of the mighty God, the Prince of Peace."[54]

REFERENCES

1 Zaun, p. 164.
2 Elvin, *Family Enterprise, The Story of Some North Country Organ Builders* (Lincoln, 1986) p. 129.
3 Conclusion Book.
4 Stones and Story, p. 295.
6 *History of Jesus College*, p. 158.
7 ibid.
8 *Parish Choir* II, p. 62; quoted Rainbow, p. 217.
9 Rainbow, *The Choral Revival in the Anglican Church 1839- 1872* – all through the book.
10 *The Cathedral Psalter Chants*, ed. Flood Jones, Troutbeck, Turle, Stainer & Barnby (London: Novello).
11 Rainbow, p. 79.
12 William Dyce, in second part of *Appendix to The Order of Daily*

Service (London: James Burns 1843).
13. It was presented in 1929.
14. By Walmisley: manuscript copies made by The Royal School of Church Music.
15. *Parish Choir* II, p. 62; quoted Rainbow.
16. Rembry, p. 494.
17. Reprinted in *Kiedricher Zeitung* IV, 1980, p. 9.
18. Quoted from *Sonderdruck aus dem Rheingauer Heimatbrief*, Folge 40 (Meier OHG, Rüdesheim; 1968) by Josef Staab in *Die Kiedricher Chorbuben und Ihre Tradition*.
19. ibid.
20. A. P. Bruck, quoted Staab, pp. 6-7.
21. Staab, p. 8.
22. Staab, p. 7.
23. Dr. A. Gottron, quoted Staab, p. 12.
24. See under "Erklärung" in *Dictionary of the Christian Church*.
25. Staab, p. 12.
26. Staab, p. 14.
27. Béthune.
28. Chorstift Archives, Kiedrich.
29. Information from the late Dekan Klippel.
30. Staab, p. 19.
31. Staab, p. 22.
32. Kenneth Clarke, *Civilization* (B.B.C. and John Murray 1969) pp. 228-229.
33. Staab, p. 13.
34. Schneider letters.
35. Schneider letters.
36. Schneider letters.
37. Zaun, p. 165.
38. Béthune.
39. In the collection of the late Mrs. Clifton-Brown.
40. Béthune.
41. Béthune.
42. Béthune.
43. Béthune.
44. Béthune.
45. Béthune.
46. Béthune.
47. Schneider letters.
48. Reproduced Staab, p. 13.
49. Walter Scott, *Ivanhoe* (New York: Airmont Publishing Co. 1964), p. 178.
50. Nicknamed "The Musical Missionary" 1820-99. *New Grove Dictionary of Music and Musicians* (London: Macmillan 1980).
51. *Ecclesiolgist* 1851, p. 24.
52. Schneider letters.
53. *Dictionary of National Biography*.
54. Béthune.

CHAPTER V

The Anglo-Belgian Seminary

Once John Sutton was settled into another faith and had found somewhere to live, there was some work waiting for him to do. Being a friend of the Béthune family, and a man of culture and learning, he seems to have become *persona grata* at the episcopal palace in Bruges quite quickly, and after about three years had elapsed, the Bishop asked him if he would help with a project suggested a while before.

When the Roman Catholic hierarchy was restored to England in 1850, the idea was mooted that Belgian priests – of whom there were many – might help forward the progress of the Church in England. The Belgian bishops were friendly with the English ones and on 28 December, 1850, Mgr. Gonella, Apostolic Nuncio in Brussels, wrote to Bishop Malou of Bruges[1] suggesting that a Scots college might be founded in his diocese.[2] The Bishop replied, not unreasonably, that he didn't see why such a college should not be founded in Scotland itself: apart from the missionary appeal of such a college in its native land, he really could not lay his hands on the "necessary resources" in his own diocese, for Belgium was going through a long period of agricultural depression just then. There the matter rested until 4 May, 1858, when Bishop Malou wrote to Cardinal Wiseman, Archbishop of Westminster[3], to introduce Fr. A. A. Boone[4], then curate of St. Gillis at Bruges, as Sir John Sutton's representative in the matter of a possible Anglo-Belgian seminary in the city. As Sir Richard, John's father, was dead, it was possible for John to promise a fair sum of money every year to underwrite the running of such a venture.

By now a good deal of the original British enthusiasm for a seminary abroad had ebbed away, especially as colleges like Oscott and Ushaw[5] were pretty well accepted in their own neighbourhoods, but eventually the idea received approval, subject to some alterations to the proposals that came from Belgium. Most of these alterations were concerned with Sutton's own relationship to the seminary, and one can understand the English bishops being rather nervous of an aristocratic convert, be he never so ready to write letters like

> "... The College of course cannot open until all matters are fully understood and arranged to the entire satisfaction of

the Cardinal, Your Lordship (Bishop Malou) and myself (15 December 1858)."

Approval from Rome was quickly forthcoming and the foundation document was signed on 19 November, 1858, by Cardinal Wiseman, Bishop Malou and the Abbé Boone. Previous to this ceremony, Wiseman had visited the town and seminary of Roulers, where Sutton had become a Roman Catholic and where Felix Béthune was Vice-Rector; then he had luncheon at Sutton's house in Bruges: a letter from George Mann to Jean de Béthune:

> "I took luncheon at Sir John Sutton's yesterday, our party was small, it consisted of His Eminence, Sir John, Mr. Boone and myself, the Cardinal and Sir John got on very well together."[6]

This foundation document provided that the Rector was to be Canon Livinus Bruneel, president of the Episcopal Seminary of Bruges, with the Abbé Felix Béthune as Vice-Rector – in fact, one supposes, Rector in all but name, as Canon Bruneel would have his hands full enough without anything more than a watching brief over the new college. Felix Béthune's father was the first to have doubts about the wisdom of this arrangement, though he seems to have got the Bishop's reasons for the appointment quite wrong: letter from Sutton to Jean de Béthune, 16 Deember, 1858:

> "... Your Father's idea, that Felix could have offend [sic] the Bishop, & on that account be removed from Roulers, and banished to the Rectorship of the new proposed English College, is a very *peculiar one*, and if carried out as far as it will go must arrive at this, that the Bishop destines the Rectorship of the English College as a refuge for the unfortunate, aristocratic, delinquent Priests of the Diocese of Bruges."

More like a bombshell was the letter from Cardinal Wiseman on 7 January, 1859, laying down very firmly the conditions upon which the English Bishops would support the seminary[7].

1) Sutton was to have no voice in appointing any of the teaching staff.

2) The Cardinal wishes that the staff would have no other teaching responsibilities.

3) "To avoid possible consequences, and because of a certain delicacy in regard to the Béthune family, it is not desirable that the Abbé Felix should be Vice-Rector."

4) The Cardinal desired the following appointments:
   Rector: Canon Dessein
   Vice-Rector: Dr. Leadbitter (a priest from the diocese of Newcastle)
   Econoom (bursar): A. Boone

One can sense the bishops' anxiety to prevent any aristocratic interference!

Sutton promised a preliminary gift of a hundred thousand francs (£4,000) and a yearly subscription of fifty thousand francs (£2,000) towards the running expenses. Students from England, West and East Flanders were eligible, and each English student would be paid for to the tune of £40 from England. Each priest ordained from the seminary was to promise to work in England for at least ten years, with the emphasis on seaport towns.

We are told that both Canon Bruneel and Felix Béthune, whose appointments had received general approval in Bruges, bore their disappointment very well. In fact, the Canon might well have been relieved and certainly Felix' career in the Church did not suffer: he moved to the major seminary at Roeselare/Roulers in 1861, was appointed a domestic prelate to the Pope in 1882, and was made archdeacon to the Bruges Cathedral Chapter in 1891.

The first four students arrived from England on 26 February, 1859, accompanied by Dr. Leadbitter[8], and they took up residence at No. 55 on the Lange Rei, not far from the major seminary of Bruges, where they were to receive instruction in philosophy and theology. Preparations had been going on for their coming, mainly as far as the letters show, in the chapel[9]. To Béthune:

> "Bruges 7 February 1859. Will you please send me a drawing for a stone frame to insert the iron doors from the Poterie Sacrament House, as we mean to set them up in the tempy. Chapel in the new Seminary."

Bishop Malou hallowed this temporary chapel on 25 March, Lady Day, the same year, and for the time being, all was in order. Ever afterwards, John Sutton would refer to this work of founding and supporting the Seminarium Anglo-Belgicum (its official name) as undertaken to save his soul (*seine Seele zu retten*)[10], and perhaps he regarded it as an offering in reparation for his early life spent as an Anglican.

For the next couple of years, nothing much can be recorded about the Seminary except the steady increase in the number of students. By Lady Day 1861 there were 28 of them, of whom 9 were Flemish and we must suppose the rest English. By now a new house had been found on the Potterierei, and another chapel had been restored and furnished. This was an ancient building, belonging originally to the bargemasters' guild of the city, and it must have retained some medieval features for Sutton to have bought it. Letter to Béthune, 6 January 1861:

> "I am now cleaning out the Schippers Chapel which is connected with the new house, and there will be room enough for all 3 altars, so I intend to put them up. The Chapel is a mere wreck, but is large and may do for a time till I can make some better arrangements. In fact I am obliged to get it ready, as there are 29 students and the place where the Altar now is, is far worse than the other was at the first house we had."[11]

The mention of three altars catches the eye; it seems that John Sutton could not resist buying a good Gothic altar with wings (what the Germans call a *Flügelaltar*), and that there were a good many such altars available. No doubt this is where the Sutton family tradition, that he made his house in Bruges into a sort of storehouse for all sorts of medieval treasures he picked up on his travels until he could find homes for them, originates.

He continued to look for "better arrangements" for the seminary chapel[12] and in 1862 toyed with the idea of moving a complete building from Ghent to serve the purpose. By 24 February, 1863, he had given this up for very practical reasons – letter to Béthune:

> "It is a very beautiful little building, but is so short, that it could not be arranged with a skreen [*sic*] and Ante-Chapel, without being added to the extent of at least 30 feet."[13]

He continued, then, to look out for a site on which he could build a seminary *de novo*, with all the features he felt necessary. This was found in 1869: a military hospital on the Vlamingdam was vacated and put up for sale[14], and, after very protracted negotiations, bought by Sutton, the Bishop of Nottingham and the Abbé Boone. Sutton was responsible for three-fifths of the purchase price, and the Bishop and Boone found one-fifth each. The building had a history, like many others in Bruges, having begun its life as a convent for Carmelite nuns, and it may well have been this history that made it so attractive – a place where prayer was wont to be made becoming just that once again. Jean de Béthune was called in on 13 October, 1871:

> "Bruges: I write these few lines to ask you to come over to Bruges some day soon if convenient to you, to go over with me the old Convent, I have bought for the English College ... I am much pleased with the old place, and think it will answer very well for the College in every respect."[15]

The Plan for the English Seminary

Sutton must soon have lost the feeling that the old convent would answer very well for the new seminary, for it is obvious that he decided to pull most or all of it down, and start again. There is a most fascinating plan in his hand, in the Béthune Archive: it may be an ideal rather than a sober estimate of what could be built on a site of a given size and shape but, whether ideal or estimate, it gives a real indication of what his hopes for the Seminary were. The sketch closely resembles Pugin's drawing of a medieval town in the 1841 edition of *Contrasts* and has numbers on the principal features and a key at the bottom of the page. Of course, medieval features find a place; for instance, even though the seminary was in the see city, there is a room or rooms for the occupation of the Bishop – one supposes for visits. This arrangement can be found in several medieval religious houses in Belgium.

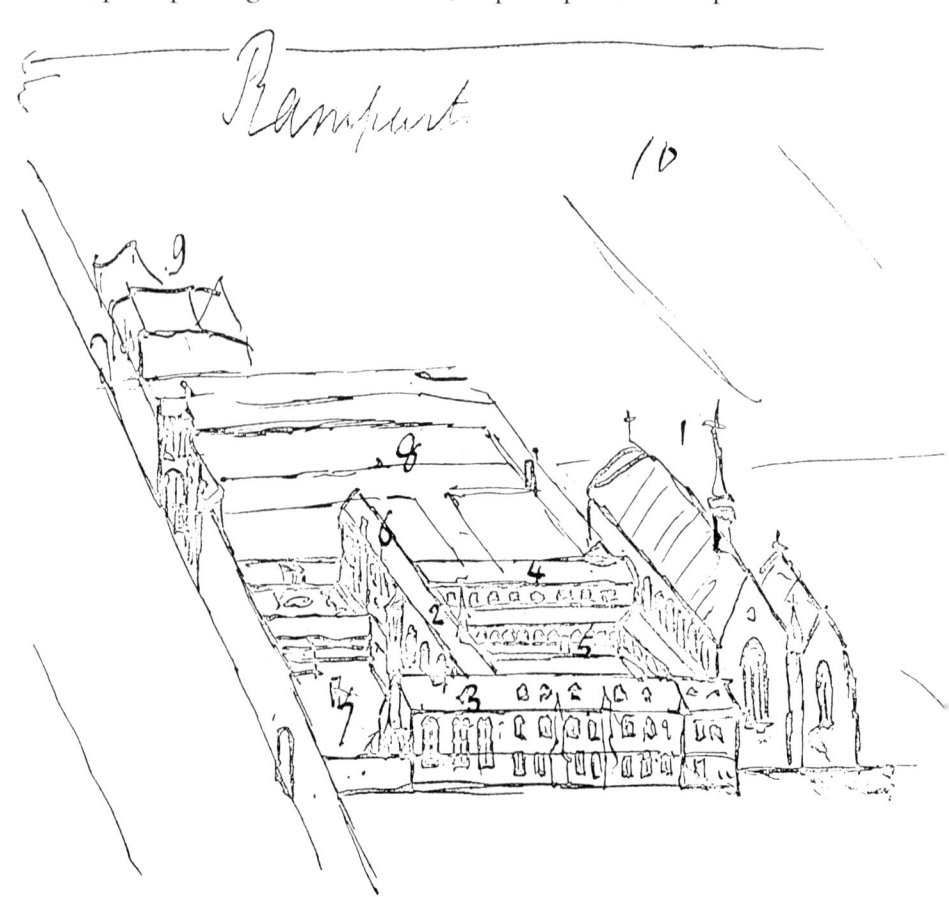

There seems to be a large garden surrounding the buildings, bounded by the *Ramparts* (a reminder that the site was once occupied by a barracks). At a little distance from the main Seminary is a *Farm house*, perhaps the gardener's house, or perhaps Sutton expected to use part of the garden as pasture for a couple of cows. The church is naturally the most imposing feature; the rest of the buildings are arranged round a *cloister court*, except the *Rector's and Bishop's Lodging* which protrudes into the *Entrance Court*, probably so that visitors could have easy access to the Rector before being permitted to see any student. It looks as though the seminarians were to have their rooms or cubicles in the east wing, which is given no title, and lecture-rooms might be included in the two-storeyed *Library*. The general appearance looks back to the plan of Oxford and Cambridge colleges as many of them must have been in the first half of the nineteenth century – but all, of course, in the most correct Gothic style.

There is the inevitable gap in writing, while the friends worked together, and then another letter on 13 January, 1872, discusses detail[15], revealing Sutton's intimate knowledge of architecture, and strong adherence to principles:

> "... I am pleased you are satisfied with all my alteration except the library windows. I own, I also feared the want of light, it is rather difficult to arrange a good outside effect (though I think *I originated* the idea of the 2 windows one over the other). Perhaps we may manage it so [sketch], but it may perhaps weaken the wall plate of the roof cutting it for the little gables."

Then another letter, dated only "Kiedrich, Monday"[15], continues discussion on another point:

> "I have been thinking much about the fire place at the end of the Refec[y] – I am getting tired of the idea, I cannot like a Fire place on a large scale except in a gable on the end of a building, So I think I shall return to my first idea & only make a thin wall between the kitchen and Refec[y] and place

1 The Church
2 Refectory
3 Kitchen
4 Library
5 Cloister Court
6 Rectors & Bishops Lodging
7 Servants back Court
8 Entrance Court
9 Farm house
10 Garden

Sutton's sketch of the proposed Anglo-Belgian Seminary

a stove in the corner with an iron pipe through the partition into the Kitchen Chim^y which can be removed in Summer ... I *cannot bear* the Chimneys breaking the backbone of the roofs. I am half inclined to make the cloister windows without foliations: I think these foliations *coming so often & so near together* give the windows in the Cloister rather too busy a look for so *plain* a *building*, & rather reduce the importance of the Chapel Windows. Please consider these ideas a little."

Reading over these letters, one feels that Sutton and Béthune between them were carrying out all the architectural work, and not employing anyone else who might have warned them of the immense costs they were incurring by so comparatively grandiose a conception. Sutton probably saw it as the crown of his work in Bruges, and a way by which the large income he secretly disliked could be used "to save his soul"[15]. Béthune cannot have been unaware of the financial side, but perhaps made one reasoned protest, and then, in true nineteenth-century aristocratic style, let the matter drop. After all, his own arts were going to be used to the full in the fitting-up of the chapel and its decoration, and he would be as personally interested in the project as Sir John himself, though for different reasons. During Sutton's stay at Amelie-les-Bains in 1872-3, looking after his Irish servant, work

Sketch by Sutton for the projected Anglo-Belgian Seminary chapel, looking north across the choir. Access to the organ appears to be from the top of the rood-screen

THE ANGLO-BELGIAN SEMINARY

progressed on the Seminary and another letter has survived, mainly about the windows and glass for them:

> "19 November 1872 ... I told him to take the measure of the panes from the lower part (*the part that opens*) of the windows in my house, which are a trifle less square than

Sutton's sketch of the interior of the projected chapel, looking west, with an alternative design for the organ-case

> those in the other 4 parts ... The fitting up of the Refec^y, Rector's lodgings – and the Bishop's apartments will require a great deal of thought ..."[15]

It seems that leaded lights were being used for the windows in question, which has at any time been a pretty expensive method of glazing.

Sutton and his man-servant returned to Bruges in the early summer of 1873, and while the man was now in no danger of death, he was still unable to work. Oddly, nobody seems to have approached Sutton with any information about the bills piling up, and his last letter to Béthune, left unfinished, gives no indication of any financial anxiety whatever[15]:

> "Bruges, Tuesday 20 June 1873 ... I am very much obliged to you for planning a little for the High Altar. I sometimes think we shall want three Standards[16] on each side, but this will shew itself when the thing is drawn out to a scale. I am very unwell & can only just walk I am so very weak. The"

Here his pen was laid down for the last time, and Mgr. Boone wrote on the back of the letter in French:

> "Sir John is indisposed and could not continue this letter. His illness presents some alarming symptoms, but the doctor could only counsel complete rest. The work at the Seminary is going very well and to the satisfaction of Sir John."

Reading this last letter, one is struck by the fact that the chapel sanctuary was to be of such a size that three pairs of standard candlesticks were even considered as a possibility. If the whole chapel was to be on this scale, it must have been of a similar size to Jesus College in Cambridge – and perhaps at the back of Sutton's mind, this too was a building whose proportions and size were something of an ideal. As work on the seminary was stopped the day after his death, Béthune never got the chance to "draw it out to a scale", so there are only Sutton's own sketches for us to evaluate as well as we can.

Had the chapel ever been built, it would obviously have shown us not only what Sutton's real architectural convictions were, but would also have been the crowning glory of all his work for God and the Church. It was to be a stately, lofty building, furnished as richly as possible and with every true principle of architecture and design followed faithfully.

There was to be a chapel proper, and an ante-chapel, divided by a massive screen. One of the sketches (from the west) shows a north aisle to both areas as well, with the screen extending from wall to wall and hence of five bays – but as the others (from the east and south) show windows and an organ where this one shows only an arcade, perhaps the serious design would have been without it. The screen is conceived on the lines of the Kiedrich one – of stone, several feet deep, with an elaborate balustrade along the top; and the two side bays were to contain a *Flügelaltar* each, while there is an indication that the centre bay was to have doors. Some feet above the screen there was to be a rood-beam, supporting a crucifix that nearly filled the apex of the chancel arch, with its accompanying figures of Our Lady and St. John. The ante-chapel itself was thought of as being empty of seating, but with a small pulpit on its south side; two windows at first-floor height were to be filled with stained glass, and a bracket between them was to support a canopied figure of a saint.

In the chancel, or chapel proper, there were to be two rows of stalls facing each other, the back ones having arm-rests, and these were returned against the screen at the west end, presumably for the

Sutton's sketch for the chapel of the Anglo-Belgian Seminary, looking east

teaching staff. A lectern stood in the centre, and the organ would be on the north side, high up, with the expected small gallery for the console, and doors to close when it was not in use. There is no sketch of the sanctuary, but if (as in the letter just quoted) it was to have three pairs of standard candlesticks, Sutton certainly thought of it as a large and dignified area. The reason for this must have been that it was customary for Minor Orders to be conferred by the diocesan bishop in seminary chapels. Plenty of room was needed for the ceremony to be carried out with dignity, and as an example of how such things could be arranged.

When the doctor told Sutton of the serious nature of his illness and its probable outcome, he set about putting his affairs in order at once. He hoped that he would have time to make some satisfactory arrangement about the financing of the seminary and its completion, but this was not to be, and when he died, the unfortunate Mgr. Boone was left as his sole representative to grapple with the fact that there were unpaid bills adding up to over a million francs (£40,000). As the whole of Sir Richard Sutton's estate had been left in trust, there could be neither saleable assets nor any further income to set against the debts, and it seems the Sutton family in England were not disposed to help in any way.

While a biography can be only marginally concerned with events after its subject's death, it is right to note very briefly that Boone's solution was to close the Seminary altogether on 16 August the same year: the students were transferred to the major seminary of Bruges. Bishop Faict of Bruges[17] was put into the embarrassing position of having to explain the state of affairs to Cardinal Manning[18], a Pharaoh who knew not Joseph, and the rest of the English Bishops:

> "18 August, 1873. [The Seminary is now closed] The reason for so doing being not to give the heirs any means of attacking the testament. My opinion is that the real cause of the suppression are the quantity of debts that are to be paid, and forbid, perhaps for long, any expense concerning the foundation."

One feels that the Bishop of Bruges' meditations on the matter must have centred round the words, "if only...", and he must have felt that the time spent in Amelie-les-Bains, when it would have been perfectly possible for Sutton to have travelled at least once to Bruges while somebody else looked after his man-servant for a week or so, was more in the nature of a holiday than anything else. In the same letter of 18 August he wrote:

> "Never have I doubted Mgr. Boone's perfect honorability. But I know that he is neglectful, at the same degree as Sir

THE ANGLO-BELGIAN SEMINARY 181

John was; and I perceive in him an inclination rather strong to independency."[19]

To cut what became a very long story short, the Belgian Ministry of Education had been looking for a site for a new *Rijksnormaalschool* or *École normale* in Flanders for some years, and Mgr. Boone's legal advisers were quick to suggest that the abandoned Seminarium Anglo-Belgicum might serve very well for this purpose. Negotiations dragged on and a report was made on 28 June, 1875:

> "*Non seulement les batiments figures aux plans comme terminés ne sont pas encore qu'à peine et imparfaitement sous toit, sans pavements, sans planchers, sans enduits ni plafonds, mais encore leur disposition les rend impropres à y installer une école dans les conditions d'hygiéne convenable.*"
>
> ("Not only is the structure of the buildings not completed according to the plans, but the part under the roof is still incomplete and defective without slabs, without floors, and the ceilings without plaster: and also their lay out makes them unsuitable to set up a school there in proper hygienic conditions.")

— which makes one wonder whether the sanitary arrangements were on a medieval scale as well as the chapel and the Bishop's lodging! A month before this, on 29 May, 1875, Cardinal Manning had written to the Bishop of Bruges:

> "The subject of the English College in Bruges is one of considerable anxiety to the Bishops of England ... Only one thing is clear, the College is a *locus pius* created by Sir John Sutton for the benefit of the Church in England. The Bishop ought therefore to possess full knowledge. But at this moment we know nothing except that Mgr. Boone possesses money and other property under Sir John Sutton's will. I cannot conceal from Your Lordship that the Bishops sensibly feel this to be an abnormal state of things. We have taken no step as yet in the hope that Mgr. Boone would spontaneously lay open the state of the accounts."[20]

— in other words, the Cardinal desired to have the accounts, and the man whose responsibility it was to have kept them, in front of him in London. If to Henry VIII's bishops, *ira principis mors est*, the wrath of this Prince of the Church must have seemed equally terrifying, if not equally fatal, and it does not seem that Mgr. Boone ever actually travelled to England with the accounts. All was done through the mediation of Bishop Faict of Bruges, who wrote illuminatingly at one point in the long correspondence,

"... Je demande à la répéter à V(otre) E(minence), Mgr. Boone n'est pas une forte tête, ni un homme d'affaires..."
("... If I may, I must tell Your Eminence again, that Mgr. Boone has not a powerful intellect, and is no man of business...")

Eventually, in 1877, the site was sold for a much smaller sum that originally hoped for, and John Sutton's brother, Charles, accepted responsibility for the two-fifths share that had belonged to the dead baronet. Was all this trouble and financial loss the reason for the fact heard from Sir John's great-niece, Mrs. Robina Clifton-Brown, that when she was very young, whenever anyone mentioned Great-Uncle John, a silence descended on the family until someone was able to produce another subject for conversation?

From the beginning to the end, the seminary had accepted 187 pupils. Certainly many of them would be ordained, and two became bishops in later years. It seems that, in sixteen ordinations from 21 October, 1859, to 7 June, 1873, forty-eight of the students were priested and no doubt more were ordained later on from the Bruges seminary.[21] Nobody knows how many actually found their way to the sea-port towns of England, but few or many, John Sutton's foundation had made a worthy mark for its short existence.

REFERENCES

1. Jean-Baptiste Malou, 1809-1864: Bishop of Bruges 1849-1864
2. Bruges Episcopal Archives, Acta 1851, copied Schepens, p. 173. In *Handelingen van het Genootschap voor Geschidenis gesticht onder de benaming Société d'Emulation te Brugge*, 1967.
3. Nicholas Wiseman, 1802-1865: Archbishop of Westminster 1850-1865
4. Aime Auguste Boone, 1823-1890: Onderpastoor, St. Gillis, Bruges 1851; Econoom (bursar) of English Seminary 1859
5. Ushaw College, Durham: students moved in 1808: *BIOS Journal* IV, 1980, p. 80. Oscott College, Birmingham.
6. Béthune.
7. Acta of Bruges Episcopal Archives.
8. William Leadbitter, D.D., 1832-1863: soon returned to England and took up a post as assistant priest at St. Mary's Cathedral, Newcastle. Pope John XXIII was also a D.D. at the age of twenty-three.
9. Béthune
10. Zaun, p. 168.
11. Béthune
12. Various letters in the Béthune Archive mention the search.
13. Béthune
14. Schepens, p. 179.
15. Béthune
16. I can only assume that standard candlesticks are meant – i.e. large ones standing on the floor.
17. Jean-Joseph Faict, 1813-1894: Bishop of Bruges 1864-1894
18. Henry Edward Manning, 1808-1892: Archbishop of Westminster 1865-1892
19. Schepens, p. 84
20. Bruges Episcopal Archives
21. Schepens, p. 197.

CHAPTER VI

Sir John Sutton and the Poor

During Sutton's lifetime, there were poor people everywhere in Europe: the novels of Charles Dickens give a good picture of the English problem in this respect, and we know of the Irish famine of the eighteen-forties. In Belgium, one can cite Vincent van Gogh's picture, *The Potato-Eaters*,[1] and a similar work was done for Tyrolean peasants by the rather later Albin Egger-Lienz;[2] these are rare examples of an art that showed, not the romantic scenery of Austria or mediaeval Flemish towns, but the actual life and hardship of those who worked on the land. There were poor and old folk in Northumberland when Sutton was at Chollerton, and his tutor was "keenly and practically" interested in their housing – which probably means that he did his best to persuade landlords to bring houses into good repair and make them up to date. Not only so, but he was quite ready to serve them with his own hands.[3] Visits to London, and to other cities and towns in England, could not fail to bring the condition of the poor to the attention of any observant person, while on the family's estates there would be plenty of opportunity to see the difference between the life-style of the Sutton family themselves, and that of many of their tenants.

What was a rich man to do? – for Christianity, and especially continental Roman Catholicism, remembered Christ's words, "Give to him that asketh thee,"[4] and "Ye have the poor with you always, and whensoever ye will ye may do them good."[5] As far as many nineteenth-century aristocrats with consciences were concerned, the example had been set in mediaeval times and had been illustrated recently by Pugin in *Contrasts*, and written up again by Kenelm Digby in *The Broadstone of Honour*: and we are wise to remember that Sutton was very friendly with Pugin, and that Digby was a contemporary of his father's at Trinity College Cambridge. The poor were to be treated as though they were Christ himself, who had said, "In as much as ye have done it to one of the least of these My brethren, ye have done it unto Me."[6] So this was the sort of thing that Sutton set out to do.

Listen to Georg Hilpisch, speaking only two months or so after Sutton's death:

"As far as his personal life went, he was so simple in his clothing that if he met a stranger for the first time, it would be very easy for him (as happened with the Kiedrich priest's housekeeper) to be offered alms; he was so moderate at table that on most days no more than ten Sgr. would supply his needs. But Herr Sutton had a heart that took part in people's concerns, and an open purse for all in need. Hundreds of gulden flowed all the year round from his hand to the poor of our village, and thousands in caring institutions, orphanages, hospitals for old people, and so on; so that the *bien public* accounts in Gand alone in Belgium for just over a year registered over a million francs (£40,000) in contributions to good works from him.

For the poor of our village he built six little well-designed houses (Zaun adds the amount of the rent – four florins a year[7]); he arranged for three Sisters of the order of the Poor Servants of Christ [In German, "*Arme Dienstmägde Christi*", a nursing order with its mother house at Dernbach] to come to nurse the sick, for whom he had a beautiful Gothic house built; he founded a centre for the care of small children, and arranged for young, talented and honest people to study at his expense – and all this in such a way, that his left hand knew not what the right hand was doing. There was hardly anything undertaken in our diocese during the shining reign of over thirty years of our present Bishop that Herr Sutton did not support. He would send princely gifts to the Holy Father as Peter's Pence."[8]

Zaun observes in addition to this list, that Sutton sent him six hundred florins (just over £85) every year, and if there was any special need, he could go to Sutton's bank and draw whatever money was necessary.[9]

As far as we know, there were no comparable foundations in Belgium – the English Seminary used up a great deal of money there – nor in England, where the clerical brothers Augustus and Frederick could be trusted to keep the family's charity going. One piece of generosity, though, appears in the West Tofts *Sunday Book*:[10] on two days every year come the entries, "Gave away John's dole of bread on the anniversary of my Mother's/Father's death". Naturally this ceased after 1873, when John was no longer there to finance it.

There are no accounts for Sutton's personal generosities; Kiedrich tradition has it that he had a bag of sovereigns on the table in his living-room, for anyone calling in need, and this would probably be true of his house in Bruges as well. If as he wrote in 1855 to Béthune, "the possession of a large income is a great grief to me,"[11] there would be no difficulty in getting rid of it with his generous habits. The final gifts of bread to twelve hundred families in Bruges, and of a franc each to eight hundred, must have made Mgr. Boone's task as executor even more difficult[12], but what matter, if the poor had what they needed and deserved?

REFERENCES

1 Vincent van Gogh, 1853-1890. See Bénézit, *op.cit.*
2 Albin Egger-Lienz, 1868-1926. See C. Henry Warren, *Tyrolean Journal*, London, Robert Hale, 1954, pp. 126-129.
3 Leaflet at Chollerton, previously cited.
4 St. Matthew 5:42.
5 St. Mark 14:7.
6 St. Matthew. 25:40.
7 Zaun, p. 171.
8 Reproduced *Kiedricher Zeitung* 5/1980, p. 10.
9 Zaun, p. 170-171.
10 Norwich Record Office, previously cited.
11 Béthune.
12 *De Gidsenkring*, April 1986, p. 33.

Memorial window to Sir John Sutton in Kiedrich Church

CHAPTER VII

The Sutton Circle

It would have been strange if John Sutton had not had one or two likeminded friends in Cambridge, during a stay of about thirteen years – who would share his enthusiasm for the organ as a means of accompanying a choir, and for Gothic as the style in which churches and all their furnishings should be designed. It has been possible to identify some of his friends and probably acquaintances; and though at this distance of time nobody answers all the questions, there are still some pointers, and one or two entirely unexpected discoveries.

John Gibson, probably 1818–1892

Gibson was elected Pensioner of Jesus College in 1836; he graduated BA as sixteenth Wrangler in 1840, and MA in 1843. He was made deacon in the same year and ordained priest in 1846. He remained at Jesus College as Fellow, Tutor and Dean from 1842 to 1857 when he was appointed Rector of King's Stanley in Gloucestershire. He retired to Brighton in 1886 and died six years later at 65 Lansdowne Place.[1]

It was said of Gibson in Cambridge that "he had considerable talent both as an artist and musician, and had expert knowledge and almost infallible taste with regard to ecclesiastical furniture and decoration. He spent much time in studying this subject both in England and abroad, and specialised in the treatment of organ cases."[2] Here was a kindred spirit indeed for Sutton; and however retired a life Sutton himself preferred, he would almost certainly have shared some of his hopes and thoughts with Gibson. Certainly they kept in touch for the rest of Sutton's life. Unlike him, Gibson was never a member of the Camden Society: his interests were very much the same as those of the members, but perhaps he disagreed on some points with the founders – who knows? – and therefore held aloof. However, he does appear as Chairman of the Society's successor in Cambridge, the Cambridge Architectural Society, in 1854;[3] this body was at once rather more practical and a good deal less strident than the Camdenians.

It seems from the rather sketchy and contradictory records of the restoration of Jesus College Chapel, that after the professional architect Anthony Salvin was asked to withdraw, Gibson and the chaplain Fisher took on the direction themselves. If so, it is to be expected that "during several years (Gibson) gave his whole mind to the work",[4] for there is a great deal more to directing building and restoration than just drawing out the details. The chapel was restored as nearly as possible to its thirteenth-century state, with series of lancet windows in the north, south and east walls of the chancel, those in the east replacing the large Perpendicular window inserted by Bishop Alcock, the sixteenth-century founder of the college. Pevsner says that Gibson collaborated with Pugin in the design for the new stalls in the chancel:[5] but there is nothing in the extant records about Pugin designing more than the roof, pavement, rose window, screen and organ – and indeed Fisher says roundly that he and Gibson worked upon the fabric and the stalls. The interior of the chapel, then, is much more a memorial to them than to Pugin, as Pevsner would have us believe.[6]

Gibson appears next in a letter from Sutton to Béthune, dated 12 September 1859: "Gibson and I have been very busy with the Kiedrich organ gallery, and I think it will turn out a very satisfactory job."[7] And in another letter dated 7 November 1860, "The Gibson gallery is now all you could wish now it is coloured and has quite lost that heavy look we all disliked when it was first done and was in oak colour."[8] And Gibson himself, writing to Béthune to inquire about a crucifix that was being repaired for him in the Gand workshop, said: "Sir John Sutton is very busy making some good improvements in the organ, in form and in colour; the details he has given me display I think excellent judgment. He is determined to have a perfect work…when a good model for a *buffet* occurs and you have opportunity to allow your workmen to do the work, it is an object I should much like to possess. A very slight sketch from your pencil would convey to me the features you would propose."[9]

Two points arise from these letters: first, that it must have been Gibson who designed the small gallery that now supports the organ at Kiedrich, and not, as we might have expected, a German architect, or Béthune. "The Gibson gallery" cannot mean anything else. As it is a polygonal affair, very like others Sutton had a hand in, it is probably right to think that Sutton himself suggested the shape and size, and Gibson designed the panels. The decorative patterns pick up something of those on the organ-case, and there is more than a suggestion of the back panels of the Jesus College chapel stalls.

Secondly, it seems that Gibson would have liked an organ-case from Béthune's designs and workshop for his church at King's Stanley (*buffet d'orgue* is the normal French term for an organ-case). Gibson never followed up this request, and Béthune perhaps forgot it for in 1876 an organ was built in the church which included no importations at all. Local tradition, repeated in an article in *Musical Opinion*[10], is that Gibson taught the local joiner, Liddiatt, to build organs and that much or all of the work on this particular organ (which became the Liddiatt firm's opus I) was done in the Rectory stables. Several years later, in 1882, Gibson wrote again to Béthune asking for:

> "two rather large figures of angels, blowing the Trumpets of the judgment, for a Gothic Organ which with advantage of long Study, in association with Sir John Sutton, I have had built in my church... The carving of figures is the only thing in Gothic work I have found myself unequal to."[11]

Gibson himself, then, designed the King's Stanley organ-case; and he must have had great influence on the tonal design of the instrument as well, for it is certainly no "music mill" and it is quite possible to accompany a choir on nearly the full 1876 organ. It is placed behind the stalls on the north side of the chancel, with a small chamber built out for the swell and pedal departments (presumably in 1895 – see below). As originally built in 1876, it was of one manual with the following stops:

Open Diapason	8	
Stop Diapason	8	
Dulciana	8	(gamut G)
Viola da Gamba	8	(grooved to Open D. at Ten. C)
Clarabella	8	(middle C up)
Principal	4	
Flute	4	
Twelfth	$2^2/_3$	
Fifteenth	2	
Mixture	III	
Cremona	8	

– and a Bourdon on the pedals.

In 1895, three years after Gibson's death, a Swell department was added on an upper manual, thus:

Bourdon	16	(the original pedal stop, with added trebles)
Horn Diapason	8	
Lieblich Gedact	8	
Salicional	8	(Ten. C)
Hohl Flute	4	
Piccolo	2	
Hautboy	8	

A new, larger Bourdon was placed on the pedals, and an Octave 8, in metal.

There is a great deal of excellent wooden pipework in the instrument which may indicate that Gibson shared Sutton's admiration for the wooden pipes made by Father Smith. The designer really spent money on the console! The stop-handles are of rose-wood, with ivory name-plates beside them on the jambs so that the names can never be

The organ in King's Stanley Church, photograph c.1930

worn away, and the natural keys have thick ivory plates. There is no manual overhang.

The organ-case is definitely based upon Kiedrich, but the resemblance is not obvious at once because there are no shutters. Moreover, Gibson placed no small pipes in the front, probably because with the amount of conveyancing that would have been necessary, the depth of the organ would have been increased. But it is a noble effort, and it seems likely that with a reputation for specialising in organ-cases, Gibson designed others during his time at Cambridge. Oddly, there is another case to this exact design, which used to be in the chapel of the convent of Dominican nuns at Stroud, and is now in the nearby Roman Catholic parish church. A typed history of the convent gives the information that the oak organ-case and the canopies for the Sisters' stalls were fixed by Thomas Liddiatt of Leonard Stanley in 1907: the Sisters claimed that the case was designed by the convent's architect, Benjamin Bucknall of Algiers, but as it is as exact a copy of King's Stanley as could be found anywhere, it must be that Bucknall approved the design Liddiatt brought out of his files.

To return to King's Stanley church: the whole chancel is of Camden Society richness (though by 1876, this would be nothing out of the way), with wrought-iron candelabra in the sanctuary, and iron single candle-holders in the choir-stalls that echo those designed by Frederick Sutton. The figures of the four evangelists on the ends of the book-boards were ordered from the Béthune workshops by Gibson when he asked for the angels for the organ-case. There is a painted ceiling in the chancel, more elaborate over the sanctuary, and in the nave there is painting on the roof-beams, and texts round the walls. The only thing of which John Sutton would not have approved is the dwarf iron chancel-screen instead of a full-sized wooden one; but by 1876 congregations were wanting to sing themselves and the acoustical block of an elaborate chancel screen was by no means so desirable.

Earlier, Gibson had felt a desire to be an author: letter to Béthune, 22 May 1861:

> "I am reckoning on a few weeks of retirement sometime during the summer, to enable me to devote myself to putting into form the valuable material I possess respecting organs. Confining myself to construction and the illustration of the Kiedrich organ – with respect to which your excellent drawings have left me without any point unsettled. My antiquarian material, also enlarged by your kindness in a former communication, together with further illustrations, I intend at present to leave to a future undertaking. If our architects and ecclesiologists are set right as to good construction on old principles, and have so good an instance as Kiedrich put before them, they will be saved from their present faults; and the faithfulness to true principles, and real gains on the part of a few, may develope into ideas in a good direction…"[12]

Sadly, there is no trace of any book written and published, nor any relics of Gibson's material to be found. Had there been, we would have had a better idea of the true principles for which he, as well as Sutton, was striving: but his work in Jesus College chapel and King's Stanley church has stood the test of time well.

Osmond Fisher, 1817-1913

Fisher was well-connected in church circles: he was grand-nephew of a Bishop Fisher of Salisbury, and his father was to become Canon of Salisbury and Archdeacon of Berkshire, and was a close friend of John Constable the artist.[13] Osmond was educated first at Eton, and then was an early student at King's College London (which was incorporated in 1829; London University received a charter for degrees in 1836). He entered Jesus College Cambridge in 1836, and graduated as eighteenth Wrangler in 1841: he became MA in 1844 and was ordained deacon, and was immediately elected Fellow of the College and Chaplain, as well as undertaking sole charge of Writhlington in Somerset. He was ordained priest in 1845 and became incumbent of All Saints Dorchester, which living he continued to hold with his College appointment (as was then common enough) until 1853. He seems to have devoted himself to University pursuits until 1858 when (perhaps on his marriage) he was given the Jesus College living of Elmstead near Colchester in Essex. He moved to Harlton a few miles from Cambridge in 1867 – where his wife died the same year – and there he remained until the close of his active ministry in 1900.

He was a man of many interests. He suffered some persecution because of his faithful adherence to the teaching of the church on Baptismal Regeneration and was one of four men who were the nucleus of a council to work for the revival of Convocation – success on this was achieved in 1852. His great love for his College and its buildings was equalled by his antiquarian knowledge, and he discovered the fine doorway to the nuns' Chapter House, covered up in the cloister wall. He took a great part in the restoration of the chapel in 1847–49, and as Chaplain preached at the re-opening service. He was also a musician and began the revival of choral services in the college with John Sutton's active collaboration. He was a great geologist, examined in geology for the Natural Sciences Tripos, and wrote a book, *The Physics of the Earth's Crust*, which said his obituary "is beyond the scope of those who are not both geologists and mathematicians". He wrote another book on rose-growing, in which art he was very successful at Harlton. One of the most interesting things about him is that he had an organ built at All Saints' Dorchester during his incumbency there, and designed the case for it himself. Some years later changes were made in that church and Fisher was able to secure the organ for Harlton Church in 1869, where it serves as his memorial to his wife. He also endowed it with a cottage, called, reasonably enough, "Organ Cottage"[14], and it is said that he had such an ear for music that he tuned the organ himself.

The late Revd. Andrew Freeman wrote of this organ case:

> "I am quite certain that the architect, whoever he was, took the case at St. Germain's, Tirlemont, which is the oldest case in Belgium (it was made *circa* 1520) as his model... there is no disguising the fact that the complex gable of the Cambridgeshire front is a deliberate reminiscence... It has departed from its model as often as it has followed it, and the result is a case as suited to an English village church as its prototype is to a large town church on the Continent."[15]

*The organ in the Church of the Assumption of Our Lady, Harlton, given by
Osmond Fisher in memory of his wife, Mary Louisa, in 1869*

The organ was built by Bishop, and is of one manual with pull-down pedals. The stops are: Open Diapason 8, Stopped Diapason 8, Principal 4 and Flute 4, with holes for three more stop-rods.

It is obvious from the above that Fisher, like many other men of his day, had travelled on the Continent; but with one successful organ-case under his belt, might he not have produced others? There are several excellent cases around Cambridge with no obvious author and, from the evidence of Harlton, Fisher was not as constricted to "correct" Gothic as were Pugin and for instance, John Gibson. He might easily, then, have designed Great Bardfield's case, with its carved wings instead of folding doors; but we shall not know until more evidence is unearthed.

John Hanson Sperling, about 1825-1894

Sperling was admitted to Trinity College, Cambridge, in 1843, and graduated BA in 1848 and MA in 1851. He was made deacon in 1849 and appointed curate of St. Mary Abbots Kensington in London. Priested in 1850, he married in 1854 and became Rector of Wicken Bonhunt in Essex in 1856. In 1862 he moved to Westbourne in Sussex, which he resigned in 1871 and was received into the Roman Catholic church. He died in 1894.[16]

Sperling has become famous in our own day because of three notebooks of specifications of English organs, now in the care of the Royal College of Organists (three other notebooks, one on foreign organs and two on heraldry, do not concern us just now). There are some thirteen hundred organs described, fifty-odd of which had been destroyed or rebuilt before Sperling could have begun his collection: and the question of where he obtained this information is discussed by Dr. Thistlethwaite in the British Institute of Organ Studies *Journal*.[17] There are also a good number of illustrations of organ-cases in another hand, pasted into the notebooks. As the collection seems to have been completed by 1854, it is of course of the utmost interest to organ historians today and indeed one of them, Dr James Boeringer of Susquehanna University, has begun publishing a complete annotated edition of it.[18]

It seems likely that Sperling and Sutton could have been introduced by Walmisley, at once organist of Trinity College, Professor of Music and resident at Jesus College. We cannot say whether there was any collaboration between the two in drawing up their lists but it is worth noting that the *Short Account* also includes several organs that had disappeared many years before its publication. Did Sutton provide their details from some source unknown to us, or did Sperling?

Sperling installed an organ at Wicken Bonhunt, bracketed form the north wall of the chancel with a reversed console below resembling a choir-stall.[19] He published *Church Walks in Middlesex*, of which a second edition appeared in 1853.

Jonathan Holt Titcomb, about 1820–1887

A contemporary of Sutton's, he was Pensioner of Peterhouse in Cambridge, graduated BA in 1841 and MA in 1845. After a curacy at St. Mark's Kennington in South London, he was appointed Perpetual Curate of St. Andrew-the-Less in Cambridge in 1845 and stayed there until 1859.[20] "In a large parish where a portion of the population were of the most disreputable and degraded character, Titcomb soon made himself popular and had large congregations attend his church."[21] He established Sunday schools and a system of district visitors. The church he served was restored in 1854, with at least the keenest interest of the Cambridge Architectural Society, if not under its direction. The minutes of the meetings of the Committee are extremely sketchy,[22] and obviously do not include a great many decisions that must have been taken by, for instance, the Chairman out of meeting times: as the chairman at this time was the Revd. John Gibson (see the first entry in this chapter), he may have felt himself above reporting to his Committee, let alone the Society! If indeed the organ was given by Sutton (see chapter II), it points to the great respect that every clergyman working in such parishes earned in those days, if he seemed to be in any way successful. Sutton, who had a great feeling for the poor even if he never shared their life, obviously admired Titcomb's work and made the sort of gesture everyone would understand.

Titcomb himself went on to become Bishop of Rangoon (1877–1882) and then of Northern and Central Europe (1884–1886).

Canon William Edward Dickson, about 1824–1910

Pensioner at Corpus Christi College, Cambridge, 1842, Scholar 1843, he graduated BA in 1846, and was made deacon in the same year: priested in 1847, he took his MA in 1852 and in 1858 took up his life's work as Precentor of Ely Cathedral. He resigned in 1895 and from that year until his death was an Honorary Canon, occupying the same house in the College. He claimed friendship with John Sutton, at Walmisley's introduction, in his book *Fifty Years of Church Music* (quoted in chapter II at p.35), being one of the select few who were invited to the musical evenings Sutton arranged in his Jesus College rooms. He does not appear in the surviving correspondence and most likely lost touch when Sutton went to live on the Continent. He was a considerable author of the sort of smallish but useful books produced in the Camden Society atmosphere – all of which, being dated, are out of print now except *Practical Organ-Building*, which was re-published in 1983 (Positif Press, Oxford). They included *Singing in Parish Churches*, *Cathedral Choirs*, and *Early Organs in Ely Cathedral*. His obituary in the *Ely Diocesan Remembrancer*[21], observed,

> "As Precentor, no one could be more zealous in the discharge of his duty. He loved it for its own sake and spared no pains to bring the choir up to the standard which his refined taste dictated. With the chorister boys he was most particular, often superintending the daily practice himself… He was known to the clergy of the diocese chiefly through the Diocesan Church Music Society, of which, some fifty years ago, he was one of the founders. He took great pleasure in its Festivals, at which, in early days, he acted as Conductor… studying Church music not only in England, but, in his holidays in Belgium, France, Germany and Italy…"

Dickson did actually build a two-manual organ himself, showing that many of the Sutton circle had a good deal of practical knowledge they were ready to exercise. Samuel Sebastian Wesley (1810-1876) had some correspondence with him in 1860-1862,[23] suggesting among other things, that Wesley himself should resign his cathedral organist's post and spend all his time composing for cathedral choirs. Wesley obviously considered Dickson the foremost Precentor of his day, for he had little use for the majority of cathedral dignitaries. Dickson seems to have left a most fragrant memory behind him in Ely.

Edmund Randolph, c.1822–1892

Randolph matriculated at Jesus College in 1840, took his BA in 1844 and MA in 1847. He was made deacon in 1845, priested in 1846 and was appointed Vicar of St. Clement's Cambridge at once. He held this post until 1849 but then disappeared from the Clergy Lists until 1855 when he held the curacy of Little Hadham, Herts, for a year. Then he was curate of Kimpton in Hampshire for five years (1865-1870) and once again is not to be found in the Clergy Lists. He died at Ryde in the Isle of Wight in 1892. We learn from Zaun[24] that he was actually Sutton's brother-in-law, for he married one of the Miss Sherlocks from Southwell, and came to stay at Kiedrich once or twice with his mother-in-law[25]. He was another of the circle who was converted to Roman Catholicism[26] – which explains his final disappearance from the Clergy Lists, but not the others. Randolph and Sutton seem often to have been together: one of the early letters in the Hardman Collection is headed "Little Hadham" in 1856[27]: in July 1859 Sutton wrote to Béthune:

"Randolph and I had a very pleasant month together, we went as far as Inspruck [sic] and returned by Saltzberg [sic] & Munich, we walked a good deal which took up much time".[28] Right at the end of his life, on 1 June 1873, Sutton wrote to Béthune that "Randolph is coming for the Holy Blood Procession on Monday, and will be staying at an hotel – as I cannot take them in, in my hospital, my man can do nothing and poor old Sophie, is more or less dropsical and very weak, and it is quite as much as she can do, to wait upon me when quite alone…"[29] (This is the only time Sophie makes an appearance: but if "old Sistra" was "by her own account not quite 70"[30] in 1866, perhaps she had either died or retired by this time. In this same letter of November 1866, Sutton observed, "I almost expect to hear that she has made a run away match.")

Randolph himself (signing as "Edmund Alban Randolph") wrote to Béthune twice after Sutton's death. On 25 April 1881 from Ryde, he wrote, "I did myself the pleasure of sending you the German history of Kiedrich with the little memoir of Sir John: I trust you received it safely?" – referring to the book we have learnt to call Zaun by now. He was still spending holidays in Kiedrich that year and in March 1882 he wrote: "I am not a rich man as our dear friend Sir John was, and I cannot do things in the princely way that he did."[31]

These, then, are the people we know Sutton associated with in Cambridge. There is no conclusion we can draw, other than the fact that most of them carried out valuable work in their various spheres and a little light is shed in some unexpected places.

REFERENCES

1 Venn, *Alumni Cantabrigienses*.
2 *Stones and Story*, p. 295.
3 Minute-Book of the Society in Cambridge University Library.
4 *Stones and Story*, p. 296.
5 *The Buildings of Britain: Cambridgeshire*.
6 Letter to Dr. Gray, 1 Dec. 1902. Jesus College Archives.
7 Béthune.
8 Béthune.
9 Béthune.
10 *Musical Opinion*, March 1957.
11 Béthune.
12 Béthune.
13 Unless otherwise noted, statements taken from his obituary in *Ely Diocesan Remembrancer*, Sept. 1914.
14 Verbal information from the Revd. B. B. Edmonds.
15 *The Organ* no. 71, p. 145.
16 Venn, *Alumni Cantabrigienses*.
17 *BIOS Journal* no.1, 1977. Oxford, Positif Press. p. 87.
18 Boeringer, *Organa Britannica* vol.1, Associated Univ. Presses, 1983.
19 Information from Revd. B. B. Edmonds.
20 Venn, *Alumni Cantabrigienses*.
21 *Ely Diocesan Remembrancer*, February 1911.
22 Quoted in Gedge, art. in *The Organ* no. 267, p. 44.
23 Venn.
24 Zaun, p. 166.
25 Schneider.
26 Zaun, p. 166.
27 Hardman Collection.
28 Béthune.
29 Béthune.
30 Béthune.
31 Béthune.

CONCLUSION

There must be a danger, particularly when a limit is set upon length, that a biography shall become merely a catalogue of things done, with explanatory notes – and that the character of the subject be lost. In John Sutton's case, his letters save us from that loss to some extent, but because they deal almost exclusively with the subjects in hand, we are left with the impression of attention to detail and correctness amounting to pernickitiness. And yet "Many will remember that particular mixture of gentleness, courtesy, sweetness, lack of guile and unbending sense of honour that characterised old-fashioned gentlemen of a certain kind."[1] There are not as many about with such memories now, and these virtues are not so generally admired. So it is right that one more "gentleman of a certain kind" should have a memorial, for when Zaun's and Rembry's words about him are read with his letters in mind, this is the sort of character that is conjured up. Added to that, though, is his immense generosity to the projects dear to his heart, and to the poor. Kenelm Digby, whom we met in Chapter I as the friend of Sutton's father, "was generally suspicious of wealth ... an answer to this difficulty was for the aristocrat in question to rid himself of his wealth by various means – the establishment and endowment of religious houses, the building of churches and almshouses, and generosity to the poor."[2]

We have here, then, the fusion of several sets of true principles – the architectural ones of Pugin and the Camden Society, and the church-furnishing ones of Pugin, Béthune and the Nazarene school, the musical ones of medieval times as in the *Kurmainzer* plainsong , – and in Sutton's early days the English cathedral tradition too: the organ traditions of each country as far back as his investigations could unearth them; and the outlook of a medieval knight, as Scott and Digby codified it.

We can rightly give this thesis the title "Sir John Sutton: a study in true principles".

REFERENCES

1   Mark Girouard, *Return to Camelot* (Yale University Press 1981) p. 14.
2   *op. cit.* p. 65.

ZUSAMMENFASSUNG

Kapitel I: Lebenslauf und geistige Einflusse

1820–1841 Kindheit und Jugend

Am 18. Oktober 1820 kam John Sutton in Sudbrooke Holme (einem Haus, das während der Jagdzeit gemietet wurde) in Lincolnshire zur Welt. Im Alter von drei Jahren erlangte sein Vater, Sir Richard Sutton, der zweite Baronet von Norwood Park (in der Nähe von Southwell, Nottinghamshire) die Baronswürde. Die umsichtige Tätigkeit seiner Vormünder brachte ihm Reichtum. Auf dem Eton College und Trinity College in Cambridge erzogen, heiratete er einige Tage nach seinem 21. Geburtstag. Er richtete sich häuslich ein, zog eine große Familie auf und betrieb die Sportarten der Fuchsjagd, des Angelns und des Schießens. Er spielte auch Flöte, liebte Bücher, und als seine Frau starb, zahlte er eine Votivkapelle bei West Tofts zu ihrem Andenken. Als ihm bewußt wurde, daß John an Nervenproblemen litt, sorgte er dafür, daß eine Orgel für ihn gebaut wurde. Sir Richard war seinen Kindern, Verwandten, Freunden und Arbeitern gegenüber immer freigiebig. Er starb in seinem Londoner Haus, 94, Piccadilly, und wurde in West Tofts beerdigt.

Johns Mutter, Lady Mary Elizabeth Sutton geb. Burton, aus der Grafschaft Carlow in Irland, war eine bedeutungslose Person, die voll in ihren Pflichten als Frau und Mutter aufging. John sprach von ihr stets voller Anhänglichkeit und mit tiefster Verehrung. Sie starb im Wochenbett am 1. Januar 1842.

Zunächst teilte John einen Privatlehrer mit den anderen Mitgliedern der Familie, dann besuchte er eine Schule in East Stoke, Nottinghamshire. Von 1834 bis 1836 ging er mit einem seiner Brüder auf das Eton College, hatte dort aber wenig Erfolg. Deshalb wurde er von 1836 bis 1841 Privatschüler von Reverend Christopher Bird, dessen Gemeinde Chollerton in der Nähe von Hexham, Northumberland, lag. Bird besaß akademische Grade sowohl von Oxford als auch von Cambridge. Er beherrschte die meisten Fächer, daher hörte man ihm respektvoll zu. Er war eng befreundet mit Lord Brougham, dem Großkanzler der 1830er-Regierung und schrieb ein Pamphlet über die Emanzipation der Katholiken. Er interessierte sich sehr für die Erziehung und die Unterbringung der Armen und gestattete keine Störung seiner priesterlichen Pflichten. Während dieser Zeit begleitete er Sutton auf seiner ersten Rhein-Reise.

Während John Sutton in Chollerton wohnte, freundete er sich mit William Henshaw an, dem Organisten der Kathedrale in Durham.

ZUSAMMENFASSUNG

1841–1844 Student des Jesus College in Cambridge

Sutton promovierte nicht, vielleicht wegen seiner Nerven oder seiner mangelhaften mathematischen Kenntnisse. Er wurde jedoch ordentlicher Student der klassischen Wissenschaften und begann die Arbeit an seinem Buch "*A Short Account of Organs*", erschienen 1847. Dadurch wurde er der College-Leitung bekannt als begeisterter Kenner des gotischen Baustils. Beeinflußt wurde er zu dieser Zeit durch die "Cambridge Camden Gesellschaft", die im Jahre 1839 gegründet worden war und deren Mitglieder sich besonders für Baukunst, Kirchenausstattung, Liturgie und Musik interessierten. Es wurde von ihnen erwartet, daß sie jede Woche eine mittelalterliche Kirche besuchten und einen Bericht darüber erstatteten. Die meisten englischen Kirchen zeigen den großen Einfluß dieser Gesellschaft, der Sutton sich während seines ersten Semesters anschloß.

T. A. Walmisley (1814–1856), Professor für Musik seit 1836, wohnte im Jesus College während der ganzen Zeit, die Sutton in Cambridge war. Er war der erste, der Musikvorlesungen einführte, die durch praktische Beispiele erläutert wurden. Als Organist der drei Colleges und der Universitätskirche vertonte er eine beträchtliche Menge Musik für Kirche und Konzerthalle und galt als guter Improvisator.

Zwei Mitglieder des Colleges – John Gibson, der Dekan, und Osmond Fischer, der Kaplan – waren ebenfalls Verehrer des gotischen Stils und dürften Sutton in seiner Begeisterung ermuntert haben.

Zu den Büchern, die Sutton während dieser Zeit wahrscheinlich gelesen hat, zählen "*The Broadstone of Honour* (eine wörtliche Übersetzung von "Ehrenbreitstein"): *Rules for the Gentlemen of England*" von Kenelm Digby (1822), der zum Katholizismus übertrat und Altersgenosse von Suttons Vater auf dem Trinity College in Cambridge war; ferner "*Contrasts*" von A.W. Pugin (1836). "*Past and Present*" von Carlyle (1843) und "*Sybil*" von Benjamin Disraeli (1845). Alle diese Schriften verfolgten die Tendenz, das mittelalterliche Rittertum wieder zu beleben, besonders unter den adeligen und besitzenden Klassen in Großbritannien. Als spirituell veranlagter Aristokrat über die damaligen Zustände in England besorgt, fühlte sich Sutton unweigerlich zur Kultur des Mittelalters hingezogen.

Am 23. Dezember 1844 heiratete Sutton Emma Helena Sherlock, die aber bereits am 26. Januar 1845 verstarb und von ihm zeitlebens betrauert wurde. Er dachte nie an eine Wiederheirat; denn die romantische Tradition von Digby bedeutete, daß ein Mann nur eine einzige Frau haben solle und ihr sein ganzes Leben lang die Treue hielt. Außer einigen Gerüchten aus Kiedrich gibt es keine Nachricht über irgendeine andere Liebschaft in seinem Leben.

Im Herbst 1845 wurde Sutton von seinem College eingeladen, seine Begeisterung und Kenntnis für die Restaurierung der College-Kapelle einzusetzen. Deshalb kehrte er zu dieser Zeit nach Cambridge zurück und blieb dort neun Jahre lang. Mit Ausnahme der Teilnahme am Dienst in der Kapelle und der Übungen mit einem Chor von Jugendlichen aus der Stadt, führte er ein sehr zurückgezogenes Leben in seinen College Zimmern.

Sutton brachte A.W.N. Pugin nach Cambridge, ursprünglich nur um beim Zeichnen des Orgelhäuses für die Kapelle zu helfen, aber schließlich um eine der Ecken des Kapellturms zu verstärken und um die von Sutton gewünschte Inneneinrichtung zu zeichnen. Der Einfluß, den Pugin auf sein Leben und seine Ansichten ausübte, war sehr stark. Wie Pugin gestaltete Sutton viele seiner Stiftungen an die Kapelle nach mittelalterlichen Vorbildern. Pugin war es auch, der ihn mit dem Baron Jean de Bethune (der als der belgische Pugin bezeichnet wurde) aus Kasteel Marke (in der Nähe von Kortrijk in Belgien) bekannt machte. Dieser schwärmte ebenfalls für den gotischen Baustil und gotische Möbel. Er hatte tatsächlich eine erfolgreiche Werkstatt für die Ausstattung von Kirchen in Gand gegründet. Seit dieser Zeit war er Suttons enger und zuverlässiger Freund.

Im Jahre 1854 verließ Sutton England, um für den Rest seines Lebens in Belgien und Deutschland zu verbringen. Natürlich kehrte er gelegentlich zurück, um den Treuhändern bei der Verwaltung des väterlichen Besitzes zu helfen. So kam er zwar besuchsweise nach England, aber das Festland wurde seine Heimat, vielleicht, weil er sich als der Fortsetzer von Pugins Arbeit sah; d.h. er führte dessen Buch über die Sammlung wertvoller europäischer gotischer Kunstwerke fort.

In 1855 trat er vor den Kanonikus Felix Béthune (Bruder von Jean de Béthune) in Rosselare, (Belgien) zum Katholizismus über. Er verbrachte einige Zeit in Bonn und übersiedelte dann nach Freiburg im Breisgau. Im November jenes Jahres starb sein Vater, und er mußte entscheiden, wie er das beträchtliche Einkommen, das ihm jetzt gehörte, nutzen würde.

In 1857 weilte er eine Zeit lang in Kiedrich, wo er das Abmontieren der alten Orgel überwachte, vielleicht auch, um seine Pläne für die Wiederherstellung der Kirche und des Chorstiftes einzuleiten.

Im Jahre 1858 kaufte Sutton zwei Reihenhäuser auf der "Gouden Hand"-Straße in Brügge und ließ sie so weit wie möglich regotisieren. Jean de Béthune half viel, besonders durch die Herstellung von Mobiliar und Stoffen, aber es scheint, daß Sutton selbst alles entworfen habe.

1849 trafen die ersten vier Studenten mit einem englischen Subregens ein, um den Anfang für eine englisch-belgische Bildungsanstalt zu machen. Diese hatte mehrer Dependencen in der Stadt, und zu Beginn der 1870er Jahre wurde mit dem Bau auf einem festen Platz nach einem prächtigen Plan begonnen. Es erfolgten jedoch keine Stiftungen, und als Sutton starb, ging das Unternehmen zuende.

1865 erheilte das Chorstift Kiedrich seine Gründungsakten und die Stiftung. Das Anfangsstadium war schwierig, hauptsächlich wegen unzulänglicher Chorregenten. Aber nach dem Tod von Sutton war ein angemessenes Niveau erreicht.

Im Jahre 1867 wurde Sutton zum "*High Sheriff of Nottinghamshire*" ernannt. Dies bedeutete, daß er die Richter der Königin bei den vierteljährlichen Assisen in Nottingham bestätigen und auch bei den sozialen Veranstaltungen, die sie begleiteten, anwesend sein mußte.

1869 kaufte Sutton drei Reihenhäuser in Kiedrich und er vereinigte sie zu einem einzigen Haus für sich selbst. Früher hatte er stets im Pfarrhaus gewohnt.

1870 wurde ihm der Orden "*Knight Commander of the Order of St. Gregory the Great*" vom Papst verliehen; offensichtlich als Anerkennung für seine Unterstützung der Bildungsanstalt in Brügge sowie für anscheinend

ZUSAMMENFASSUNG 201

geheime Geschenke an die katholische Diözese Plymouth in England.

Während des ganzen Winters 1872/73 nahm er seinen schwindsüchtigen Dienstboten mit nach Amelie-les-Bains in Südfrankreich.

Am 6. Juni 1873 starb Sutton an rheumatischem Fieber in Brügge. Am 2. November 1974 wurde sein nach Kiedrich überführter Leichnam dort auf der nördlichen Seite des Kirchhofs beigesetzt.

Kapitel II: Der Orgelfreund

Keine einzige Orgel gleicht genau einer anderen. Der Grund hierfür ist vielleicht, daß Schwärmer für dieses Instrument ihn ganzes Leben lang so bleiben. Als John Sutton 13 Jahre alt war, wurden bereits Verhandlungen zum Kauf einer Orgel geführt. Er verbrachte als Student in Cambridge (1841-1844) viel Zeit mit der Vorbereitung seines Buches *A Short Account of Organs*, das sehr wichtig ist für das Verständnis seiner Ansichten über dieses Instrument. Die Cambridger Richtung der Oxford-Bewegung verfaßte viele Bücher über Bau und Einrichtung von Kirchen und über die Durchführung der Gottesdienste. Sie zeichnen sich durch Vollständigkeit und sorgfältige Beobachtung aus. Die Grundlage bildete die Theorie der Camdener Gesellschaft, nach der die mittelalterlichen Kirchen nach bestimmten Regeln gebaut wurden, die wiederentdeckt werden konnten, indem man anhand verschiedener Beispiele, z. B. eines Lettners, die Stilmerkmale einer bestimmten Epoche verglich. Die auf diese Weise ermittelten Regeln konnten dann nicht nur beim Bau neuer Gotteshäuser für die wachsende Bevölkerung in den Industriestädten angewendet werden, sondern auch beim Restaurieren der vielen vorhandenen, aber reparaturbedürftigen Kirchen. Die Gesellschaft sorgte für die Suche nach Informationen und für die Anfertigung von Skizzen, nach denen die Details dieser "Regeln" ermittelt, vergleichen und beurteilt werden konnten. Dies geschah mittels Blank Forms for the Description of a Church, die jeweils eine Reihe von Schlagwörtern enthielten nebst Leerzeilen, die von den Kirchenbesuchern auszufüllen waren. Auf diese Weise erhielt man ein umfassendes Bild von den Stilmerkmalen eines Kirchenbaues und seiner Einrichtung.

Sutton wandte diese Methode auf den Orgelbau an und unternahm viele Reisen, bei denen er Details der Instrumente aufschrieb. Die übrigen Mitglieder der Camdener Gesellschaft notierten alle Einzelheiten über eine ganze Kirche. Die einzelnen Kapitel des *Short Account* entsprechen diesen Einzelheiten. Suttons Ideal für Orgelneubauten war die Orientierung am Klang der ihm bekannten Instrumente von Smith und Harris aus dem späten 17. Jahrhundert. Sie sollten so klein sein wie möglich und den musikalischen Erfordernissen der Kirche entsprechen, für die sie errichtet wurden, sei es eine Kathedrale, eine College-Kapelle oder eine Pfarrkirche. Die Prospekte sollten denen alter Orgeln auf dem europäischen Kontinent nachgebildet werden, das heißt mit Flügeltüren, und zwar in der Form eines Tryptichons zur Symbolisierung der Dreieinigkeit.

Zu jener Zeit galt in England bei Orgelneubauten der Grundsatz; "Je größer, desto besser!" Nur wenige Leute interessierten sich für teure Gehäusekonstruktionen, wenn das Instrument im Altarraum neben den

Sängern in einem Kasten aufgestellt werden konnte, wie es die Meinung der Camdener Gesellschaft war. Daher wurden Suttons Ansichten nur von seinen Freunden und Brüdern geteilt. Die Orgeln, welche er in England hatte bauen lassen, entsprechen strikt den Prinzipien des *Short Account*.

1. Jesus College Chapel, Cambridge
Ursprünglich, im Jahre 1846, suchte Sutton eine ältere, von Bernard Smith erbaute Orgel. Da aber keine verfügbar war, wurde 1847 eine Orgel ähnlicher Bauart bei J. C. Bishop in London bestellt und im Oktober desselben Jahres nach Cambridge geliefert. Fünf Arten der Holzpfeifen stammen noch aus dem 17. Jahrhundert, und es scheint, als suchte man sich so eng wie möglich an den Orgeln des 17. Jahrhunderts zu orientieren, Das Orgelgehäuse wurde wahrscheinlich von Sutton entworfen, da es unwahrscheinlich is, daß der Baumeister Pugin für mehr als die detaillierten Zeichnungen verantwortlich war. Die Orgel befindet sich auf einer Empore im östlichsten Bogen des Kirchenschiffes und ist klanglich kaum verändert worden.

2. West Tofts I
Diese kleine Orgen, die heute in der Pfarrkirche zu Great Walsingham, Norfolk zu sehen ist, scheint ein Probstück des jungen Orgelbaumeisters George Dawson aus Cambridge gewesen zu sein, dem Sutton bei seiner Neiderlassung behilflich war. Der Überlieferung nach existierte sie bereits vor dem großen Wiederaufbau der Kirche und hätte damals als Notbehelf bei den Gottesdiensten gedient. Sie besitzt nur vier Register, die Pfeifen sind sämtlich oder größtenteils aus Holz. Viele Merkmale deuten auf Sutton als Urheber, und obwohl die ursprüngliche Malerei überdeckt worden ist, sind die erhaltenen Spuren ebenfalls sehr charakteristisch.

3. West Tofts II
Als die Kirche in West Tofts im Jahre 1941 geschlossen wurde, baute man diese Orgel ab und lagerte sie ein. Sie befindet sich jetzt auf der winzigen Westempore der Pfarrkirche zu South Pickenham in der Grafschaft von Norfolk. Der Briefwechsel von 1856/57 über diese Orgel ist nicht mehr vorhanden, aber anscheinend wurde das Gehäuse in der Werkstatt von Bethune in Gent angefertigt und bemalt, schließlich reguliert von Zimmermann, dem Hauptregulierer der Firma Hooghuys in Brügge (die Sutton für alle seine Orgelprojekte auf dem Kontinent in Anspruch nahm). Das Gehäuse gleicht dem von Kiedrich, das Sutton soeben kennengelernt hatte; darüber hinaus gibt es auch klangliche Ähnlichkeiten. Höchstwahrscheinlich handelt es sich hier im ältesten Stadium um den Idealtyp einer Dorforgel, wie er im *Short Account* (S.107) beschrieben ist. Pedal und das kleine Schwellwerk (als Brustpositiv) wurden 1888 von Miller aus Cambridge hinzugefügt.

Nachstehend sind einige Hausorgeln aufgeführt, die Sutton kennengelernt hatte:
4. Die Organ, die sein Vater 1833 für ihn kaufte, wurde im Musiksalon bei Lynford Hall in der Nähe von West Tofts in Norfolk gebaut. Sie bestand aus zwei Manualen und Pedal mit neun oder zehn klingenden Stimmen. Im

ZUSAMMENFASSUNG 203

Jahre 1856, nach dem Tod von Sir Richard Sutton, wurde sie an die Heiliggrabkirche in Cambridge verkauft, wo man sie 1879 durch ein anderes Instrument ersetzte.

5. Die Hausorgel in Northampton
1847 kaufte Sutton diese seiner Meinung nach im späten 17. Jahrhundert von Bernhard Smith erbaute Orgel, die in seinem Zimmer in Cambridge aufgestellt wurde. Später kam sie in Suttons Haus in Brügge, wo sie von seiner Schwester gezeichnet wurde. Nach seinem Tod gelangte sie in das Pfarrhaus seines jüngsten Bruders zu Brant Broughton in der Nähe von Newark. Jetzt ist sie im Besitz des Marquis von Northampton, der in Compton Wynates, Warwickshire wohnt. Das Werk hat zwei Manuale mit sechs Registern.
6. Eine einmanualige Orgel mit sechs Registern von demselben Erbauer kaufte Sutton 1845 für zehn Pfund vom New College in Oxford. Sie wurde im Jesus College zu Cambridge für die während der Restaurierung der Kapelle im Speisesaal stattfindenden Gottesdienste benützt und befindet sich jetzt bei "*St. Peter's Organ Works*" in London.
7. Die Tragorgel König Jakobs II. wurde 1848 auf einer Auktion des Inventars vom "*Stowe House*" für dreißig Pfund von einem im übrigen unbekannten Herrn Robert Sutton ersteigert. Sie gleicht den Instrumenten Nr. 5 und 6 und besitzt ein Manual mit fünf Registern, von denen drei geteilte Schleifen haben. Seit 1924 befindet sie sich in Amerika.
8. 1860 schenkte Sutton der Kirche in Chollerton, wo er einst als Privatschüler im Pfarrhaus geweilt hatte, eine kleine Orgel. Sie wurde 1903 grundlegend umgebaut, so daß man heute nicht mehr feststellen kann, warum sie ihn so interessierte, abgesehen von dem noch vorhandenen Gehäuse, das in die zweite Hälfte des 18. Jahrhunderts zu datieren wäre.

Orgeln in Europa

9. Kiedrich im Rheingau
Diese Orgel ist bereits mehrfach an anderer Stelle beschrieben worden, daher befassen wir uns nur mit den Ideen der Restaurierungsarbeiten von Sutton und Hooghuys in der Zeit von 1857 bis 1859 (bzw. 1861, wenn man die Bedeutung der von August Martin gemalten Flügeltüren einbezieht).

Da das Hauptwerksgehäuse von 1492 immer noch existierte, meinte Sutton, daß es aus optischen Gründen unbedingt mit Flügeltüren versehen werden müßte. Das Positivgehäuse erschien ihm nicht als gleichwertig; denn nach den Theorien von Pugin und der Camdener Gesellschaft hörten die Künstler nach 1500 auf, zur Ehre Gottes zu bauen und zu malen. Gab es Pedalpfeifen, so durften sie nicht gesehen werden. Deshalb wurden die Pfeifen des Rückpositivs und des Pedals unsichtbar im Turm aufgestellt. Das Pedalwerk wurde mit sieben Registern disponiert, da nach Suttons Meinung (*A Short Account*, S. 11) eine derartige Disposition "einen eindeutigen Erfolg haben könnte". Die zwei vermutlich nicht mehr restaurierbaren Manualzungen wurden durch Flöte 4' im Hauptwerk und Gedact 8' im Positiv ersetzt. Beide waren als Begleitregister sehr nützlich. Die neue Orgelempore wurde von John Gibson, dem ehemaligen Dekan des Jesus College entworfen, und Sutton leistete zweifellos Hilfe bei der farblichen Gestaltung.

Die Kiedricher Orgel ist heute ein wertvolles Denkmal aus verschiedener Sicht: durch das mittelalterliche Orgelgehäuse, durch die Disposition aus der Mitte des 17. Jahrhunderts und durch die Restaurierung nach den optischen und klanglichen Grundsätzen des 19. Jahrhunderts.

10. Die Hausorgel in Kiedrich

Man nimmt an, daß das jetzige Chor-Positiv in Kiedrich im späten 17. Jahrhundert von einem belgischen Meister erbaut wurde. Sie ähnelt den englischen Hausorgeln (vgl. Nr. 5, 6 und 7) und besitzt ein Manual mit fünf Registern. Sie dient hauptsächlich zur Belgleitung des Chorgesanges und alljährlich im August bei der Wallfahrt im Freien als Prozessionsorgel.

11. Vijvekapelle bei Brügge in Flandern

Die Kapelle wurde 1865-1867 von Béthune erbaut. Daß Sutton sich mit dem Orgelprojekt beschäftigte, beweist die Bestellung von nicht bemalten Flügeltüren aus Birmingham. Das Gehäuse wurde in der Werkstatt von Béthune in Gent hergestellt, das Werk selbst von Hooghuys. Die Gehäusebekrönung ähnelt der an der Orgel in St. Andrew-the-Less in Cambridge. Die Planung erfolgte nach den Grundsätzen von Kiedrich, wurde aber gemäß belgischen Traditionen abgeändert. Die Orgel hat ein Manual mit acht Registern und ein angehängtes Pedal mit elf Tasten.

12. Eltville am Rhein

Das wahrscheinlich in Gent erbaute und mit Flügeltüren (von August Martin bemalt) versehene Gehäuse wurde mit einem Werk von Hooghuys und im Jahr 1868 aufgestellt. Es zeigt die gleichen Merkmale jene im benachbarten Kiedrich und in Sion/Sitten im schweizerischen Kanton Valais. Daraus kann man schließen, wieviele Reisen Suttons uns nicht bekannt sind. Diese Orgel stand ursprünglich auf einer Empore im östlichen Bogen des Kirchenschiffes.

13. Freiburg im Breisgau, Münster

Die Geschichte der Münsterorgel ist lang und kompliziert. 1867 bot Sutton 3.000 Taler für die Restaurierung der Orgel an, bei der alle originalen Pfeifen verwendet werden sollten. 1870 wurde das Gehäuse um ein Rückpositiv erweitert und beide Teile hatten Flügeltüren mit Malereien von Martin erhalten. Durch Suttons frühen Tod wurde das Werk selbst lediglich im damaligen Zustand konserviert. Es wäre zu wünschen, daß die Flügeltüren wiedergefunden werden.

14. Frauenstein bei Wiesbaden

Diese Orgel wird in Briefe von Prälat Schneider erwähnt und ist auch in den Verzeichnissen von Hooghuys zu finden, daher dürfte Sutton die Kosten getragen haben. Verwunderlich ist nur, daß Sutton die Aufstellung mißverstand. Er schreibt, sie stehe auf einer Schwalbennestempore wie in Sion, Freiburg/Breisgau oder Kiedrich. Tatsächlich ist die Orgel in Frauenstein aber von der Nordwand der Kirche aus durch Kragsteine gestützt. Sie ähnelt stark dem Rückpositiv einer großen Orgel, und soll aus dem benachbarten, im Jahre 1803 aufgehobenen Zisterzienkloster Eberbach stammen. Sie hat ein Manual mit sieben Registern nebst einem Pedal von einer Oktave Umfang mit drei Registern und zwei Ersatzzügen, offenbar eine Synthese von deutscher und belgischer Pedalbauweise. Als Ergänzung zu der vorstehenden Liste folgen einige Orgeln, bei denen eine Verbindung mit dem Namen Sutton sehr wahrscheinlich ist:

15. Cambridge, St. Andrew-the-Less
Am 14. November 1853 wurde im Protokollbuch der Architekturgesellschaft aus Cambridge der Vorschlag notiert, es würde eine Orgel gestiftet, wenn die Lettnertreppe als Zugang zur Orgel restauriert würde. Ein Name wird nicht genannt, aber wenn man diese Protokollnotiz mit dem von John Sutton vorgeschlagenen Aufstellungsplan für die Kapelle der Bildungsanstalt in Brügge vergleicht, ist Suttons Mitwirkung zumindest möglich. Außerdem ähnelt die Bekrönung des vorhandenen Gehäuses so sehr jener in der Vijvekapelle (vgl. Nr. 11), daß sie wahrscheinlich von derselben Hand gezeichnet wurden, nämlich von dem Belgier Jean de Bethune. Obwohl die Höhe des Altarplatzes völlig ungeeignet war, um das Versetzen des Lettners durchzusetzen, damit er und seine Treppe als Zugang zur Orgel dienen konnten, wie Sutton es wünschte, verlangte das Prinzip der Wahrheit, daß er die Orgel stiftete. Sie hat ein Manual mit Pedal und acht Registern.

16. Cambridge, Kapelle des Christ's College
Diese Orgel wird hier mit aufgeführt, weil Sutton vermutlich dafür sorgte, daß die sehr alten Pfeifen des damals verwaisten Instrumentes 1849 herausgenommen und sicher in Kisten gelagert wurden, bis eine Restaurierung im Jahre 1865 möglich war, da ihm zunächst die Mittel fehlten, die er damals gerade für die Restaurierungen im Jesus College und West Tofts benötigte.

17. Die Hausorgel von Osmond Fisher
Zwei Inschriften im Innern behaupten, daß Sutton die Restaurierung dieser kleinen Orgel überwacht habe, und der gegenwärtige Besitzer glaubt, das Instrument sei zwischen 1660 und 1665 von Robert Dallam erbaut worden. Die Pfeifen der Register Diapason, Open Diapason Treble und Principal stammen aus dem 17. Jahrhundert, die übrigen sind als Arbeit von George Dawson aus den frühen 1850er Jahren einzuschätzen. Manche ungewöhnliche Merkmale, vor allem ein System der Stimmkontrolle, können kaum durch Sutton eingeführt worden sein.

18. Die Gebetstischorgel
Auf der Rückseite des Fotos einer verlorengegangen Orgel, das dem Verfasser weitergeleitet wurde, heißt es: "von James Scott aus West Tofts für Sir John Sutton". Dies ist höchst unwahrscheinlich, da der Name James Scott erst 1863 in den Norfolker Adreßbüchern erscheint, also lange Zeit, nachdem John Sutton England verließ. Das Instrument gleicht keiner anderen von Sutton betreuten Orgel, die alle schön und geschmackvoll gestaltet sind. Das Instrument hat nur eine einzige Pfeifenreihe mit 29 Tönen. Vielleicht war sie für die von August Sutton entworfene Kapelle für die Ortsarmen bestimmt.

19. Brügge, St. Gillis
Hier, wo Sutton seine Andacht verrichtete, wenn er daheim war, wurde 1850 eine Orgel aus der ehemaligen Jesuitenkirche in Tournhout angeschafft, von der man nur weiß, daß sie oft repariert werden mußte. Fünf Jahre nach Suttons Tod ersetzte Hooghuys sie durch eine neues Instrument.

20. Brügge, Kathedrale St. Salvator
Suttons Ruf als kenntnisreicher Orgelfreund verbreitete sich bald in Brügge. Im Juni 1856 stiftete er für das Positivwerk der Kathedralorgel eine neue Hohlpfeife 8' "nach der Art und dem Stil der uralten Stimmen", und am 24. November desselben Jahres erstattete er einen Bericht über die restaurierte Orgel, worin er sagt, sie sei in so gutem Zustand, als wäre sie neu für die Kirche gebaut worden.

21. Brügge, Kapelle der Bildungsanstalt
Es kann fast als sicher gelten, daß Sutton seinen Prinzipie gemäß Orgeln für jene Kapellen besorgte, die von der englisch-belgishen Bildungsanstalt verwendent wurden. Ein Hinweis auf die Vorsorge ist in zwei kleinen Orgeln zu Kasteel Marke zu finden. Sie sehen aus wie kleine aufrechtstehende Klaviere (Pianinos), ohne sichtbare Pfeifen und mit Tretvorrichtungen für den Blasbalg wie bei einem Harmonium. Die Instrumente dienten ausschließlich für die Begleitung des gregorianischen Chorals und haben ein Manual mit zwei oder drei Registern. Wenn die Zeichnungen, die in Marke erhalten sind, Suttons letzte Vorstellungen sind, wäre die Kapellenorgel der ständigen Bildungsanstalt hoch an der Nordwand befestigt und hätte auch ein gotisches Gehäuse mit Flügeltüren erhalten. Sie war nicht so groß, deshalb hatte sie nur ein einiges Manual. Eine Zeichnung zeigt uns, daß der Zugang zur Orgel von oben über den Lettner führen sollte, genau so, wie es einige Jahre zuvor für St. Andrew-the-Less in Cambridge vorgeschlagen worden war.

Kapitel III: Der Kirchenrestaurator

Das 19. Jahrhundert war in England eine bedeutende Zeit für Kirchenbau und Kirchenrestaurierung. Die Oxford-Gruppe hatte eine starke religiöse Erneuerungsbewegung innerhalb der Geistlichkeit und der begüterten Schichten erweckt. Auf dem europäischen Festland herrschten natürlich andere Bedingungen, aber John Suttons Vermögen (nach 1855 die horrende Summe von ca.40.000£ pro Jahr), seine Kenntnisse und sein Enthusiasmus waren überall willkommen. Doch sollte niemand erfahren, wieviel er auf diese Weise ausgab. Deshalb kann hier nur eine unvollständige Liste aufgestellt werden.

1. Lady Suttons Votivkapelle und West Tofts
Aus einer Eintragung im Tagebuch der Firma Hardman über Malerarbeiten im Jahre 1846 wissen wir, daß die Sutton-Familie zwischen 1844 und 1846 eine Votivkapelle zum Andenken an Lady Mary Elizabeth Sutton bauen oder zumindest ausstatten ließ und daß darin der von Augustus Pugin

entworfene Sarg stand. Es ist durchaus möglich, daß John Sutton und Pugin sich kennenlernten, als Pugin an der Oxborough Hall arbeitete, die nur 15km von Lynford entfernt ist. Sicher ist, daß beide bereits 1845 eng befreundet waren. Sobald Johns Bruder, Augustus Sutton, im Jahre Pfarrer von West Tofts wurde, begann auch der Wiederaufbau des im 17. Jahrhundert zestörten Nordschiffs der Kirche. Die Arbeiten wurden mit einigen Unterbrechungen, die der Geldbeschaffung durch John Sutton dienten, fortgesetzt, bis die Kirche am 13. August 1857 neu geweiht werden konnte. Als letzter Teil wurde die Kapelle fertig. Den ursprünglich vorhandenen Sarkophag beließ man darinnen. Die Kapelle ist zwar sehr klein, aber der Platz reicht gerade aus, damit man um den Sarkophag herumgehen kann. Die Wände sind wunderschön bemalt und der Boden ist mit herrlichen, buntglasierten Kacheln belegt.

Heute ist die St. Mary's Kirche nicht so leicht zu erreichen; denn seit 1941 wird das ganze Gebiet als Truppenubüngsplatz verwendet. Dennoch ist sie eine der besten schöpferischen Leistungen von A. W. N. Pugin. Er war als Architekt für das Nordschiff, den Altarraum, das Südportal und die Sakristei verantwortlich, eigentlich – mit Ausnahme des Turmes und des Hauptschiffes – für das ganze Gebäude, dessen Fenster er erneuerte. Von außen vermittelt die Kirche deshalb – bis auf den Turm – den Eindruck einer architektonischen Einheit. Innen war sie reich ausgestattet, dieser Reichtum wuchs noch im Laufe der Jahre. Hauptschiff und Nordschiff erhielten noch während der Lebenszeit von Sir Richard Sutton ihr Kirchengestühl, wodurch vielleicht die ursprüngliche Kanzel zu erklären, ist die mit einem Schreibtisch kombiniert war, von dem der Pfarrer im Stil des 17. und 18. Jahrhunderts – genau vor dem Gutsherrenstuhl – Frühgebet und Abendgebet leitete. Dies stand so völlig im Gegensatz zur Anschauung der *Camden Society*, daß diese oder eine ähnliche Erklärung dafür gefunden werden muß. Pugin starb im Jahre 1852, hatte aber tatsächlich den Entwurf für das gesamte Gebäude beendet; sein Sohn Edward beaufsichtigte den Rest der Arbeiten. Der Altarraum war an jeder Seite mit einer Reihe gegen die Ostseite des Lettners gerichteter Kirchenstühle versehen; denn es gibt hier drei kostbare, verzierte Holzschranken. Die beiden anderen umschließen das, was die Fakultät als einen "abgeschirmten Ort mit Plätzen für die Familie" beschrieb. Sutton brauchte einen Lettner, wenn er sich in einer Kirche wohl fühlen wollte. In mehreren seiner späteren Briefe beklagt er die Zerstörung der Lettner in deutschen Kathedralen durch die Domkapitel. Die Innenausstattung lehnt sich weitgehend an Vorbilder aus benachbarten Kirchen an. Suttons Zahlungen an die Kirche endeten im Jahre 1860. Er hatte versucht, den Sarg seiner Frau vom West Tofts-Friedhof in einen römisch-katholischen Friedhof umbetten zu lassen. Dazu gab jedoch der Bischof von Norwich keine Erlaubnis. Glücklicherweise waren die Kirche und ein Großteil der Innenausstattung bis zu jenem Jahre fertig. Zwei von Suttons Brüdern hatten Fachkenntnisse in der Herstellung von gemalten Kirchenfenstern und konnten somit diesen Teil der Ausschmückung selbst vollenden.

2. Jesus College – Kapelle in Cambridge
Das College wurde 1497 durch Bischof Alcock von Ely unter verwendung der Stiftungen und Gebäude des St. Radegund-Klosters gegründet. Die

Klosterkirche wurde – ohne das Nordschiff und den größten Teil des Mittelschiffs – Kapelle des College. Sie ist anscheinend immer gut gepflegt worden und war auch schön ausgestattet. Das *Fellows' Conclusion Book*, eine Protokollsammlung über die Besprechungen des Lehrkörpers und des Vorstandes, ist leider unvollständig und gibt keinen Aufschluß über Zeit und Art von Maßnahmen. Doch konnten folgende Tatsachen ermittelt werden: Die Restaurierung dauerte drei Jahre, nämlich von 1846 bis 1849. Der führende Architekt Anthony Salvin erhielt am 20. Dezember 1844 den Auftrag für die Arbeiten. Als aber achtzehn Monate später die Arbeiten am Turm gerade begonnen wurden, zeigte sich, daß manche Teile gefährdet waren. Sutton, der nach Cambridge zurückgekehrt war, um bei der Restaurierung zu helfen, hatte A. W. N. Pugin zur Bestätigung der Maße für die Orgel mitgebracht, die er stiften wollte. Pugin bot sofort seine Hilfe bei diesem Problem an, wurde jedoch nicht mit der Leitung der Arbeiten beauftragt, obwohl Salvin des Auftrag verlor. Stattdessen beaufsichtigten Gibson und Fisher, zwei in gotischer Architektur erfahrene College-Mitglieder, das Projekt mit der vollen Unterstützung von Sutton bis zur Fertigstellung.

Außer der Restaurierung des gesamten Gebäudes wurde auch ein neues Nordschiff gebaut. Das Ostfenster im Perpendicularstil, das einst unter Bischof Alcock eingesetzt worden war, wurde durch drei Spitzbögen ersetzt und die Kapelle völlig neue ausgestattet mit Altar, Ambo, Gestühl, Lettner, Orgel, Fußboden und Dachdekorationen, die größtenteils von Pugin entworfen und von Sutton bezahlt wurden. Als der Bau 1849 zu Allerheiligen endlich wieder in Gebrauch genommen werden konnte, wurde er allgemein gelobt - sogar vom *Ecclesiologist*, der Zeitschrift der *Camden Society* und deren Nachfolger, der *Ecclesiological Society*, der selten etwas lobte und der das Werk als "abgerundet und korrekt" bezeichnete.

3. Kiedrich im Rheingau

Die Kirche St. Valentinus und St. Dionysius in Kiedrich ist ein sehr imposantes und mit bedeutenden historischen Gegenständen ausgestattetes Bauwerk. Ihre jetzige Gestalt erhielt sie im Jahre 1480. Bis in die zweite Hälfte des 19. Jahrhunderts war sie durch die Folgen der in jener Gegend besonders heftigen napoleonischen Kriege sehr vernachlässigt und bot einen bedauernswerten Anblick, zumal jede Regeneration eine gewisse Zeit benötigt. Wahrscheinlich besuchte Sutton Kiedrich zum ersten Mal, als er noch ein sehr junger Mann war. Das erste sichere Datum über einen dortigen Aufenthalt ist 1857. Obwohl er oft recht lange Zeit in dem Dorf verbrachte, kaufte er erst 1869 dort ein Haus und wohnte bis dahin im Pfarrhaus. Er gestattete keine Aufzeichnungen über die in der Kirche auf seine Kosten ausgeführten Maßnahmen und deren finanzielle Höhe, weil dies seinem Verdienst Abbruch getan hätte. Aus diesem Grunde müssen wir auf Zauns Geschichte und auf eine erst kürzlich entdeckte, wenige Monate nach Suttons Tod gehaltene Ansprache des Chorregenten Hilpisch züruckgreifen. In ihr ist die Rede von der Restaurierung der Außenfassade, der fast vollständigen Erneuerung der Fenster und dem Einsetzen farbiger Glasmalereien, vom Wiederaufbau des Lettners (aber nach einem neuen Plan mit drei statt vier Unterteilungen), von der Instandsetzung des Gestühls, der

Altäre und des Sakramentshauses, von der Ausschmückung der Kirche sowie der Beschaffung neuer oder alter Meßgewänder; insgesamt eine weitreichende Liste. Alles wurde von Sutton bezahlt. Ferner wurde auch an der Michaelskapelle auf dem Friedhof gearbeitet.

Suttons persönliche Briefe über die Restaurierung veranschaulichen, wie er und Jean de Béthune die neuen Glasmalereien für die Kirchenfenster herstellten, immer in der Nachahmung oder auch unter Verwendung von mittelalterlichen Vorbildern. Einige Gegenstände wurden in Antiquitätenläden gekauft, wenn Sutton sie irgendwo entdeckte: denn er unternahm lange Reisen, um gotische Architektur oder Ausstattungsgegenstände zu skizzieren und zu kopieren, weil er der Überzeugung war, daß er Pugins Arbeit auf diesem Gebiet in Europa weiterführen müsse.

Nur wenig bzw. nichts ist über Kirchenrestaurierungen durch Sutton in Belgien bekannt. Das rührt daher, daß St. Gilles, seine dortige Kirche in Brügge, keinen Lettner hatte. Uns stehen jedoch einige Briefe über den Umbau und die Einrichtung des Hauses zur Verfügung, das er sich dort in der Gouden-Hand-Straat kaufte. Auch hier zeigt sich das gleiche Interesse für das Detail und sein Festhalten an den Prinzipien der gotischen Baumeister.

Kapitel IV: John Sutton als Musiker

Trotz der Unkenntnis der Fakten, müssen wir versuchen die Frage zu beantworten: "Wer brachte dem kleinen John Sutton das Orgelspielen bei?"

Wir wissen, daß er eine geraume Zeit bei seinem Großvater in Lincoln verbracht hat, und so ist es möglich, daß der Dom-Organist George Skelton (1794–1850) sein Lehrer war. Suttons Vater kaufte ihm im Alter von 13 Jahren eine Orgel. Dies zeigt uns, daß er wohl recht gute Fortschritte machte. Während er als Privatschüler im Pfarrhaus zu Chollerton von 1836 bis 1841 lebte, freundete er sich mit William Henshaw an, der von 1819-1862 Organist der Kathedrale von Durham war und wahrscheinlich seine musikalische Ausbildung weiterführte. Wir wissen, daß Henshaw sehr streng zu den Chorknaben war und viel von ihnen forderte. Wenn er genauso entschlossen mit anderen Schülern war, können wir sehr wohl verstehen, warum Suttons Spiel in späteren Jahren in Europa bewundert wurde und wie er es vermochte, Chöre in Cambridge und Kiedrich mit solchem Erfolg zu führen. Auch T. A. Walmisley, Professor für Musik in Cambridge, muß ihn beeinflußt haben, denn er war stets bereit, an den Kirchen- und Oratorien-konzerten mitzuwirken, die Sutton in seinem Haus für seine Freunde organisierte.

Ansonsten konzentrierte sich Suttons Musizieren am Jesus College auf die Kapelle. 1846 gründete er einen Chor, bestehend aus sechs Knaben (später erweitert auf acht) aus der Stadt und bildete sie aus, damit sie die Gottesdienste zumindest an Sonntagen und Heiligenfesten vormittags und abends singen konnten. Während die Kapelle restauriert wurde, hielt man die Gottesdienste in der Aula des College. Der Chor wurde vom Kollegium sehr geschätzt, wie die Aufzeichnungen zeigen. Sutton entschädigte die

Jungen für ihren Zeitaufwand, indem er sie die Grundschulfächer lehrte. Auch blieb er während der Semester-ferien in Cambridge, um sicherzustellen, daß sie nicht vernachlässigt wurden. Die Knaben sangen ohne Zweifel in der Aula und in der Kapelle, denn in jenen Tagen galt es für Männer mit Universitätsstatus nicht als gesellschaftsfähig, selbst zu singen.

Es gibt gegensätzliche Darstellungen über die Methode Psalmen und Lobgesänge zu singen. Die Tatsache, daß die Berichte nicht übereinstimmten, bedeutet wahrscheinlich, daß eine Anzahl einstimmiger anglikanischer Kirchenmotetten gebraucht wurde. Sutton veröffentlichte 1850 ein Textbuch zu den orgelbegleiteten Motetten, die er mit dem Chor zu lernen beabsichtigte. Es wurde von Charles Whittingham of Chiswick mit demselben schönen Schriftsatz gedruckt, der auch für "*Short Account*" Verwendung fand, es erscheint dem Autor aber wahrscheinlich, daß die vierstimmigen. Motetten mit Orgelbegleitung, die es beinhaltet, selten – wenn überhaupt – zur Zeit Suttons gebraucht wurden. Anlaß hierfür war die Wiedereröffnung der College-Kapelle nach ihrer Restaurierung 1849 mit dem Motette "*Ponder my Words*" für vier Knabenstimmen mit Orgel, speziell für den Gottesdienst geschrieben von Prof. Walmisley. Die Wiedereröffnung einer Kultstätte pflegt in der Regel ein festliches Ereignis mit einem stark besetzten Chor zu sein, aber offensichtlich waren keine Männerstimmen verfügbar. Das Orgelmotettebuch zeigt Suttons musikalischen Konservatismus: die meisten Motetten stammen aus dem 17. und frühen 18. Jahrhundert und natürlich zumeist englischer Herkunft. Aber es findet sich ein kleiner Teil mit Bearbeitungen von Sätzen italienischer Komponisten sowie eine Komposition von Sutton selbst ("*Haste Thee, O God, to deliver Me*"). Seltsamerweise wurde kein Motette von Purcell aufgenommen.

In Brügge St. Gillis gab es bereits einen etablierten Chor und ein Orchester, welche ohne Zweifel die gebräuchliche Musik der Zeit aufführten. Auf irgendeine Weise wurde Sutton 1858 von der Vortrefflichkeit und sakralen Würde der Musik Palestrinas überzeugt. Daher überredete er den Gemeindepfarrer, ihm zu erlauben, die völlige Umwandlung der Kirchenmusik zu bezahlen. Das Orchester wurde entlassen und ein Chor aus Knaben und Männern zum Singen von Palestrinas Messen und anderen Kompositionen. Er bat darum, daß der Chorleiter Priester sein sollte. Da dies nicht geschah, wählte man einen Studenten des Hauptseminars von Brügge. In der Tat sang man brillant, und der Chor wurde der berühmteste der Stadt. Der nachfolgende Chorleiter, ein Schüler, führte die Arbeit bis zu Suttons Tod 1873 fort. Als dann die Zahlungen zur Unterstützung des Chores aufhörten, war sein Requiem der letzte Gottesdienst, in dem der Chor zu hören war.

Zu Kiedrich im Rheingau jedoch findet man bleibende Monumente von Suttons Musikalität und seiner Musikauffassung (die Orgel ist im Kapitel II beschrieben). Als Sutton 1857 dem Dorf seinen ersten längeren Besuch abstattete, entdeckte er dort die reiche musikalisch-liturgische Tradition von der Zeit Karls des Großen bis ins 18. Jahrhundert, speziell bis 1817, als der durch Napoleon ernannte Mainzer Bischof Joseph Colmar, die deutschen Choralbücher durch französische ersetzte.

Sutton war entschlossen, die alte Mainzer Tradition soweit wie möglich wiederzubeleben, sowohl hinsichtlich der Musik als auch deren Ausführung. Den ersten Schritt unternahm er am 27.12.1865, als Chor und

Chorschule wieder gegründet und finanziell ausgestattet wurden im Einvernehmen mit dem Bischof und der Diözese Limburg, zu der Kiedrich mittlerweile gehörte. Das Gründungsdokument zeigt eine umfangreiche Liste aller Gottesdienste in der Pfarrkirche, bei denen der Chor im Laufe des Jahres singen sollte (gekleidet in englisch geschnittenen Chorhemden, die man seitdem trägt). Auch hier legte sich Sutton auf einen Priester als Chorregent fest, und die Diözese Limburg reagierte anders als in Brügge, indem man die Kapläne in Kiedrich auch zu Chorregenten ernannte. Dies verlangte natürlich eine voll dotierte Stelle, jedoch wurde Kiedrich als eine einfache Pfarrei für einen Priestergehilfen erachtet, in die man oft junge Männer sandte, um ihre Gesundheit nach Krankheiten verschiedener Art wiederherstellen zu lassen. Natürlich erwuchsen manche Schwierigkeiten, aber mit der Ernennung des Kanonikers Johannes Zaun zum Gemeindepfarrer 1869 und durch Übernahme eines großen Teils der Chorarbeit durch Sutton selbst verbesserte sich die Lage. Bei Suttons Tod 1873 hatte sich der Chor auf einem starken Fundament etabliert und stand in der Obhut eines musikalisch fähigen Chorregenten. Der Chor hat heute professionelles Niveau, und wenn auch die finanzielle Unterstützung aus Suttons Stiftung verloren ging, so hat doch der Stolz der Einwohner von Kiedrich auf ihre Tradition zur Folge, daß Männer und Knaben immer noch bereit sind, ihre Zeit und ihr Talent zur Verfügung zu stellen.

Nachdem das Motettenbuch für die Jesus-College-Kapelle in Cambridge gedruckt vorlag, begann Sutton mit den Editionen für die Kiedricher Chormitglieder, bestehend aus Graduale und Manuale. Das Graduale ist ein großer Foliant, welcher auf ein Pult gelegt wird, aus dem der Chor singt. Sutton bediente sich bei der Restaurierung des Kurmainzer Chorals der Hilfe des Mainzer Domkapellmeisters Weber; die Briefe an Kanonikus Schneider schließen den regelmäßigen Dank für dessen Arbeit ein. In der Tat handelte es sich bei der kopierten Version um jene, die unter der Herrschaft des Mainzer Erzbischofs Johann Philipp von Schönborn 1671 gedruckt worden war, also eine barockisierte Fassung. Die Arbeit beanspruchte fünf Jahre. Da, der gesamte Druck und die künstlerische Aufmachung neu gestaltet werden mußten, waren die Kosten gewiss extrem teuer. Das Manuale wird im Briefwechsel nicht erwähnt, dafür aber ein anderes Buch – offenbar Kirchenlieder – von dem es keine Spur gibt. Die Korrespondenz zeigt, wie Sutton sich weit mehr für die antikisierende Aufmachung eines Objektes als für dessen praktischen Nutzen interessierte.

Schließlich noch ein Wort über John Suttons eigene musikalische Begabung und sein Stilempfinden: mehr als einmal wird über seine Fähigkeiten auf der Orgel oder dem Klavier berichtet, über seinen Interpretationsstil und sein großes improvisatorisches Können. Er konnte anscheinend die Stile bekannter Komponisten (besonders der von ihm hoch geschätzten J.S. Bach, Händel, Mozart und Beethoven) nach Belieben reproduzieren. In seinem Zimmer in der Gouden-Hand-Straat in Brügge standen ein großer Flügel und die "Northampton"-Hausorgel. In einem seiner Briefe an Madame Bethune spricht er davon, wie er zum Einüben eines Stückes von Mozart zwei Stunden benötigte, ein Zeichen für seine hohe Begabung. Er spielte eine Zeit lang die Orgel in Kiedrich, nahm aber niemals eine regelmäßige musikalische Verpflichtung an. Gegen Ende seines Lebens wohnte er gelegentlich musikalischen Zusammenkünften bei, wie er sie während seines Lebens in Cambridge gepflegt hatte.

Kapitel V: Das anglo-belgische Seminar

Sutton war bald "persona grata" am bischöflichen Palast in Brügge und wurde um 1857 von Bischof Malou gebeten, bei der Gründung eines dortigen Seminars, das Priester für ihre Arbeit in England und insbesondere den Hafenstädten ausbilden sollte, behilflich zu sein. Die Idee war kaum neu und der Enthusiasmus für ein Seminar außerhalb Englands war schon länger abgeflaut. Rom gab gedoch seine Zustimmung und die englischen Bischöfe unter der Leitung von Kardinal Wiseman unterstützten das Vorhaben, so daß am 19. November 1858 die Grüdungsurkunde unterzeichnet wurde. Sutton stiftete gleich zu Beginn 100,000 Franc und versprach weitere 50,000 Franc pro Jahr; doch bemühten sich die englischen Bischöfe, soweit wie möglich sicherzustellen, daß er weder die Besetzung der Lehrerstellen noch die Ausbildung beeinflussen konnte.

Das erste Gebäude befand sich in der Lange Rei 55, und Sutton widmete sich sogleich der Aufgabe, in ihm eine gotische Atmosphäre zu schaffen, indem er die Inneneinrichtung der Kapelle selbst auswählte. Die Absicht war, die jungen Gemüter auf diese Art zielstrebig auf die Gotik als den wahren Stil für Kirchen auszurichten, so daß junge Priester, denen beim Bau neuer Kirchen in England die Wahl der Architekten und Stilarten oblag, fähig wären, diese Aufgabe korrekt durchzuführen. Nach zwei Jahren war die Studentenzahl derartig gestiegen, daß ein neues Heim gefunden werden mußte; dies lag in der Potterierei, und für das Gotteshaus erwarb Sutton die alte Schifferkapelle. Einen Großteil der Räumungs – und Reinigungsarbeiten führte er selbst aus und fand für die Einrichtung natürlich Altäre u.ä. in seiner Sammlung.

Dieses Haus war niemals als endgültige Behausung des Seminars gedacht, und als 1869 ein Lazarett am Vlamingsdam, ein formaliges Karmeliterkloster, verfügbar wurde, kauften Sutton, der Bischof von Nottingham und Msgr. Aime Boone, Suttons Vermittler bei den meisten belgischen Angelegenheiten, es im Jahre 1871. Usprünglich war beabsichtigt, es nur zu ändern, aber Sutton erstellte bald Skizzen und Zeichnungen für ein völlig neues Gebäude im rein gotischen Stil, dessen Plan und Ausstattungen stark vom flämischen Mittelalter beinflußt waren. Diese Skizzen befinden sich noch im Béthune-Archiv und veranschaulichen, wie dies die Krönung aller von ihm entworfenen Bauprojekte werden sollte. Die Kapelle sollte besonders großzügig bemessen sein, mit kunstvoller, reicher Ausstattung.

Die Arbeiten am Seminargebäude zogen sich über Jahr 1872 hinaus bis zum Frühjahr 1873 hin. Im Winter hatte Sutton sich aber der Pflege seines schwindsüchtigen Dieners in Amelie-les-Bains, Südfrankreich, gewidmet und wurde anscheinend nicht gewarnt, daß sich die Auslagen in der Zwischenzeit häuften. Als er dann bei seiner Rückkehr nach Brügge an Gelenkrheuma erkrankte und der Arzt von Todesgefahr sprach, versuchte er noch, Vorkehrungen zur finanziellen Sicherung für die Vollendung des Baues zu treffen. Dies erwies sich jedoch als unmöglich, und am Tage nach seinem Tode wurden die Arbeiten eingestellt, wobei die ausstehenden Rechnungen sich auf eine Million Franc beliefen. Das Seminar wurde im August des gleichen Jahres geschlossen und die Studenten in das Hauptseminar in Brügge umgesiedelt. Nach ausgedehnten Verhandlungen wurde das Gelände schließlich für ein viel kleinere Summe verkauft, als ursprünglich gefordert war, und diente danach als "Rijksnormaal"-Schule. Suttons Bruder Charles mußte swangsläufig fur 3/5tel – d.h. den Anteil des Verstorbenen – gerade stehen, der von der römisch-katholischen Kirche in England verlangt wurde – ein Tatsache, die die Familie nie vergaß. Die ganze Sache befriedigte die englischen Bischöfen wenig, deren Führung jetzt Cardinal Manning oblag, der Sutton nie kennengelernt hatte. Der für uns heute recht unterhaltsame Briefwechsel zeigt dies in aller Deutlichkeit.

Das "*Seminarium Anglo-Belgicum*" hatte während seines Bestehens 187 Schüler, von denen später 48 Priester und zwei sogar Bishöfe wurden; Ein wahrlich überzeugender Nachlaß für eine derart kurze Wirkungsdauer.

Kapitel VI: Der Kreis um Sutton

Die Colleges an den Universitäten waren um die Mitte des 19. Jahrhunderts viel kleinere Gemeinschaften als heutzutage. Vor allem wohnten alle Studenten in den College-Gebäuden. Obwohl Außenstehende gelegentlich eingeführt wurden, bestand nur wenig Verkehr mit Studenten anderer Colleges, und eine Universitätsvereinigung wie die *Camden Society* zog meist Gleichgesinnte an. Sutton selbst war ein sanfter, schuchterner Mensch, der nur wenige enge Freunde hatte. Bekannt sind die nachstehend genannten:

John Gibson (1818-1892) war Mitglied, Dozent und Vorstand des Jesus College von 1842 bis 1857, anschließend Rektor von King's Stanley in Gloucester, wo er bis zur Pensionierung 1886 blieb. Er war Künstler und Musiker mit Fachkenntnissen in Fragen des Kirchengestühls und der –ausschmückung und spezialisierte sich auf Orgelgehäuse. Er gehörte nie zur *Camden Society*, wird aber 1854 bei deren Nachfolger in Cambridge, der *Cambridge Architectural Society*, als Vorsitzender aufgeführt.

Anscheinend übernahmen Gibson und sein Kollege Fisher 1846 die Leitung der Restaurationsarbeiten an der Kapelle des Jesus College, als der Berufsarchitekt Salvin gebeten wurde zurückzutreten. Sie waren (mit Beiträgen von John Sutton!) für alle Arbeiten am Gebäude und dem neuen Gemeindegestühl verantwortlich.

Als Sutton von England zum europäischen Festland übersiedelte, blieb er mit Gibson in Kontakt und bat ihn sogar, die neue Orgelempore für die Kirche in Kiedrich zu entwerfen. Diese fand nicht sofort Beifall, da man sie für zu dunkel hielt. Doch wurde sie einstimmig befürwortet, als sie farbig gestrichen war.

1876 wurde eine neue Orgel von Liddiatt, einem ansässigen Tischler, für die Kirche in King's Stanley gebaut. Ein Brief von Gibson an Béthune läßt keine Zweifel aufkommen, daß Gibson das Gehäuse selbst entwarf, und es ist eindeutig dem in Kiedrich nachgeahmt. Das Instrument selbst zeigt zahlreiche Merkmale der von John Sutton entworfenen Orgeln: viele Holzpfeifen, ein milder Gesamtklang und sehr weiche Baßtöne. Der

Spieltisch ist wohl der prächtigste – und der bequemste – den der Kreis jemals entworfen hat. Gibson hatte beabsichtigt, ein Buch über Orgelgehäuse mit Kiedrich als Ideal zu schreiben, jedoch ist keine Spur davon zu finden.

Osmond Fisher (1817-1913): Mitglied und Geistlicher des Jesus College von 1844 bis 1858. Er war ein Mann mit zahlreichen Interessen: Einer von jenen Theologen, die für die Wiederaufnahme der Provinzialsynode in der anglikanischen Kirche arbeiteten; Altertumsforscher und "Freund" seines College und dessen Gebäuden – u.a. war er an der Restaurierung der Kapelle beteiligt. Er war ursprünglich Geologe und veröffentlichte ein Standardwerk mit dem Titel "*The Physics of the Earth's Crust*". Aber was sein Person betraf, war er vor allem Musiker und Orgelliebhaber. Er entwarf eine Orgel für die All-Saints-Kirche in Dorchester, wo er zwischen 1845 und 1853 Pfründeninhaber war; der Orgelbauer war Bishop und das Gehäuse basiert auf der Orgel von St. Germaine in Tirlemond (Belgien). Als die Kirche in Dorchester umgebaut wurde, konnte Fisher die Orgel für seine Kirche in Harlton, in der Nähe von Cambridge, sicherstellen, wo sie bis zum heutigen Tag blieb. Er reiste offensichtlich in andere europäische Länder; da er aber ein Orgelgehäuse erfolgreich entworfen hat, liegt es nicht nahe, daß er auch für andere auf ihn zurückgehen? In der Gegend um Cambridge gibt es mehrere vorzügliche Orgelgehäuse aus der Mitte des 19. Jahrhunderts, deren Urheber nicht bekannt sind, aber von Fisher oder Gibson stammen könnten.

Jonathan Holt Titcomb (*ca.*1820-1887): Pfründeninhaber von St. Andrew-the-Less 1845-1859. Es handelte sich um eine große Gemeinde mit vielen armen und sozial benachteiligten Mitgliedern. Titcomb war bald sehr beliebt, seine Kirche wurde stark besucht und die Gemeinde hatte für die damaligen Zustände eine sehr aufopfernde und geschätzte Betreuung. Als die Kirche 1854 restauriert wurde, war die *Cambridge Architectual Society*, bei der Gibson Vorsitzender und John Sutton Gründungsmitglied waren, zumindest aktiv daran interessiert. Wie im Kapitel Orgelliebhaber dargelegt, war die Orgel wahrscheinlich ein Geschenk von Sutton und das Gehäuse ein belgischer Entwurf. Wir haben hier ein Beispiel für den Respekt, den Gemeinden aus Arbeiterständen für den Klerus hatten, wenn er in seiner Arbeit irgendwie erfolgreich war.

John Hanson Sperling (*ca.*1826-1894): Wegen seiner drei Notizbücher mit Spezifikationen von englischen Orgeln, die er anscheinend um 1854 abschloß und die für Orgelhistoriker von großen Interesse sind, ist er heutzutage verhältnismäßig berühmt. Er kann bei Sutton durch T. A. Walmisley eingeführt worden sein, der am Trinity College, wo Sperling Student war, gleichzeitig Musikprofessor und Organist war und der im Jesus College zusammen mit Sutton wohnte. Nur wenig scheint die Notizbücher von Sperling mit dem *Short Account* zu verbinden... außer der Tatsache, daß Sperlings Bücher mehr als fünfzig Orgeln behandeln, die zu seiner Zeit bereits zerstört oder umgebaut worden waren. Diese Kenntnisse könnten mit Sutton während der ersten Monate ihrer Bekanntschaft geteilt worden sein.

BIBLIOGRAPHY

Addleshaw, G. W. O. and Etchells, F., *The Architectural Setting of Anglican Worship* (London: Faber & Faber, 1948).
Baron, J., *Scudamore Organs* (London: Bell & Daldy, 1948).
Bénézit, E., *Dictionnaire des Peintres, Sculpteurs, Dessinateurs et Graveurs* X (Paris: Gründ, 1976).
Bernhard, H. and Staab, J., *Kiedricher Chortradition – lebendig für die Zukunft* (Chorstift Kiedrich, 1965).
Bettenson, H., *Documents of the Christian Church* (Oxford University Press, 1943).
Bösken, Franz, art. "Die Orgel von Kiedrich" in *Acta Organologica* VIII (Berlin: Merseburger, 1974).
Anon. (though must be ed. William Brougham) *The Book of Anthems for the use of the Chapel at Brougham* (London: William Pickering, 1835).
Burke, *Peerage, Baronetage and Knightage*.
Clarke, K., *Civilization* (London: B.B.C. and John Murray, 1969).
Clutton, C. and Niland, A., *The British Organ* (London: Batsford, 1963).
Cobb, I. F., *A Brief History of the Organ in the Chapel of Trinity College, Cambridge* (Cambridge: Fabb & Tyler, 1913).
Complete Baronetage ed. George E. Cokayne.
Dearmer, P., *The Parson's Handbook* (Oxford University Press, 1932).
Dickson, W. E., *Fifty Years of Church Music* (Ely: Hills, 1894).
Digby, K., *The Broadstone of Honour: Rules for the Gentlemen of England* (1822).
Dyce, W., *The Order of Daily Service* (London: James Burns, 1843).
Einsingbach, W., *Kiedrich Im Rheingau* (Köln: Rheinische Kunststätten, 1974).
Elvin, L., *Bishop & Son, Organ Builders* (Lincoln: 1954).
Elvin, L., *Family Enterprise, The Story of Some North Country Organ Builders* (Lincoln: 1986).
Faber, G., *Oxford Apostles* (London: Pelican, 1936).
Ferrey, B., *Recollections of A. W. N. Pugin*, 1861: republished with introduction by Clive and Jane Wainwright (London: Scholar Press, 1978)
Forster, H. R., ed. *The Stowe Catalogue* (London: David Bogue, 1848).
Fowler, J. T., *Life and Letters of John Bacchus Dykes, Vicar of St. Oswald's Durham* (London: John Murray, 1897).
Freeman, A., *Father Smith* (London, Musical Opinion 1926), revised Rowntree, J. (Oxford: Positif Press, 1977).
Freeman, A., *English Organ Cases* (London: Mate, 1921).
Fulford, R., *Royal Dukes* (London: Duckworth, 1933).
Girouard, M., *Return to Camelot* (Yale University Press, 1981).
Gray, A. and Brittain, F., *A History of Jesus College Cambridge* (London: Heinemann, 1960).
Grove, *New Dictionary of Music and Musicians* (London: Macmillan, 1980).
Helbig, J., *Le Baron Béthune, Fondateur des Écoles Saint-Luc* (Lille/Bruges: 1906).
Honey, J. R. de S., *Tom Brown's Universe* (London: Millington, 1977).
Hopkins, E. and Rimbault, E., *The Organ* (London: Robert Cocks, 1855).

Moortgat, G., *Oude Orgels in Vlaanderen* (Brussels: BRT, 1963) II.
Morgan, I. and Morgan, G., *The Stones and Story of Jesus College Chapel, Cambridge* (Cambridge: Bowes & Bowes, 1914).
Ollard, S. L., *A Short History of the Oxford Movement* (London: Faith Press, 1963)
Pearce, C. W., *Notes on English Organs* (London: Vincent Music Co., 1905).
Pevsner, N., *The Buildings of Britain – Cambridgeshire* (London: Penguin, 1954).
Pevsner, N., *The Buildings of Britain – North West and South Norfolk* (London: Penguin, 1962).
Quoika, R., *Das Positif in Geschichte und Gegenwart* (Kassel: Bärenreiter 1957).
Rainbow, B., *The Choral Revival in the Anglican Church 1839-1872* (London: Barrie & Jenkins, 1970).
Rembry, E., *De Bekende Pastoors van St. Gillis te Brugge* (Bruges, 1896).
Roose, O., art. "Werklijst anno 1885 van L. B. Hooghuys", *Orgelkunst* (Brussels, 1983).
Schepens, art. "Het Engels Seminarie te Brugge", *Handelingen van het Genootschap voor Geschiedenis*, (Bruges, 1967).
Schnell and Steiner GMBH, *Kiedrich im Rheingau* (Kunstführer 1465, Munich 1984).
Scholes, P. A., *Oxford Companion to Music* (O.U.P., 1947).
Scott, W., *Ivanhoe* (New York: Airmont Publishing Co., 1964).
Smets, P., *Die Orgel der St. Valentinuskirche zu Kiedrich* (Mainz: Rheingold-Verlag, 1945).
Staab, J., *Die Kiedricher Chorbuben und Ihre Tradition* (Chorstift Kiedrich, 1985)
Staab, J. and Bibo, W., *1,000 Jahre Kiedrich im Rheingau* (Gemeinde Kiedrich, 1979).
Stanton, P., *Pugin* (London: Thames & Hudson, 1971).
Sumner, W. L., *The Organ* (London: MacDonald, 1952).
Sutton, J. (pub. anon), *A Short Account of Organs built in England from the Reign of King Charles II to the Present Time* (London: Masters, 1847; rep. Oxford: Positif Press, 1979).
Sutton, J., *A Collection of anthems used in Divine Service upon Sundays, Holy-days & their Eves, in Jesus College Chapel Cambridge* (London: Whittingham, 1850).
Thistlethwaite, N., *The Organs of Cambridge* (Oxford: Positif Press, 1983).
Tricker, R. W., *St. Mary's West Tofts Norfolk, History and Guide* (pamphlet) (Ipswich, 1984).
Venn, John, and Venn, J. A., *Alumni Cantabrigienses* (C.U.P., 1924).
Wainwright, C., *Notes for the Victorian Society's Tour of Norfolk 1978* (typescript).
Walgrave, A., *Het leven van Guido Gezelle, Vlaamsche priester en dichter* (Amsterdam, 1923) II.
Wand, J. W. C., *A History of the Modern Church* (London: Methuen, 1952).
Wedgwood, J. I., *Continental Organs and their Makers* (London: Reeves, 1910).
Wedgwood, A., *A. W. N. Pugin and the Pugin Family* (London: Victoria & Albert Museum, 1985).
White, J. F., *The Cambridge Movement* (C.U.P., 1962).
Wilson, M. I., *The English Chamber Organ, 1650-1850* (London: Cassirer, 1968).
Zaun, J., *Geschichte des Ortes und der Pfarrie Kiederich* (reprinted Gemeinde Kiedrich, 1979).
Dictionary of National Biography (London: Macmillan, 1921-2).

Periodicals

British Institute of Organ Studies: *BIOS Journal*, annually, from 1977; *BIOS Reporter*, three or four times a year, from 1977.
Musical Opinion, monthly (London).

BIBLIOGRAPHY 217

Parish Choir (Ollivier, 1846-51).
The Christian Remembrancer – or The Churchman's Biblical, Ecclesiastical and Literary Miscellany (London, 1819-1840).
The Ecclesiologist (London: Rivington & Masters, 1841-1868).
The Organ, quarterly, from 1921 (London).

Background Books

Betjeman, J. ed., *Guide to English Parish Churches* (London: Collins, 1958).
Bond, F., *Screens and Galleries* (O.U.P., 1908).
Bourke, J., *Baroque Churches in Central Europe* (London: Faber, 1958).
Clutton, C. and Dixon, G., *The Organ* (London: Grenville, 1950).
Cross, F. L., *Oxford Dictionary of the Christian Church* (O.U.P., 1957).
Eberstaller, O., *Orgeln und Orgelbauer in Österreich* (Graz: Bohlaus, 1955).
Ellis, C. D. B., *Leicestershire and the Quorn Hunt* (Leicester: Backus, 1951).
Leech, A. ed. A. Sutton, *Rural Rides of the Bristol Churchgoer* (Gloucester: Alan Sutton Pub. Co., 1982).
Medici, N. and Hughes, R., *A Mozart Pilgrimage* (London: Novello/Eulenburg, 1975).
Moorman, J. R. H., *A History of the Church in England* (London: Black, 1953).
Pacey, R., *The Organs of Oxford* (Oxford: Positif Press, 1980).
Scholes, P., *The Great Dr. Burney* (O.U.P., 1948).
Surtees, R. S., *Handley Cross* (London: Folio Society, 1951).
Whiffen, M., *Stuart and Georgian Churches outside London* (London: Batsford, 1948).
Williams, P., *The European Organ 1450-1850* (London: Batsford, 1966).
Wood, H., *My Life of Music* (London: Gollancz, 1938).

Manuscript Sources

Letters of Sir John Sutton to Baron J. de Béthune, at the Béthune Archive, Kasteel Marke, Kortrijk, Belgium: no. 1230.
Letters of Sir John Sutton to Pralat Schneider, at the Staatliches Hochschulinstitut für Musik, Mainz.
Letters of Sir John Sutton to John Hardman & Co., Hardman Archives, the Central Library, Birmingham.
Jesus College Conclusion Book, and documents relative to the 1846-49 Restoration of the Chapel, Jesus College Old Library, Cambridge.
Minute-book of the Cambridge Architectural Society, Add. Mss. 2758-2762, University Library, Cambridge.
The Bursars' Long Books, New College, Oxford.
Vestry Minute-books and other documents of All Saints', Northampton, at Northamptonshire Record Office, Delapre Abbey, Northampton.
Registers and Records of West Tofts, Norfolk County Record Office, at the Central Library, Norwich.
Records of Bishop and Son, Organ-builders, at Beethoven Street, London.
The foundation documents of the choir school, at Chorstift Kiedrich, 6229 Kiedrich/Rhg., Germany.
Papal grant of the Order of St. Gregory-the-Great, Vatican Archives.
The note-book of organ visits of the Revd. Andrew Freeman, in the care of the Revd. B. B. Edmonds, Clare, Suffolk.
Sperling Notebooks at the Royal College of Organists, London.
Crace Papers, R.I.B.A.

INDEX

A
Adcock, E. E. 77
Alcock, Bishop 187
Aldeburgh Festival 156
altar-bequests 148
Amelie les Bains 160, 176, 180
Anglican chants 140
Anglo-Belgian Seminary 170-182
Anthems, Book of (1850) 141-146, 156
Armstrong, Revd. Benjamin 13, 121
Attwood, Thomas 19, 48, 65

B
Bach, J. S. 40
Baron, John 37, 41, 105
Berger, Andries Jacob (ob) 102
Berrow, Jim 43
Béthune, Baron Jean de 22, 24, 26, 27, 30, 31, 33, 43, 53, 87-9, 97, 116, 129, 131, 133, 134, 162, 168, 173, 178, 187, 195, 196
Béthune, Felix 23, 24, 33, 171, 172
Béthune workshops 60, 62, 79, 187, 190
Bicknell, Stephen (ob) 48, 51
Bird, Revd. Christopher 17, 22
Bishop, J. C. (ob) 48, 49, 51, 52, 56, 60, 65-8, 70, 71, 99, 105, 193
Bishop, Son and Starr (ob) 67
Bodley, G. F. 14, 125
Boeringer, Dr. James 193
Boone, Mgr. A. A. 29, 130, 133, 170, 171, 173, 178, 180, 181, 185
Bösken's, Franz 77
Boucquillon, Bruno 62, 63
Box of Whistles, The 43
Brant Broughton 14, 70
Bremhill Church 99
Britten, Benjamin 29
Brougham Anthem Book 145
Brougham, Lord 67
Brougham, William 123
Bruges 24, 27- 30, 32
Bruges:
    Cathedral 103, 104, 172
    House 70, 134, 135, 162, 163, 184
    St. Gillis 102, 103, 133, 146, 147, 163
    Schippers' Chapel 120, 173
    Seminary 104, 170, 182
Bruneel, Canon Livinus 171, 172
Buckingham, Duke of 73
Bullen, J (ob) 105

INDEX

C
Cambridge:
    Architectural Society 21, 95, 97, 186, 194
    Christs College 98, 99
    Duke of 18
    Jesus College 13, 18, 20-3, 36, 41, 47-54, 70, 71, 88, 97, 121-6, 139, 140, 178, 186, 191
    Jesus College chapel restoration 121-6
    Jesus College choir school 139-41
    Jesus College organ 47-54
    Professor of Music 19
    Round Church (Holy Sepulchre) 67, 68
    St. Andrew-the-Less 59, 90, 95-8, 194
    St. John's College Chapel 121
    Trinity College 18, 19, 193
Camden Society 18, 19, 21, 33, 36, 38, 39, 41, 47, 54, 56, 58, 68, 105, 112, 118, 126, 140, 148, 156, 186, 190, 194
Canons Ashby 72
Canterbury, Dean Bargrave organ 100
chamber organs 37, 65, 88, 99
chancel screens 116, 117, 131, 132, 133, 178, 179
Cheadle, St. Giles' Church 56, 80
Chiswick Press 37
Chollerton 17, 75, 76, 77, 138, 139, 183
choral services 139, 140, 191
Clifton-Brown, Robina 68, 182
Collins, Benjamin (ob) 105
Compton Wynyates 69
Cooper, George (2) 47, 48
Corps, James (ob) 105

D
Dallam family (ob) 72, 75, 100
Dawson, George (ob) 54, 56, 58-60, 97, 99, 100
Dearmer, Dr. Percy 122
Dickson, Canon W. E. 37, 69, 145, 194
Digby, Kenelm 19, 20, 183, 197
Dorchester, All Saints 191
Durham Cathedral 17, 49

E
Eagles, James (ob) 65, 66
Earls Colne 14
East Stoke 16
East Walton 105
Ecclesiologist, The 39, 41, 42, 126, 166
Edmonds, Revd B. B. 21, 77
Eltville-am-Rhein 90, 91, 92, 133
Elvin, Laurence 48, 49, 51
Ely, Precentor of 194, 195
English Seminary 29, 170-182, 184
Erkes, Kurt 29
Eton College 16, 67, 190

F
Faict, Bishop of Bruges 180, 181
Fisher, Osmond 21, 47, 99-101, 122, 123, 139, 190-193
Forster & Andrews (ob) 67
Freeman, Revd Andrew 53, 56, 69, 71, 73, 95, 99, 191

Freiburg im Breisgau 162
    Cathedral 92-4
French, Dr. William 123

G
Gauntlett, Dr. Henry John 40, 41
Gibson, John 21, 26, 47, 80, 84, 85, 122, 123, 186-190, 193, 194
Gray, Dr. Arthur 124
Gray, R. (ob) 75
Great Bardfield 193
Great Walsingham 54, 55, 57, 62, 80
Gonella, Mgr. 170
Gwynn, Dominic (ob) 72

H
Hardman, Mrs 33
Hardmans (John Hardman of Birmingham) 90, 110, 111, 120, 121, 124
Harlton Church 21, 191, 192
Harris family (ob) 72, 75, 100
Harrison & Harrison Ltd (ob) 52, 75, 77
de Hearne, Canon 27
Hearst, William Randolph 73
Helmore, Frederick 166
Henshaw, William 17, 139
Hill, Dr. A. G. 91, 94
"Hill-Gauntlett Revolution" 41
Hill, William (ob) 40, 41, 51, 99
Hilpisch, Georg 129, 167, 183
Holdich, G. M. (ob) 105
Hooghuys (Louis-Benoit) (ob) 59, 60, 79-84, 90, 92, 97, 103, 104,
Hooghuys Family 106, 107

I
Institut Städel, Prof. 82

J
James II, King, travelling organ 73-5

K
Kiedrich 17, 21, 24-31, 54, 56, 60, 65, 77-88, 90, 107, 110, 126-132, 147-50, 161, 187
    chamber organ 88
    choir 148, 152-7, 161, 164, 166-8
    church restoration 126-132
    Graduale 151
    house 135, 136, 162, 184
    music books 159, 160, 161, 165, 166
    organ 77-88
King James II's travelling organ 73-5
King's Stanley church 21, 186-8, 190
Kirchner, Johann Wendelin (ob) 79
Kuhn, Th, of Männedorf (ob) 80
Kurmainzer plainsong 140, 148, 150, 152, 156-9, 164, 165

L
Lady Sutton's Chantry 110-12, 114, 115, 117
Lane, Capt. J. 72
Leadbitter, Dr. 172
Ley, Jonas (ob) 75
Liddiatt, Thomas (ob) 187, 189

Limburg, Bishop of 30, 152, 153, 155, 156
Lincoln Cathedral 14, 119
London, St. Paul's Cathedral 19, 48, 65
Lynford Hall 18, 24, 65-67, 111

M
Mainz, Archbishop of 149, 150, 157, 164, 165
Mainz, plainsong 30
Malou, Bishop 24, 170-2
Mander, N. P. Ltd (ob) 37, 49, 52, 53, 70-2
Mann, Dr. A. H. 141
Mann, George 26, 27, 29, 168
Manning, Cardinal 180, 181
Martin, August 44, 45, 59, 79, 82, 85, 87, 90, 94
Meason, George 43
Mendelssohn, Felix 19, 40
Miller, A. T. (ob) 59, 60, 62, 97
Moortgat, Gaby 90

N
Napoleonic Wars 150, 165
Nazarene school of painting 82
Neale, J. M. 18, 36
Newman, Dr. Harding 71, 72
Newman, Revd. John 18, 23
New York, St. David's School 73
Nicholai, Nicholaus (ob) 79
Nichols, Richard 38
Noble, Mark (ob) 104
Norbury, John 43, 93
Northampton, Marquess of 68
"Northampton" organ 68-70, 162
Norwood Park (Southwell) 15
Nottingham, Bishop of 173

O
Oscott College 170
Overbeck, Johann Friedrich 82
Oxburgh Hall 21, 112
Oxford:
    Magdalen College 72
    Movement 18, 36, 110, 115
    New College 70-2
    St. Mary Magdalene church 118
    University College 20

P
Paget, Canon Gordon 102
Perpignan Cathedral 45, 46
Perth, St. Ninian's Cathedral 166
Pevsner 97, 187
plainsong 140, 148, 150, 152, 156-9, 164-6
Plymouth, Bishop of 28, 110
poor, helping the 183
Practical Organ-Building 194
Pratt, John 145
prayer-desk organ 101
Pugin, Augustus Welby 13, 19, 21-3, 33, 37, 43, 53, 59, 60, 80, 95, 97, 111-4, 116, 117, 121-4, 132, 183, 187, 193

Q
Quarles, Charles (ob) 98, 99
Quoika, Rudolph 88

R
Railway Guides 43
Rainbow, Dr. 140
Randolph, Edmund 20, 33, 160, 195
Rattee's (Builders) 121
Roman Catholicism 23, 32, 37, 116, 118-20, 170, 183, 195
Roman Catholic Liturgy 148, 152, 161
Rome, St. Peters 163
Rüdesheim, St. Hildegard-Kapelle 164
Russen, Michael (ob) 59

S
Salvin, Anthony 21, 186
Samuels & Twyford (ob) 105
Santon Downham 54
Schmidt, Bernard (ob) (Father Smith) 37, 38, 47, 48, 51, 68, 70, 72, 77, 79, 99, 188
Schneider, Prälat 28, 30, 32, 44, 45, 156, 159
Scots college, Belgium 170
Scott, James (ob) 104, 105
Seminarium Anglo-Belgicum 27, 170-182
Shaw, F. W. (ob) 69, 70
Sherlock, Emma Helena (Sutton) 20, 112, 119
Short Account of Organs... 36-43, 53, 60, 68, 69, 71, 138, 145, 193
Simmons, H. & J. 73
Sion/Sitten 90, 91
Skelton, George 138
South Pickenham Church 59, 61-3
Sperling, John Hanson 193
Sperling Notebooks 98, 193
stained glass 119, 131
Stanton, Prof. 112
Steinle, Edward 82
Stowe Catalogue 73
Stroud, RC Parish Church 189
Sudbrooke Holme 15
Sumner, Dr. W. L. 77
Sutton, Revd. Arthur Frederick 14, 68, 73
Sutton, Revd. Augustus 13, 24, 102, 105, 111, 113, 114, 116, 118, 119
Sutton, Charles 182
Sutton, Revd. Frederick Heathcote 14, 41, 70, 73, 118, 119, 190
Sutton, Judith 162
Sutton, Lady (Chantry) 110-12, 114, 115, 117
Sutton, Mary Elizabeth 15, 16, 18, 110-12, 114
Sutton, Sir Richard 15, 16, 18, 19, 23, 24, 26, 65, 66, 68, 75, 111, 118
Sutton, Robert 73

T
Theddingworth 14
Thistlethwaite, Revd. Dr. Nicholas 68, 193
Titcomb, Jonathon Holt 194
Tractarian Movement 18, 115

U
Ushaw College 53, 132, 170

INDEX

V
van Coillie, M. 29
Van Robaeys 90
Vienna Masses 150
Vijvekapelle 77, 88, 89, 90, 96, 97

W
Wainwright, Clive 112
Walmisley, Thomas Attwood 19, 22, 48, 193
Walmsley, Nick (ob) 56, 57
Webb, Benjamin 18
Wesley, Samuel Sebastian 195
West Tofts (St. Mary's) 13-15, 20-2, 41, 53, 54-65, 88, 97, 99, 101, 102, 111, 112-121, 156, 184
Whittingham, Charles 37, 141
Wilson, M. I. 77
Wiseman, Cardinal 170, 171

Z
Zaun, Canon 20, 26, 29, 32, 33, 110, 129, 138, 162, 184, 195
Zimmermann, Heinrich (ob) 60
Zimmermann, Pfarrer 79, 82